STUDIES IN INDUSTRIAL GEOGRAPHY
THE USSR

STUDIES IN
INDUSTRIAL GEOGRAPHY

-THE USSR-

John C. Dewdney

Department of Geography
University of Durham

WESTVIEW PRESS · BOULDER · COLORADO

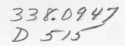

WESTVIEW SPECIAL STUDIES IN INDUSTRIAL GEOGRAPHY

Library of Congress Cataloging in Publication Data

Dewdney, John C.
   The USSR.

   (Westview special studies in industrial geography)
   Bibliography: p.
   Includes index.
   1. Russia—Industries.   2. Industries, Location of—Russia.
I. Title.
HC336.24.D49   338'.0947   76–16744
ISBN 0–89158–616–4

Printed and bound in Great Britain.
Produced by computer-controlled phototypesetting,
using OCR input techniques, and printed offset by
UNWIN BROTHERS LIMITED
The Gresham Press, Old Woking, Surrey

To Jean, Peter, Nicholas and Alexander

Contents

List of Illustrations

TABLES

FIGURES

Introduction

THE INTENTION OF this volume is to provide a picture of the industrial geography of the Soviet Union in the early 1970s, paying particular attention to the location of industrial activities and the resources on which these are based. In many respects the USSR is unique among the nations of the modern world, not least in the vast size of her territory and the tremendous resources at her disposal, both of which are far greater than those of any other country. Despite these advantages, only since World War II has the Soviet Union emerged on the world scene as a 'super-power', her one rival the United States. Before 1940 her economic strength was clearly less than that of the USA, and was generally considered inferior to those of the leading West European powers – Britain and Germany. The relative weakness of the Soviet Union in the 1930s was largely a product of her late start in the industrialisation process, which began only in the latter part of the nineteenth century and had reached but a modest level at the time of the Bolshevik Revolution in 1917. While World War I can be said to have revealed the weakness of the Russian Empire in its closing decades, World War II can equally be said to have shown the growing strength of the Soviet Union some 25 years after its foundation. The immense physical destruction and loss of life experienced between 1941 and 1945, like those of the period 1914 – 21, were a major setback to the country's economic development. By the late 1940s reconstruction was complete, but the structure of Soviet industry still had a somewhat old-fashioned appearance, with a strong emphasis on capital goods industries and a relatively low stage of development in the technologically more complex branches and in the production of consumer goods. Over the past two decades, however, and particularly since the early 1960s, continued expansion of the industrial sector of the economy has been accompanied by major qualitative changes in the nature of industrial production. Soviet industry has become more diverse, with an ever-widening range of products and, in many branches, has shown rapid technological advance.

The present patterns of industrial geography in the USSR, or for that matter in any country, can only be fully comprehended if the present situation is considered as the product of the sequence of changes that have gone before. Consequently a good deal of attention is paid in this book to phases of industrial development as well as to the current situation. Important changes have occurred over the past 100 years not only in the scale and nature of industrial production in the Russian Empire/USSR but also in its geographical location. Put in simple terms, these changes have involved an expansion of industrial activities from their nineteenth-century base in the European part of the country to various locations in the Asiatic regions. It must be emphasised, however, that in terms of population and industrial production, though not perhaps in terms of industrial resources, the European section remains over-whelmingly predominant in the Soviet economy.

Any discussion of the Soviet economy, from whatever point of view, inevitably poses the question of the extent to which the achievements of the USSR since 1917 are a product of the Soviet economic and political system. No definitive answer can be given to this major ideological question. Soviet writers invariably suggest, specifically or by implica- tion, that only under the 'socialist' system could the present level of development have been achieved in the period that has elapsed since the Revolution. Favourable comparisons are made between current rates of Soviet economic growth and those of 'leading capitalist powers', with little or no mention of the very rapid rates of growth achieved by the latter during the nineteenth century and more recently by newer recruits to the 'developed' world such as Japan. Defenders of the capitalist system, on the other hand, are prone to emphasise the failures rather than the achievements of the Soviet regime, pointing to the undoubtedly higher standards of living prevailing at present in the United States and elsewhere. A dispassionate assessment is difficult if not impossible, and one is forced to return a verdict of 'not proven' in the case of either system. The geographer may well conclude that, so great are the industrial resources contained within the boundaries of the Soviet Union, any vigorous effort directed at their exploitation, under whatever political and economic system, could hardly fail eventually to establish the USSR as a leading, perhaps the leading, world industrial power. The rate of industrial growth achieved over the half century since the Revolution is as much a reflection of the low stage of development reached in the Tsarist period as it is an advertisement for the efficacy of Soviet economic planning. Possibly the next 50 years will give a clearer answer. This said, it must be remembered that the difficulties placed in the way of Soviet economic development by an adverse physical environment are very much greater than those experienced by the United States, or indeed by most other capitalist economies, and are a major factor in the cost of all forms of development.

To many people capitalist and socialist economies, particularly those of the USA and the USSR, which are each the epitome of its group, are so different that any search for similarities becomes pointless. Socialist economies are, by definition, 'command' economies, where the nature of production is planned by central government organs, whereas capitalist economies are 'market' economies, in which production is determined by consumer demand. This dichotomy, never wholly valid, has become much less clear cut during the period since World War II. In capitalist countries government intervention, direct or indirect, in economic affairs has become more and more common and is increasingly accepted as normal, while in socialist countries the voice of the consumer is now heard, though still rather faintly, in the land. Thus the methods and objectives of economic planning under the two systems become more rather than less similar. Government investment in and control of industry become more common in the capitalist world; cost effectiveness and the profit motive play increasingly important roles in socialist economies. With this convergence, basic considerations tend to override ideological differences. A national economic unit, to whichever system it belongs, comprises three basic elements – territory, population and resources – and the relations between these three are the substance of economic geography. Differences in territorial extent, resource endowment, and population size and composition are, it is suggested, of greater and more lasting significance than ideological differences.

This said, it must be admitted that certain features specific to the USSR must be ascribed primarily to political decisions. One such has been the heavy concentration of effort, in economic development, on industry at the expense of agriculture and, within the industrial sector, on extractive and heavy manufacturing industry at the expense of consumer goods production. Another has been the emphasis on economic self-sufficiency, which contrasts so strongly with the majority of capitalist economies' deep involvement in the world market. Both these goals were physically attainable only by virtue of the Soviet Union's rich industrial resource base; both were operationally feasible only under a highly centralised and authoritarian system of political and economic control. They were emphasised from the beginning of the first

Five Year Plan in 1928 and retained their emphasis until the middle 1950s. They have become less marked over the past two decades, during which time the production of consumer goods has risen rapidly and trading contacts with the outside world have multiplied. Both have had a strong influence on the structure and location of Soviet industry, and account for much of the present-day pattern.

The text that follows has been arranged in three parts. In the first part (Chapters 1-3) a number of general features relevant to the development of the Soviet industrial economy as a whole are discussed. These include the physical environment, natural resources, population geography and the transport system. This part concludes with a consideration of the problems and processes of industrial development, and attempts to identify phases in the growth and distribution of Soviet industry. The second part (Chapters 4-7) adopts a sector-by-sector approach and again emphasises, for each sector, the phases of development that have produced the present-day pattern. Inevitably, particular attention is paid to the extractive and heavy manufacturing industries, which still form the dominant element in the Soviet economy in terms of capital and labour employed and final output. The third part (Chapters 8-11) deals with regional contrasts. After a general discussion of the regionalisation process, this part attempts to indicate the main features of the industrial economy of each region and its contribution to the Soviet industrial economy as a whole.

As the Bibliography indicates, a wide variety of sources, both Soviet and western, have been used in the preparation of this volume. It must be admitted that, to a certain extent, the nature of the information available influenced the final form of the text, particularly as regards the amount of detail given on the volume of production and the precise location of productive sites in the various branches of industry. Numerous official statistical handbooks at all-Union and republican level are now available, but their coverage is extremely uneven. While figures of production in some industries are given at the level of administrative divisions, others are published only for republics, some only for the Soviet Union as a whole and some (eg non-ferrous metals) not at all. Furthermore, while some data are given in absolute quantities, there are several cases where only indices are available. Although the amount of information freely available on the economy of the Soviet Union has increased enormously over the past 20 years, there are still serious deficiencies, some of which are discussed at the appropriate points in the main body of the text.

Most of the information on the location of economic activities is derived from Soviet sources, mainly from textbooks of economic geography and atlas maps. Among the western sources consulted, special mention should be made of the debt all students of Soviet geography owe to Theodore Shabad. The latter's book, *Basic Industrial Resources of the USSR* (1969), together with his 'News Notes', published regularly in *Soviet Geography*, are major stores of factual information on industrial location and production painstakingly assembled over the last 20 years from a mass of Soviet sources. Any errors of fact or interpretation in the present volume are of course entirely the present writer's responsibility.

Finally, tribute must be paid to the skill and devotion of the secretarial and technical staff of the Department of Geography, University of Durham, particularly to Mrs Brenda Billinghurst, Mrs Suzanne Eckford, Mrs Florence Blackett and Miss Cythia Perkins, all of whom typed sections of the manuscript, and to Mr George Brown, who prepared the final versions of all the maps.

J.C.D.

PART ONE

FACTORS IN
THE DEVELOPMENT OF
SOVIET INDUSTRY

1
Environment and Resources

Physical Factors

A VOLUME DEVOTED to the industrial geography of the USSR is not the place for a full, systematic treatment of that country's physical geography: for such a treatment the reader is referred to the several comprehensive regional texts which have appeared during the past decade.[1] Nevertheless, some reference must be made at the outset to the nature of the physical environment, which presents problems and difficulties more daunting than those faced by any other major industrial power, existing or potential, with the possible exception of Canada. These problems are derived from the simplest geographical characteristics of the USSR – its size, shape, latitudinal position and surface configuration – which in turn have a profound influence on the patterns of climate, drainage, soils and natural vegetation.

The physical factors might appear more relevant to a study of the country's agriculture than to a consideration of her industrial geography, but the two main sectors of the economy – agriculture and industry – cannot be completely divorced from each other, particularly in view of the avowed objective, dominant over most of the period since the Revolution, of attaining self-sufficiency in both. Agriculture has generally played a secondary, supporting role to that of the favoured industrial sector, particularly in the earlier stages of industrialisation, when capital for state-directed industrial growth was largely derived from the agricultural sector. Agriculture received only a very limited allocation of investment funds and, as a consequence of this and a complex of other factors, developed only slowly. Not until quite recently could the requirements of agriculture be numbered among the factors influencing industrial growth. (An example was the expansion of the chemical industry during the 1960s.) One consequence of this situation has been that, in terms of population and employment at least, agriculture has occupied a more prominent place in the Soviet economy than in that of her rival 'super-power', the United States, or for that matter in those of the middle-rank industrial powers like Britain and Germany, whose industrial output the Soviet Union has now surpassed. Slow development of agriculture, reflected in the low productivity of a vast rural population, has in turn affected industrial development by keeping down the rate at which labour has been transferred from the agricultural to the industrial sector. Not until 1961 did the urban element in the Soviet population exceed 50 per cent, and even today it is only 58 per cent.

With more than 40 per cent of the population classed as rural and some 30 per cent of the labour force engaged in agriculture, it is not surprising that the pattern of population distribution is strongly influenced by the availability and quality of agricultural land and thus, quite obviously, by the physical environment. This relationship is reinforced by the fact that a large part of the present pattern of industrial location was established before 1940, at which date two-thirds of the population were rural. Although there are noteworthy exceptions, few major industrial zones developed in areas that previously lacked a sizeable rural population. Thus the rigours of the physical environment, acting primarily on the rural population but also affecting the areas chosen for industrial development, have tended to confine the population of the USSR, like that of its predecessor, the Russian Empire, to a limited part of the national territory, leaving vast areas virtually uninhabited, with their industrial resources almost untouched.

Another feature in which the physical environment has been a major, though not the only, factor is the long-established concentration of population and economic activity in the European section of the country, where the earliest developments in modern industry took place during the nineteenth century. Only during the last 50 years has there been any large-scale movement of industry outwards from this European base to the more hostile environment of Siberia, and even today the European section contains the greater part – some 70 per cent – of the Soviet Union's population and industrial capacity, as it does of the country's agricultural land and production.

Among the basic physical constraints on both the development and the operation of the Soviet economy, none are more important than those imposed by climate, whose basic features are derived from the country's form and position as a large, compact land mass in high latitudes. The largest political unit in the contemporary world, the USSR covers no less than $22 \cdot 4$ million sq km, one-sixth of the earth's land surface. The forty-ninth parallel of latitude, which forms the northern boundary of the United States (excluding Alaska), passes only about 250km north of the Black and Caspian seas. About three-quarters of the Soviet Union is north of this line, including virtually the whole of Siberia and the Far East, as well as the greater part of the European plain. Moscow is about the same latitude (56°N) as Port Nelson on Hudson's Bay, and Leningrad (60°N), which can be said to mark the northern limit of the continuously settled part of the USSR, is as far north as the southern tip of Greenland and Anchorage, Alaska. Latitude alone would suggest a preponderance of cold climates, which is in fact intensified by other factors. Bounded on the north by the Arctic Ocean, which is frozen for much of the year, and hemmed in on the south and east by high mountain ranges, which present a barrier to the ingress of Indian Ocean or Pacific air masses, the Soviet Union is characterised by an intense continentality, the severity of which increases eastwards towards the centre of Siberia.

As one writer has put it, 'the Russian landscape is stamped in the image of its climate'[2] and it is climate rather than relief which is the main aspect of regional contrasts in the physical environment. Among the climatic elements (Fig 1), special importance attaches to temperature extremes (especially to winter cold) as having the greatest impact on human activities, industrial as well as agricultural. The map of temperature conditions in January (Fig 1A) shows how heavily the 'burden of winter' lies on most of the Soviet land. Vast areas are rendered useless for agriculture by virtue of their short growing season, and their small population, coupled with their remoteness, presents special difficulties in the exploitation of their industrial resources, however rich these may be. Cold of itself has obvious effects on such activities as hydro-electric power generation, navigation and the provision of industrial water supplies. It also has a general effect in making all types of machinery more difficult to operate and maintain. Special types of equipment are necessary for use at temperatures below −25°C, when some metals become brittle and normal lubricants freeze. Cold also hinders all kinds of outdoor work, which must by law cease when the thermometer falls to −40°C, and is a major hindrance in construction work. While few activities are actually made impossible by low temperatures, the majority are carried out less efficiently at a much greater expense. Temperature conditions have a strong seasonal effect on industry, as Hutchings has shown,[3] and output in many branches varies greatly as between the winter and summer seasons. 'The eastward march of industry into climatically severer regions has probably accentuated the seasonality of industrial output.'[4] Over something approaching half the territory of the USSR, winter

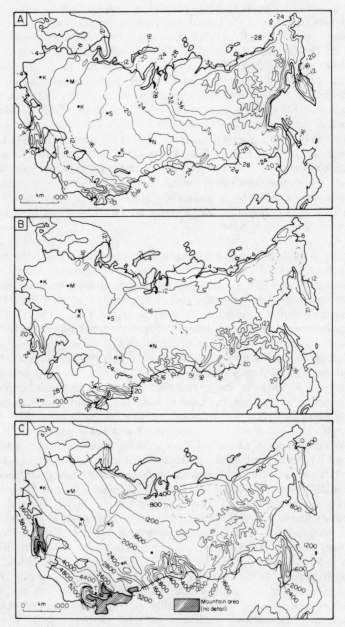

Fig 1. CLIMATIC ELEMENTS
SOURCES: A and B: *Atlas SSSR* (Moscow, 1969), 81

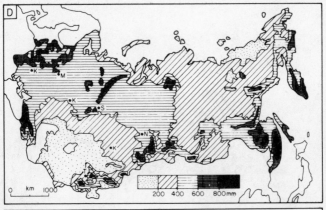

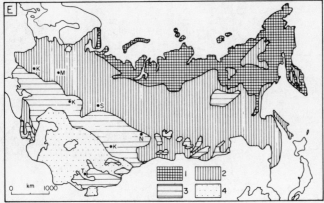

A. January mean temperatures °C

B. July mean temperatures °C

C. Accumulated temperatures: day-degrees above 10°C

D. Annual precipitation

E. Moisture availability

    1. Very humid – aridity index <0·45
    2. Humid – aridity index 0·45–1·0
    3. Sub-humid – aridity index 1·0–3·0
    4. Arid – aridity index >3·0

C: *Fiziko-Geograficheskiy Atlas Mira* (Moscow, 1964), 202
D: *Atlas SSSR*, 84   E: *Atlas SSSR*, 80

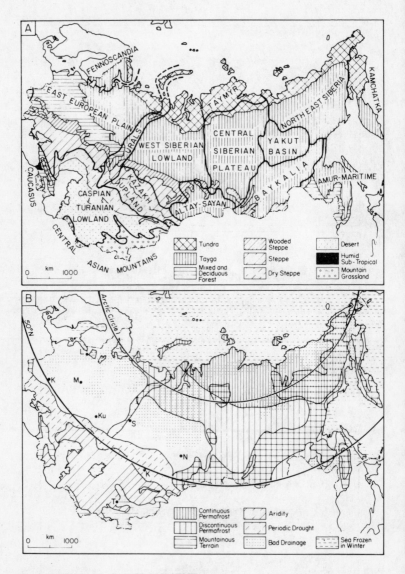

Fig 2. PHYSICAL ENVIRONMENT
A. Natural vegetation and physiographic regions. SOURCE: *Fiziko-Geografiches-kiy Atlas Mira*, 248–9
B. 'Anti-resources': based on W. H. Parker, *The World's Landscapes, 3. The Soviet Union* (London, Longman, 1969), Fig 4, p 8, by permission of the author and publisher

temperatures are low enough to maintain the condition of permafrost. This obviously presents additional difficulties in all types of construction work. Mining, the laying of pipelines and underground cables, and the building and maintenance of roads and railways all require the use of special techniques under permafrost conditions.

While winter cold is undoubtedly the main climatic problem, it is by no means the only one. Over most of the Soviet Union, annual rainfall amounts are small (Fig 1D), and low precipitation and high summer temperatures (Fig 1C) combine to present serious problems of aridity in many areas (Fig 1E). Once again the main direct effect is on agriculture, and thus on the established pattern of population distribution, but shortage of water often presents problems in industrial development that can only be overcome by expensive construction projects like the 400km-long canal built to convey water from the Irtysh river to the Karaganda industrial complex.

As far as the relief factor is concerned, the situation at first sight appears favourable in that the Soviet Union contains vast expanses of flat or gently sloping terrain, and mountainous territory is dominant only in the extreme south and in the eastern part of the country beyond the Yenisey. This situation, however, is by no means wholly advantageous. Most lowland areas north of about latitude 50°, despite their small annual precipitation, have a large moisture surplus owing to low evaporation rates. A combination of moisture surplus, particularly severe after the melting of the winter snow cover, and gentle relief leads to major drainage problems that are exacerbated by the results of the Pleistocene glacial deposition and, in Siberia, by the presence of the permafrost layer.

Parker[5] has coined the graphic term 'anti-resources' to embrace such negative aspects of the physical environment as permafrost, aridity, bad drainage and mountainous terrain, which tend to repel human settlement and economic activity. One or more of these features is present over very large areas of the USSR (Fig 2B). Areas relatively unaffected are largely confined to the European section of the country, particularly the wooded steppe and mixed forest zones, and these have long been the most densely settled of the natural regions.

In addition to all this, we cannot ignore the direct human response to a hostile physical environment. One important facet of Soviet industrial development has been the extension of industrial activity into progressively more difficult physical environments, particularly those of Siberia. In the past a significant proportion, though by no means all, of the movement of population towards such areas was achieved by the direction of labour. Today, with the element of direction largely removed, the impetus of migration to the east has perceptibly slackened, migrants from the densely settled areas of European Russia much preferring more pleasant southerly climatic zones. Considerable difficulty is now being experienced in maintaining an adequate permanent labour force in areas of harsh climate, a factor which presents problems in the economic development of Siberia in particular.

One final feature should be mentioned in this brief assessment of the influence of the physical environment on the USSR's economic development, and this is the shortage of ice-free ports. In the past, at least, this hindered the growth of trading contacts with the outside world, and was one of several factors favouring the development of an inward-looking economy and society. This attitude was strengthened by a desire for self-sufficiency dictated, particularly during the Stalin period, by Soviet ideology and political relations with the rest of the world. Over the last two decades the situation in this respect has radically changed, and trading and other contacts between the Soviet Union and other countries are more widespread than at any time since the Revolution. Nevertheless, the effects of the winter freeze on maritime transport are still considerable, reducing, for example, the possibility of regular maritime contacts between different parts of the country, and increasing the isolation of such remote areas as the Far East and the Siberian north. Lack of maritime contacts has also affected the general location of industrial activity, in that large coastal agglomerations of industry, common in western Europe and the United States, are quite rare in the Soviet Union.

All in all, the problems of distance and remoteness, inevitable in a country the size and shape of the USSR, are greatly intensified by the dominance of hostile physical environments, which constitute an added burden in the economic development of the country.

Natural Resources

A country which covers one-sixth of the earth's land surface yet contains only about one-fourteenth of the world's population may confidently be expected to contain a large share of the planet's resources and to display a favourable balance between its resources and population. In general terms this is undoubtedly the case with the USSR. While it is not a practical proposition to attempt a precise evaluation of the Soviet Union's total resource endowment, there can be little doubt that, in volume and variety, it is superior to that of any other state in the modern world, certainly in absolute terms and probably in per capita terms as well. In comparison with the United States, for example, the USSR is superior in practically every type of resource and, in most of them, measures up to or surpasses North America as a whole rather than the United States alone. This even applies to agricultural resources, the amount of land available for agriculture being equal to that of the United States and Canada combined, though the value of much of this land is reduced by the environmental constraints already discussed. In industrial resources, where the environmental constraints are less rigid, the Soviet Union's wealth is particularly outstanding. Details of the distribution and development of individual industrial resources will be found in subsequent chapters, our attention at present being confined to the general situation.

The Soviet Union is especially favoured as regards her energy resources, which have been estimated to represent as much as a quarter of total world energy supplies. Foremost among these vast reserves is coal, which is present in quantities far in excess of those likely to be required by the Soviet economy in the foreseeable future, particularly in view of the rapidly increasing importance in the Soviet energy budget of alternative sources of power such as oil, natural gas and hydro-electricity. Writing more than a decade ago, Hodgkins[6] was able to assert that 99 per cent of all non-renewable energy resources in the USSR were in the form of coal, and this fuel was the basis of Soviet industrialisation until the mid-1950s. Over the past two decades, however, although coal production has continued to expand, increasing attention has been paid to oil and natural gas, output of which has risen extremely rapidly, and here too the USSR has proved to be extremely well endowed. Although, at any given point in time, oil and gas may represent only a very small fraction of the country's proven energy reserves, new discoveries are constantly being made and estimates revised upwards, whereas the coal reserves are more completely known and major new discoveries are much less likely. Furthermore, the Soviet Union has an enormous hydro-electric potential, only a small part of which has so far been realised.

In short, the USSR would appear to possess energy reserves in the form of coal, oil, gas and water power sufficient to supply her needs for a very long time to come. Indeed, present policy envisages a growing export of energy, in the form of oil and natural gas, as a prime source of the foreign currency needed for imports of equipment vital in the industrialisation programme. When the inevitable stage is reached that oil and gas resources in the USSR, as throughout the world, are approaching exhaustion, the Soviet Union will be among those fortunate countries still possessing very large untouched reserves of coal and water power, though the physical difficulties involved in their exploitation will be much greater than those experienced at present. Today the country has no problem of shortage in energy production. On the contrary, there is something of an *embarrass de richesses* and the possibility of choice among a wide variety of alternatives. Such problems as do arise in the field of energy production, and they are important ones, are concerned with the geographical location of energy resources and the fact that a large proportion occur in remote, inaccessible and environmentally hostile parts of the country. While more than 70 per cent of total Soviet energy is consumed in the European section of the country[7], it has been estimated that some 90 per cent of the energy resources, including 93 per cent of the coal, 80 per cent of the hydro-electric potential, 60 per cent of the natural gas, and 20 per cent of the oil, are to be found in the Asiatic regions. Recent discoveries of oil and gas are likely to increase the latter's share of proven reserves. Sixty per cent of the country's coal reserves lie in the arctic and sub-arctic zones of Siberia and these in particular constitute a vast energy reserve, at present virtually untouched and lying, quite literally, in cold storage for possible future use as and when this becomes necessary through the depletion of more accessible supplies.

Thus, although there is no general energy problem in the Soviet Union, which remains unaffected by the current world energy crisis, certain difficulties have arisen as a result of the widely differing patterns of resource location and demand. This has led to a somewhat paradoxical situation in which there has been intensive exploitation of low-grade fuels like lignite and peat in regions where resources are in short supply, while high-grade coal deposits have remained untouched in areas remote from the main industrialised zones. The power resources of the Asiatic regions, and particularly those of Siberia, present special problems if they are to support, as they may well be required to in coming decades, an increasing share of total industrial production. Their utilisation will require either the establishment of large industrial complexes in their vicinity, which implies a large-scale migration of labour towards the east, or the exploitation of the energy resources by a relatively small local population and the movement of coal, gas, oil and electricity westwards to the main consuming areas, a process involving massive investment in railways, pipelines and electricity transmission systems. While Soviet policy over most of the period since the Revolution has tended to favour the first alternative, it has found it increasingly necessary in recent years to have recourse to the latter. This problem applies particularly in the sphere of energy supply, not only because of the location of energy resources but also because of their fundamental role in the continued growth of industrial capacity. The problem is also readily apparent with regard to a variety of other industrial resources, and the great distances that separate resources from consuming areas, a function of the size of the Soviet Union and the uneven distribution of both resources and population,

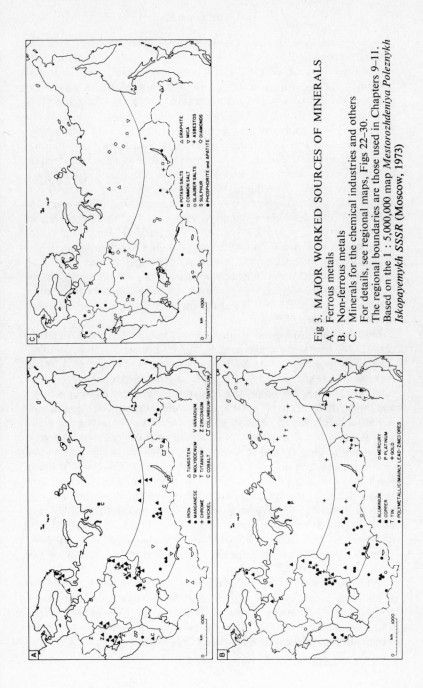

Fig 3. MAJOR WORKED SOURCES OF MINERALS

A. Ferrous metals
B. Non-ferrous metals
C. Minerals for the chemical industries and others

For details, see regional maps, Figs 22–30.
The regional boundaries are those used in Chapters 9–11.
Based on the 1 : 5,000,000 map *Mestorozhdeniya Poleznykh
Iskopayemykh SSSR* (Moscow, 1973)

A

IRON ■ MANGANESE ● CHROME + NICKEL ◆
TUNGSTEN △ MOLYBDENUM ▽ TITANIUM ◁ COBALT C
VANADIUM V ZIRCONIUM Z COLUMBIUM-TANTALUM CT

B

ALUMINIUM ▲ COPPER ■ TIN T GOLD +
MERCURY ○ PLATINUM P
POLYMETALLIC (MAINLY LEAD-ZINC) ORES ●

C

POTASH SALTS ■ COMMON SALTS □ GLAUBER SALTS ○
SULPHUR S PHOSPHORITE and APATITE ●
GRAPHITE △ MICA ▽ ASBESTOS + DIAMONDS ◇

have been a major source of difficulty in the planned development of the industrial economy.

Turning to metallic minerals (Fig 3), we find a rather different situation. The most basic of these, iron ore, is available in very large quantities and a wide variety of locations, and the Soviet Union has experienced no difficulty in supplying all her own requirements. Indeed, until recently, it proved possible to support a continuously increasing output of steel from a small number of high-grade iron ore deposits: until the 1950s the average iron content of ores consumed in Soviet furnaces was roughly double that of the ores used in most western countries. Over the past two decades, however, some of the major sources of high-grade ore have been approaching exhaustion, and increasing use has been made of newly developed sources of lower-grade ores, which are available in abundance. Despite plans to move steel production towards the resources, however, the industry has tended to remain concentrated in districts developed before 1950. The distribution of iron ore resources in relation to population would appear to be more favourable than that of energy resources, for an estimated 70 per cent of extractable reserves of industrial quality lie in the European section of the country.[8]

Data on the production of non-ferrous metal ores are difficult to obtain, this fact alone suggesting that there have been problems in this sphere. A number of these ores have had to be imported on a considerable scale until very recently, and the development of home supplies of others has involved expensive mining operations in remote and inhospitable districts. Imbalance between resources and population is particularly marked in this sector of the economy, since the main settled zone of the European USSR, apart from the Urals, has relatively few deposits of non-ferrous metal ores and there is heavy reliance on outlying areas such as Siberia, Middle Asia and the Caucasus. Despite these problems, it would appear that the Soviet Union is now self-sufficient in the great majority of the commodities required by modern industry. Any dependence on imports for these vital raw materials is considered by Soviet economic planners to be particularly undesirable, and this has stimulated the exploitation of home supplies, even of those items that might well be obtained more cheaply on the world market.

With the possible exception of a few of the rarer minerals, the USSR has adequate supplies of all the raw materials necessary for an advanced and diversified industrial economy. Whatever problems she may have to face in achieving further industrial growth, a declining resource base will not be among them in the foreseeable future.

2
Population and Transport

Population

General Background

IN A DEVELOPED country with a strong resource base and a great
potential for further economic expansion, a large and steadily growing
population is a major asset, providing that economic growth can be
maintained at a higher rate than population increase, and the structure
and distribution of population match the nature and location of
economic activities. At the most recent census, held on 15 January
1970, the population of the USSR numbered 241,720,000, and in 1974
passed the 250 million mark, a total exceeded only by China (760
million) and India (550 million). The Soviet population exceeded that of
the United States by about 18 per cent, a fact of considerable
importance when comparing the two countries, and was more than four
times that of the United Kingdom (56 million).

During the present century the population of the territory that now
constitutes the Soviet Union has roughly doubled, but this general
impression of fairly vigorous growth conceals a good deal of variation
in the rate of increase over the past 75 years (Table 1). Since
international migration has had a minimal effect on Soviet population
growth, these variations have resulted almost entirely from fluctuations
in the rate of natural increase (Table 2). In the years preceding World
War 1 the population of the Russian Empire was growing steadily at an
annual rate of about 1·7 per cent, and increased by more than a quarter
between 1897 and 1913. Fertility was still high by west European
standards, but a good deal of this was offset by high mortality. Between
1913 and 1926, however, the numerical increase amounted to only 5·8
million as against nearly 35 million in the preceding 16 years, a

Table 1

POPULATION GROWTH, 1897-1972

| | Population (millions) | | | Change (per cent) | | |
	Total	Urban	Rural	Total	Urban	Rural
1897	124. 6	18. 4	106. 2	—	—	—
1913	159. 2	28. 5	130. 7	+27. 8	+54. 9	+23. 1
1926	165. 0	33. 0	132. 0	+3. 6	+15. 8	+1. 0
1940	194. 1	63. 1	131. 0	+17. 6	+91. 2	−0. 8
1950	178. 5	69. 4	109. 1	−8. 0	+10. 0	−16. 7
1955	194. 4	86. 3	108. 1	+8. 9	+24. 4	−0. 9
1960	212. 4	103. 6	108. 8	+9. 3	+20. 0	+0. 6
1965	229. 6	120. 7	108. 9	+8. 1	+16. 5	+0. 1
1970	241. 7	136. 0	105. 7	+5. 3	+5. 7	−2. 9
mid-1972	247. 5	143. 8	103. 7	+2. 4	+5. 7	−1. 9

Source: *Narodnoye Khozyaystvo SSSR,* various years

dramatic decline attributable to the disastrous demographic effects of World War I, the Revolution and the ensuing Civil War, during which mortality was extremely high and fertility dropped below pre-war levels. A 'population deficit' of 28 millions has been attributed to this period, comprising 16 million additional deaths, a shortfall of 10 million births and a migration loss of 2 million. By 1926 the birth rate was again very high, mortality had fallen well below the pre-war level and rapid growth was taking place. During the inter-war years there were considerable fluctuations in the rate of natural increase but the trend was downwards, the result mainly of declining birth rates. This decline, however, was a good deal slower than that which occurred in western Europe, and in 1940 the Soviet population was still expanding at roughly twice the west European rate.

World War II was an even greater setback to population growth in the USSR than the events of 1914-21. Even in 1950 the population was still some 15 million below the 1940 level, and the deficit attributed to 1940-45 exceeds 40 million: 10 million deaths in the armed forces, a similar number of additional civilian deaths and a birth deficit in excess of 20 million.

Population growth during the late 1940s and the 1950s was again quite rapid. The birth rate continued its slow decline and there was a very marked reduction in the death rate, which fell to half the pre-war level, partly because of the youthful age structure of the post-war population. Thus the rate of natural increase, at 1·7 per cent, remained well above that of the 1930s until about 1960. During the 1960s a further major change took place. While mortality remained fairly stable,

Table 2

VITAL RATES (PER 1000) 1913-71

	Birth rate	Death rate	Natural increase
1913	47. 0	30. 2	16. 8
1926	44. 0	20. 3	23. 7
1940	31. 2	18. 0	13. 2
1950	26. 7	9. 7	17. 0
1955	25. 7	8. 2	17. 5
1960	24. 9	7. 1	17. 8
1965	18. 4	7. 3	11. 1
1970	17. 4	8. 2	9. 2
1971	17. 8	8. 2	9. 6

Source: *Narodnove Khozyaystvo SSSR,* various years

save for a slight increase due to the ageing of the population, the decline in fertility accelerated and the birth rate fell to much the same level as that of western Europe. As a result, the rate of natural increase is now less than 1 per cent and is kept at this level only by the exceptionally low death rate. In the early 1970s there was a slight recovery, the birth rate rising from a trough of 17·0 in 1969 to 17·8 in 1971 and the natural increase rate from 0·89 per cent to 0·96 per cent, but is is doubtful if a growth rate much above 1 per cent per annum will be achieved in the foreseeable future. As a result of these trends, there has been a marked reduction in the annual growth of the Soviet population, which reached a peak of 3·9 million in 1960, but fell to only 2·2 million in 1969 and 1970. The economic implications are considerable in that, from 1975 onwards, when those born after 1960 start to reach working age, the annual addition to the labour force will inevitably become smaller.

Another feature of note in this general review of twentieth-century population trends is urbanisation. At the beginning of the century Russia was still a predominantly agricultural country. In 1897 only 15 per cent of the population was classed as urban, and by 1940 the proportion had risen only to 33 per cent. The 50 per cent urban level was reached in 1961, and even today the figure is only 58 per cent. In numerical terms the urban population has increased more than fivefold since 1913. The rural element remained fairly stable at about 130 million during the inter-war years, but between 1940 and 1950 it fell sharply, partly as a result of war losses and partly because of changes in the definitions of urban and rural population. From 1950 to 1960 there was little change in its size, but there has since been a slow decline. Nevertheless, the great number of rural inhabitants, still in excess of

Table 3

POPULATION DATA FOR REGIONS AND SUB-REGIONS, 1970

	Area+ 000 sq km	Per cent	Population 000	Per cent	Density per sq km	Urban per cent	Growth 1959-1970 (per cent)
Centre*	485.1	2.2	27,653	11.4	57.0	71.3	7.5
Volga-Vyatka*	263.3	1.2	8,348	3.5	31.7	52.9	1.2
Black Earth Centre*	167.7	0.8	7,997	3.3	47.7	40.2	2.9
CENTRE	916.1	4.1	43,998	18.2	48.0	62.1	5.4
Donets-Dnepr*	220.9	1.0	20,059	8.3	90.8	67.6	12.9
South-west*	269.5	1.2	20,694	8.6	76.8	41.1	8.8
South*	113.3	0.5	6,383	2.6	56.3	57.1	26.1
Moldavia	33.7	0.2	3,572	1.5	106.0	31.7	23.8
Rostov obl	100.8	0.5	3,832	1.6	38.0	63.0	15.7
SOUTH	738.2	3.3	54,540	22.6	73.9	53.6	13.5
W. Kazakhstan[1]	729.6	3.3	1,562	0.7	2.1	47.1	46.0
Volga*	680.0	3.1	18,377	7.6	27.0	57.0	15.0
Ural*	680.4	3.1	15,184	6.3	22.3	68.7	7.1
VOLGA-URAL	2,090.0	9.4	35,123	14.5	16.8	61.7	12.5
N. Kazakhstan[2]	1,276.6	5.7	6,820	2.8	5.3	53.0	35.7
W. Siberia (S)[3]	923.3	4.2	11,392	4.7	12.3	62.2	5.8
E. Siberia (S)[3]	1,901.9	8.6	6,859	2.8	3.6	62.6	13.5
N. KAZ-S. SIB	4,101.8	18.5	25,071	10.4	6.1	59.6	14.8
FAR EAST (S)	1,233.2	5.6	4,277	1.8	3.5	74.2	15.9

Belorussia*	207.6	0.9	3.7	9,003	43.4	43.4	11.8
Baltic*	189.1	0.9	3.1	7,583	40.1	58.9	14.7
North-west (pt)[4]	196.5	0.9	2.9	6,984	35.5	80.0	13.4
BALTIC	593.2	2.7	9.7	23,570	39.7	59.2	13.2
North-west (pt)[5]	1,426.3	6.4	2.2	5,276	3.7	63.0	14.5
W. Siberia (N)[6]	1,503.9	6.7	0.3	718	0.5	47.3	47.4
E. Siberia (N)[6]	2,220.9	10.0	0.3	605	0.3	52.4	41.0
Far East (N)[6]	4,982.7	22.4	0.6	1,503	0.3	63.7	31.4
NORTHLANDS	10,133.8	45.5	3.4	8,102	0.8	60.9	21.5
S. Kazakhstan[7]	708.9	3.2	1.8	4,468	6.3	48.1	39.1
Middle Asia*	1,279.3	5.8	8.3	19,954	15.6	38.0	44.3
MIDDLE ASIA	1,988.2	8.9	10.1	24,422	12.3	39.8	43.4
N. Caucasus (pt)[8]	254.3	1.1	4.3	10,453	39.5	46.7	26.1
Transcaucasus*	186.1	0.8	5.1	12,292	66.1	51.1	29.3
CAUCASIA	440.4	2.0	9.4	22,745	51.6	48.2	27.8
U.S.S.R.	22,234.9	100.0	100.0	241,720	10.9	56.3	15.8

+ excluding water bodies. * official Major Economic Regions
1 Aktyubinsk, Guryev and Uralsk oblasts
2 East Kazakh, Karaganda, Kokchetav, Kustanay, North Kazakh, Pavlodar, Semipalatinsk, Tselinograd and Turgay oblasts
3 South of latitude 58°N
4 Leningrad, Novgorod and Pskov oblasts
5 Arkhangelsk, Murmansk and Vologda oblasts, Karelian and Komi ASSRs
6 North of latitude 58°N
7 Alma-Ata, Chimkent, Dzhambul, Kyzyl Orda and Taldy-Kurgan oblasts
8 Excluding Rostov oblast

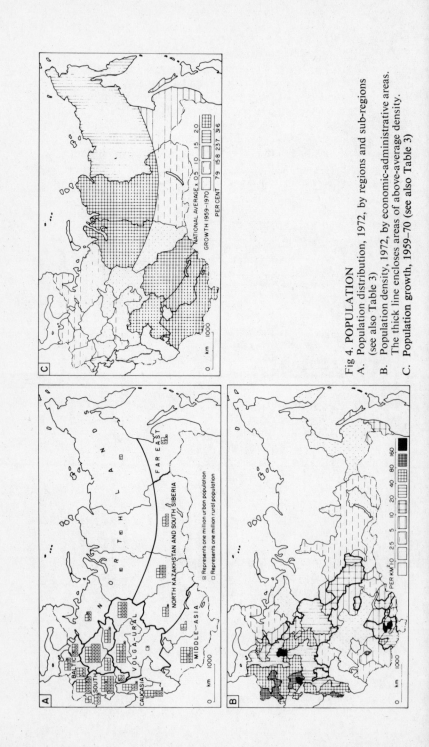

Fig 4. POPULATION
A. Population distribution, 1972, by regions and sub-regions
(see also Table 3)
B. Population density, 1972, by economic-administrative areas.
The thick line encloses areas of above-average density.
C. Population growth, 1959–70 (see also Table 3)

100 million, is an outstanding characteristic of the country's population geography.

The present century has also witnessed a significant redistribution of the population among the various regions – most strikingly in the growth of the Asiatic sector, which contained less than 20 per cent of the total in 1913 but nearly 30 per cent in 1970. Over most of the period this change has been due mainly to migration, but in recent years, while migration has continued, its nature and significance have changed. At the same time regional differences in fertility have become more marked and are now a major factor in regional contrasts in the rate of population growth. With these general features in mind, we can now proceed to a more detailed examination of the present distribution of the Soviet population and the most significant recent trends as exemplified by the inter-censal period 1959-70.

Distribution and Density

The Soviet Union as a whole is a thinly settled country, with a density in 1972 of only 11·1 persons per sq km. This may be compared with densities of 30 per sq km in the United States, 80 in China, 170 in Japan and 227 in the United Kingdom. Furthermore, the Soviet population is very unevenly distributed; vast areas are virtually uninhabited and contrast vividly with the relatively limited areas of densely settled territory. The general situation is depicted in Fig 4A, which shows the distribution of population among the various regions and sub-regions used in later chapters of this book (see also Table 3). Of the 242 million people living in the USSR in 1970, about 70 per cent were to be found in the European sector, which constitutes slightly less than a quarter of the national territory. This relatively densely settled section is continued southwards into the Transcaucasian republics, whose population of 12·3 million represents another 5 per cent living in less than 1 per cent of the area. The Middle Asian and North Kazakhstan/South Siberia regions, although they include large stretches of empty desert land, are the homes of some 50 million people. All these regions, and particularly the European USSR, form a striking contrast to the Siberian northlands, where less than 3 million people occupy 8·7 million sq km, an area whose size approaches that of the United States (9·4 million sq km) but whose population is close to that of New Zealand or Wales.

Fig 4B shows variations in population density at the level of the smallest administrative devisions for which appropriate data are available (see Chapter 8). A heavy line encloses those divisions in which the density is greater than the national average, and it is immediately apparent that these cover only about a quarter of the national territory. The largest such area, forming the main settled zone of the USSR and containing the great bulk of the Soviet population, stretches from the western frontier eastwards beyond the Urals to terminate in the Kuzbass district of western Siberia. This zone is broadest in the west, where it extends from Leningrad to the Transcaucasus; in the east it is confined to a relatively narrow belt between the northern Tayga and the central Asian desert. Within this main settled zone there are considerable variations. The highest densities are recorded in the heavily urbanised and industrialised oblasts such as Moscow, Leningrad and those of the eastern Ukraine, but high figures are also recorded in the most favourable agricultural areas, like Moldavia and the western Ukraine, where the population is predominantly rural. Outside this main settled zone, districts with above average densities include the Karaganda oblast of central Kazakhstan and the hill-foot zone of Middle Asia, between the southern mountains and the desert. In the latter, whose size is somewhat exaggerated owing to the arrangement of administrative boundaries, intensive irrigated agriculture supports large concentrations of rural population. At the other extreme are the very low densities of the Turanian desert, Siberia and the Far East. In Siberia and the Far East the size of the administrative units masks local variations in population density: in these regions, small concentrations strung out along the Trans-Siberian railway would, on a more detailed map, stand out as islands of settled land in a vast expanse of near-empty territory.

As has already been indicated, the distribution of population is closely associated with the type of physical environment. The Soviet ecumene is essentially confined to the mixed and deciduous forest, wooded steppe and steppe zones (Fig 2A), whereas settlement in the tundra, tayga and desert is only sporadic. Within the ecumene, however, population distribution, and particularly the contrast between the European and Asiatic sections of the country, owes much to historical and economic factors. The early Russian state, precursor of the Russian Empire and the Soviet Union, was established in the European mixed forest zone, whence it spread eastwards across Siberia to the Pacific and southwards across the steppe and desert to Caucasia and Middle Asia. Settlement, agriculture and industry have followed a similar pattern of diffusion from a European core, so that the outlying territories are less densely populated and less developed economically for historical as well as for environmental reasons. The urge to develop the eastern territories has been a recurrent theme, not least during the Soviet period, and a transfer of population from the European to the Asiatic part of the country has long been in progress. The effect of this movement during the present century can be seen in the data displayed in Table 4 although, owing to the problem of internal and international

Table 4

POPULATION CHANGE BY MAJOR GEOGRAPHICAL DIVISIONS, 1897-1970

(a) Population (millions)	1897	1913	1926	1940	1959	1970
European USSR	102.5	131.6	132.3	152.9	153.7	171.2
Siberia and Far East	7.2	10.0	12.5	16.6	22.6	25.4
Kazakhstan and Middle Asia	10.0	11.6	13.7	16.6	23.0	32.8
Transcaucasia	4.9	6.0	6.6	8.0	9.5	12.3
Total	124.6	159.2	165.0	194.1	208.8	241.7
(b) Population growth (per cent)						
European USSR	—	28.4	0.5	15.6	0.6	11.4
Siberia and Far East	—	38.9	25.0	32.8	36.1	12.4
Kazakhstan and Middle Asia	—	16.0	18.1	21.2	28.6	42.6
Transcaucasia	—	22.4	10.0	21.2	18.8	29.3
Total	—	27.8	3.6	17.6	7.6	15.8
(c) Share of total (per cent)						
European USSR	82.2	82.7	80.2	78.8	73.7	70.9
Siberia and Far East	5.8	6.3	7.6	8.6	10.8	10.5
Kazakhstan and Middle Asia	8.0	7.3	8.3	8.6	11.0	13.6
Transcaucasia	3.9	3.8	4.0	4.1	4.5	5.1

boundary change, the figures given can only be approximate. Since 1897, while the population of the country as a whole has nearly doubled, that of the European sector has risen by about 70 per cent while that of the Asiatic regions combined has increased more than threefold. Before 1959 the most rapid growth occurred in Siberia and the Far East, which, during a period when natural increase was fairly uniform throughout the country, benefited the most from net migration gain. Over the past decade, however, there has been a marked change, as will be apparent from an analysis of trends during the intercensal period 1959-70.

Recent trends

Regional variations in the rate of population growth between 1959 and 1970 are given in Table 3 and mapped in Figure 4c. Between the two censuses the Soviet population increased by 32.9 million or 15.8 per cent. The urban population rose by 36 million (36 per cent), while rural numbers declined by 3·1 million (2·8 per cent). Although the growth achieved between 1959 and 1970 was much greater than that of the preceding inter-censal period of 1939-59, which included the war years, it slowed down considerably during the 1960s, mainly because of declining fertility. The decline was not, however, uniform throughout the country. In particular there were marked differences between the various ethnic groups, reflected in strong regional contrasts in the rate of natural increase. The biggest contrasts were those between the peoples of European origin, including the Russians and other related groups, among whom fertility fell to levels similar to those of western Europe, and the non-Slav peoples of Middle Asia and the Caucasus, among whom very high birth rates were maintained. In the Russian republic, for example, the birth rate in 1970 was only 14·6 per 1000, while the death rate, at 8·7, was slightly above the Soviet average, giving a natural increase rate of only 5·9 per 1000. At the other extreme, the Turkmen republic recorded a birth rate of 35·2, a death rate of 6·6 and thus a natural increase rate of 28·6, nearly five times that of the RSFSR (Russian Socialist Federated Soviet Republic). Such regional differences in fertility would now appear to be the dominant factor underlying regional variations in the rate of population growth.

Although migration continues to play an important role, its nature and direction have changed. Movement from the old settled areas of Europe to the Asiatic regions continues, but Siberia benefits little, if at all, and the most important inter-regional migration flows are towards Kazakhstan and the Middle Asian republics. Thus the two components of population change – migration and natural increase – tend to supplement each other: areas experiencing large-scale migration losses are also areas of slow natural increase, while regions with a high natural increase also have high rates of net migration gain. As a consequence, regional variations in the rate of population growth have, during the past decade, been very great indeed, ranging from as little as 1.2 per cent in the Volga-Vyatka region to as much as 44·3 per cent in the Middle Asian republics.

As Fig 4c shows, the zone where growth is particularly slow (less than half the national average) now includes not only the European centre but also the Urals and western Siberia, regions which in earlier periods were characterised by rapid population increase. In addition, growth rates below the national average were recorded in the remaining European regions, with the exception of Moldavia, the southern Ukraine and the North Caucasus, and in eastern Siberia, while the Far East showed growth only slightly above average. In contrast, Middle Asia and Kazakhstan experienced growth at a rate more than double that of the USSR as a whole; and there was rapid growth in the Transcaucasus and the Asiatic northlands, though in the latter the absolute numbers, of course, were small. A more detailed examination, based on smaller territorial units, would obviously reveal a good deal of diversity within each of these major divisions. Nevertheless, the most

Table 5

VOLUME OF FREIGHT MOVEMENT, 1913-70
Thousand million ton-km
(Figures in brackets are percentages of total freight movement)

	1913		1940		1950		1960		1970	
Railway	76.4	(60.6)	415.0	(85.1)	602.3	(84.4)	1504.3	(78.8)	2494.7	(65.1)
Road	0.1	(0.1)	8.9	(1.8)	20.1	(2.8)	98.5	(5.2)	220.8	(5.8)
Inland waterway	28.9	(22.9)	36.1	(7.4)	46.2	(6.5)	99.6	(5.3)	174.0	(4.5)
Sea	20.3	(16.1)	23.8	(4.9)	39.7	(5.6)	131.5	(7.0)	656.1	(17.1)
Air	—			(n)	0.1	(n)	0.6	(n)	1.9	(n)
Pipeline	0.3	(0.2)	3.8	(0.8)	4.9	(0.7)	51.2	(2.7)	281.7	(7.4)
Total	126.0	(100.0)	487.6	(100.0)	713.3	(100.0)	1885.7	(100.0)	3829.2	(100.0)

Source: *Narodnoye Khozyaystvo SSSR 1922-72, 293*

Table 6

VOLUME OF PASSENGER MOVEMENT, 1913-70
Thousand million passenger-km
(Figures in brackets are percentages of total passenger traffic)

	1913		1940		1950		1960		1970	
Railway	30.3	(92.7)	98.0	(92.2)	88.0	(89.5)	170.8	(68.5)	265.4	(48.4)
Road	—		3.4	(3.2)	5.2	(5.3)	61.0	(24.4)	198.3	(36.1)
Inland waterway	1.4	(4.3)	3.8	(3.6)	2.7	(2.7)	4.3	(1.7)	5.4	(1.0)
Sea	1.0	(3.0)	0.9	(0.8)	1.2	(1.2)	1.3	(0.5)	1.6	(0.3)
Air	—		0.2	(0.2)	1.2	(1.2)	12.1	(4.8)	78.2	(14.2)
Total	32.7	(100.0)	106.3	(100.0)	98.3	(100.0)	249.5	(100.0)	548.9	(100.0)

Source: *Narodnoye Khozyaystvo SSSR, various years*

striking feature of current population trends is the dichotomy between, on the one hand, Europe and Siberia, where general growth is slow, urban growth is below average and rural numbers are declining, and, on the other hand, Middle Asia, Kazakhstan and the Transcaucasus, where rapid growth of both rural and urban elements continues.

Some of these recent developments raise serious problems for the planned growth of the Soviet economy. The slow-down in the rate of population growth will inevitably lead to a less rapid growth or even a decline in the size of the labour force, while the distribution of population growth among the regions is at variance with their potential for economic development. Middle Asia, for example, which has the most rapid population increase, already has a surplus of labour, especially in rural areas, and a somewhat limited industrial resource base. Siberia, on the other hand, has vast untapped resources, but slow population growth makes it more difficult to exploit them.

Transport

In a country the size of the Soviet Union, where great distances separate industrial resources from manufacturing centres and manufacturing centres from markets, transport costs, both capital and recurrent, assume an infinitely greater scale and significance than they do in smaller economic entities. This is particularly so where heavy industry constitutes a very large part of the total industrial economy and requires the movement of enormous quantities of bulky materials over long distances. In such a situation it is not surprising that the development of the Soviet economy has involved a huge increase in the volume of freight movement, which has multiplied more than thirty-fold since the Revolution. The transport sector employs some 8 million workers, approximately 10 per cent of all non-agricultural employment, and has received about 10 per cent of all capital investment in the Soviet period. According to Lydolph,[1] 'the transport system regularly consumes about one fourth the fuel and steel production of the country'. Transport costs have been a major preoccupation of Soviet economic planners, and their desire to minimise such costs has had a considerable effect on patterns of economic development.

While the layout of the Soviet transportation network is to some extent influenced by environmental factors, it is for the most part a product of the patterns of population distribution already described and of the industrial developments that form the main theme of this book. Such adverse physical factors as poorly drained land, unconsolidated and easily eroded surface deposits, broad river crossings and permafrost all add to construction costs and may have a local effect on the alignment of routes, while floods, frost, snow and aridity may hinder operations.[2] Nevertheless, the layout of routes is determined primarily by economic necessity, and physical difficulties are overcome by the transport engineer where the volume of traffic, actual or potential, warrants the expenditure involved. Because of the heavy demands for capital in extractive and manufacturing industry, funds available for investment in transport have always been limited. As a result, 'added transport capacity has been made available only to the minimum necessary extent. This policy stands in marked contrast to American and Russian policy prior to the First World War, when thousands of miles were laid down with the hope that they would stimulate industrial and agricultural growth. In the nineteenth century, transport was considered a prime mover: in Soviet practice it has always been a handmaiden of industrial growth'.[3] This has meant among other things that, with the possible exception of a few areas of European Russia developed during the nineteenth century, wasteful competition between alternative routes has largely been avoided. Similarly, during the Soviet period, there has been little or no competition for traffic among the various transport media.

Rail Transport

Railways, throughout the present century, have remained over-whelmingly predominant in the transport system of the USSR, particularly for the movement of freight. As Table 5 shows, railways were still responsible in 1970 for nearly two-thirds of all freight movement and nearly half the passenger traffic (Table 6). Even these high figures represent a marked decline in the relative, though not in the absolute, position of the railways over the last decade, for in 1960 they were responsible for nearly 80 per cent of the freight and 70 per cent of the passenger movement. These changes reflect the growing importance of road transport and, in the case of passengers, the airlines. Nevertheless, though the railways' share of traffic has declined, the volume of movement by rail has continued to increase rapidly: between 1960 and 1970, rail-freight movement on a ton-kilometre basis rose by no less than 65 per cent. In any case, the great bulk of movement by road is still over very short distances. While the average length of rail-freight hauls has steadily increased and in 1970 stood at 861 km, road freight consignments moved on average less than 20km. In addition, there can be little doubt that freight traffic provides the great bulk of the railways' income, there being more than 9 ton-km of freight movement for every kilometre of passenger travel. All this is in striking contrast to the situation in North America and most of western Europe, where, in the absence of national transport policies, the movement of

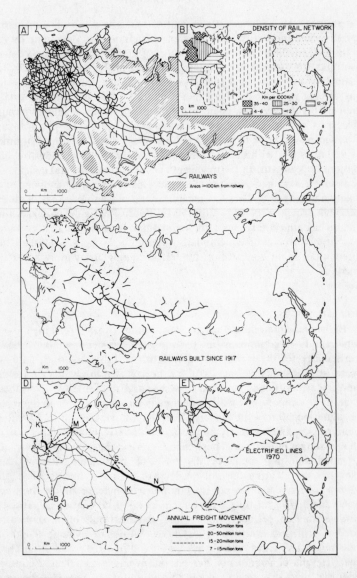

Fig 5. RAILWAYS

SOURCES: A, B and C based on *Atlas Razvitiya Khozyaystva i Kultury SSSR*
(Moscow, 1967), 82–3

D. Data from I. V. Nikolskiy, *Geografiya Transporta SSSR* (Moscow, 1960)

E. N. P. Nikitin, E. D. Prozorov, B. A. Tutykhin (eds), *Ekonomicheskaya
Geografiya SSSR* (Moscow, 1973), 314–15

goods and passengers by road has presented a serious challenge to the very existence of the railways.

Despite the predominant role played by the railways, the Soviet network is a relatively open one, with 1 km of track for every 165 sq km and 1800 people (cf United States: $27 \cdot 6$ sq km and 600 people). Although Soviet railways carry nearly twice as much traffic as those of the United States, their route length, at 135,400 km, is only 40 per cent of the United States'. Consequently, the Soviet system carries the heaviest freight loads of any in the world, with an annual average movement of $18 \cdot 5$ million ton-km for every kilometre of track. A few major bulk commodities make up a large proportion of the total traffic. On a ton-kilometre basis the main items are coal and coke (18 per cent), petroleum products (14 per cent), ores and metals (14 per cent), timber (12 per cent), mineral building materials (12 per cent), grain (5 per cent) and mineral fertilisers (3 per cent).

A number of characteristics of the railway network are illustrated in Fig 5. The first and most obvious feature is the general relation between population distribution and railway provision, the great bulk of the network lying within the main settled zone identified earlier in this chapter. The density of the network bears a clear relation to population density, and there is a marked contrast between the areas to west and east of the Volga river. West of this divide the network is relatively close, though much less so than in western Europe. Radial routes centred on Moscow and the high density of lines in the Ukraine are striking features. East of the Volga, the Urals, western Siberia and northern Kazakhstan now have fairly complete networks, though these are much more open than in the western regions. Elsewhere the system comprises a series of trunk routes with numerous short branch lines.

Much of the present network, particularly in the west, was constructed during the last 50 years of the Tsarist period, the Soviet Union inheriting some 70,000 km of railway. About 80 per cent of this was in the European section of the country, but it also included the Trans-Caspian and Trans-Aral routes to Middle Asia and the Trans-Siberian to Vladivostok. During the Soviet period the route length has almost doubled, reaching 135,400 km in 1971, and continues to grow at the rate of several hundred kilometres annually. Fig 5c shows all the railways built since 1917. From this it will be observed that, in the lands to the west of the Volga, construction has been on a relatively small scale, consisting chiefly of short cuts designed to reduce the length of many of the more devious routes between the cities of the European plain. The great bulk of Soviet railway building has taken place in the middle zone between the Volga and Lake Baykal, providing better connections within and between the Volga, Ural, West Siberian,

Kazakh and Middle Asian regions, and reflecting the great importance
of the economic developments that have occurred in this section of the
country over the past 50 years.

Very little construction has been undertaken in the thinly settled
northern regions, a major exception being the line to Vorkuta, built to
open up the Pechara coalfield in the 1940's, and, until recently, there
was little building to the east of Lake Baykal. In the latter region
however a major new development was announced in 1974.[4] This is the
Baykal-Amur railway, a line some 3,150 km long, designed to link the
existing Tayshet-Ust Kut and Komsomolsk-Sovetskaya Gavan sections.
Such a project was first mooted in the 1930's, but the relatively low
level of investment in the Far East delayed its realisation. The new line
will run parallel to and several hundred kilometres north of the
Trans-Siberian, thus strengthening the links between the Far East and
the rest of the country and permitting the exploitation of a variety of
industrial resources along its length. By early 1975, several hundred
kilometres had been built.

An immense volume of freight traffic, coupled with a rather limited
route length, give the extremely heavy loadings referred to above. Even
so, there are major contrasts in the volume of freight carried over
different parts of the system, and Mellor has estimated that 86 per cent
of all freight is carried on 46 per cent of the route length, the most
heavily used quarter of the system carrying nearly two-thirds of the
traffic.[5] Thus certain sections have loadings several times the high
average figure (Fig 5D). The most heavily laden sections of all,
carrying well over 50 million tons of freight annually, are those
associated with the major heavy industrial 'combines' of the Urals-
Kuzbass and Donbass-Dnepr Bend. Very high densities of 25-50
million tons occur on lines linking Moscow with the Donbass and Urals,
on the Karaganda-Magnitogorsk link and on the section of the
Trans-Siberian from Novosibirsk to Irkutsk. Lines with near-average
loadings (15-20 million tons) join Leningrad, the western Ukraine and
Baku with the areas already mentioned.

The heavy and constantly rising pressure on these major routes led to
large-scale investment during the 1960s in improvements to the system.
Steam traction has been almost entirely replaced by diesel and electric,
and there have been major advances in signalling and other operational
techniques. About a quarter of the route length is now electrified,
compared with a mere five per cent in the 1950s. Electrified lines are
shown in Fig 5E, and it will be seen that these correspond very closely
with the most heavily used routes identified in Fig 5D.

Throughout the Soviet period, great emphasis has been laid upon the
need to plan industrial development in such a way as to minimise the

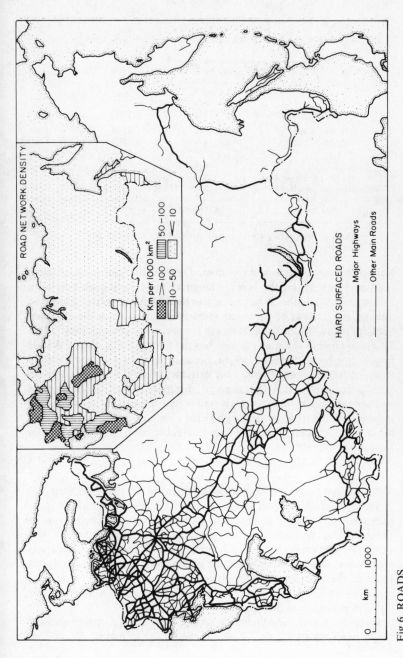

Fig 6. ROADS
SOURCE: *Atlas Razvitiya Khozyaystva i Kultury SSSR* (Moscow, 1967), 86–7

Table 7

AVERAGE LENGTH OF RAIL-FREIGHT HAULS (KM) 1940-70

	1940	1950	1960	1970
Coal	694	659	681	692
Coke	839	916	617	707
Petroleum products	1234	1205	1360	1169
Iron and steel	1039	1213	1163	1357
Timber	750	842	1387	1647
Grain	734	795	1152	1050
Ores	612	574	552	690
Mineral building materials	253	296	364	434
Mineral fertilisers	1496	1307	1207	1000
All freight	700	722	798	861

Source: *Narodnoye Khozyaystvo SSSR v 1970 godu*, 432

load placed on the transport system. Despite this, rail loadings have risen very rapidly and the average length of rail-freight hauls continues to increase. While the former is an inevitable consequence of economic growth, the latter is of particular interest as a measure of the distances between areas of supply and demand for particular commodities (Table 7). At one end of the scale, timber has the longest hauls, nearly double the average for all types of freight, because lumbering is almost wholly confined to the tayga. At the other extreme, mineral building materials are carried only half the average distance, a reflection of their widespread availability and high bulk/value ratio. Changes with time indicated in the table include significant increases in the length of haul for timber and grain, a result of increased reliance on the eastern regions for these commodities.

Road Transport

As we have already seen, the significance of road transport has increased considerably in recent years and it now accounts for more than one-third of all passenger movement but less than 6 per cent of freight traffic. In both cases the vast majority of movements are over very short distances. Long-distance transport of goods by road on any significant scale occurs only where rail transport is not available, so that some of the most important highways are in very remote areas – for example, the Aldan Highway, which runs for about 1000 km from Yakutsk to the Trans-Siberian railway at Never.

Over the past decade there has been a good deal of improvement to major inter-city road links, at least in the European part of the country.

Even so, in 1970 the Soviet Union still had only 511,000km of hard-surfaced road, compared with about 6 million km in the United States. The densest road networks in the western part of the country rarely exceed 100km for every 1000 sq km of territory, and throughout practically the whole of Siberia, the Far East and Kazakhstan, the average is below 10 km (Fig 6).

The sparseness of the road network and the relatively minor role played by road transport are of course the result of Soviet policies, which have persistently favoured the railways as the chief medium for freight transport, a natural choice in view of the basic requirement for bulk movement over long distances. A big increase in the use of road transport may be predicted for the 1970s. Production of motor vehicles has increased rapidly in recent years and private car ownership is rising. Long-distance movement of freight by road, however, is most unlikely to approach American levels in the foreseeable future.

Inland Waterways

Despite the obvious difficulties presented by the winter freeze, inland waterways have traditionally played an important role in the transport system. Before the Revolution they were responsible for one-fifth of all freight movement, and although by 1970 the proportion had fallen below 5 per cent, the volume carried had increased fivefold. There has been large-scale investment in river improvement and canal building during the Soviet period, mostly on the Volga and associated waterway systems in the European plain, which together carry about two-thirds of all water-borne freight. Timber and building materials are by far the most important items carried, followed, particularly in the case of the Volga system, by petroleum products and foodstuffs.

3
Industrial Development

DESPITE THE SEVERAL valid criticisms that may be levelled at such a procedure, there is considerable merit in a simple division of the history of modern economic development in the USSR into three phases, which for convenience we can label 'pre-revolutionary', 'inter-war' and 'post-war', separated by the traumatic upheavals of World War I, the Revolution and Civil War, and World War II. Assigning dates to these phases, however, is a separate issue and major turning points in the process of economic development do not precisely coincide with those historical events.

In 1917, without doubt, there were fundamental changes, but a decade of confusion in the economic as well as in the political sphere followed the Bolshevik Revolution, and the planned development of the Soviet economy, with its apparently orderly progression of Five Year Plans, did not begin until 1928. Ten years later, the approach of World War II was already distorting economic plans, and recovery from that conflict was not achieved until at least 1948, giving another decade during which economic growth was distorted by external forces. The late 1940s and early 1950s constitute a phase in which development continued along lines very similar to those of the inter-war period, a fact which may be attributed in large measure to the continuing dominance of 'Stalinism' in all aspects of Soviet life. In the latter half of the 1950s, with the beginning of what may well be termed the 'post-Stalin' period, major changes occurred both in the organisation of the Soviet economy and in the nature of the country's economic development. In emphasising change, however, one should not lose sight of the element of continuity or inertia, particularly as regards the location of economic activities. Patterns established in the pre-revolutionary period had a considerable effect on the location of industrial capacity during the inter-war years, and developments during the latter period have influenced the patterns of the post-war era. Thus the location of economic activities in the Soviet Union of the 1970s can only be understood in the light of a sequence of developments extending back for at least 100 years. In Hooson's well chosen words, 'the nation-state of Russia, to which the Soviet Union has become heir, is both old and new – a Europe and a North America rolled into one'[1], with many of the problems and possibilities of both those continents.

The Pre-revolutionary Period

Although the general level of industrial production on the eve of World War I was low, and although in many fields industrialisation began almost from scratch after the Revolution, it would be wrong in any assessment of the Soviet achievement to ignore the progress made in the Tsarist period, particularly during its closing half century. In the 50 years before 1913 important industrial developments took place within the Russian Empire, and these had a considerable influence on the nature and distribution of Soviet economic development in the inter-war period.

An initial phase of industrialisation can be said to have occurred as early as the first quarter of the eighteenth century, during the reign of Peter the Great (1696-1725). With the aid of imported technicians, chiefly from central Europe, numerous ironworks were established, most of them in the Ural and Moscow-Tula regions, and Russia became the world's leading producer of iron, with an annual output of some 150,000 tons. Copper was mined and smelted on a considerable scale, also mainly in the Urals, and metal-working centres were established in and around St Petersburg, Moscow and Nizhniy Novgorod. Extensive linen and woollen textile manufactures were set up, chiefly in the zone between the upper Volga and Oka rivers, and there were several other important developments, notably in the production of glass, paper and leather goods. There was further expansion in all these fields during the remainder of the eighteenth century but, by the early part of the nineteenth, the rate of industrial growth and technological progress had fallen far behind those of contemporary western Europe and North America. Not until about 1860 can the nineteenth-century industrial revolution be said to have reached the Russian Empire, but between that date and 1913 progress was rapid: there are conflicting estimates as to the rate of industrial expansion during this period but it would appear that production increased tenfold and was rising by at least 5 per cent per annum during the last 25 years of the Empire.[2]

The achievements of this period can be measured by the performance of a number of major industries. The output of coal, for example, rose

from 300,000 tons in 1861 to 29 million tons in 1913 and that of pig
iron from 484,000 tons to 4·5 million, and steel production reached 4·6
million tons. The output of oil, which in 1861 was a mere 30,000 tons,
stood at 9 million tons in 1913, and indeed for a few years around the
turn of the century Russia was the world's leading producer. In the light
industrial sector a large-scale factory-based textile industry, processing
middle Asian and imported cotton as well as the traditional local flax
and wool, became firmly established in the European centre, and in
1913 it accounted for one-third of all Russian industrial production by
value.

The same period also saw the construction of the basic elements of
the railway network. Although the first short line, from St Petersburg to
Pushkin, was built by 1837, the first trunk route (St Petersburg-
Moscow) was not in operation until 1851 and the second (Moscow-
Warsaw) until 1861. Thereafter, growth of the system was rapid and by
1913 Russia had 70,000km of railway. Eighty per cent of this was in the
European part of the country, but long-distance trunk routes to Siberia,
the Far East, Middle Asia and the Transcaucasus were all available by
the beginning of World War I.

However, although the rate of industrial growth during the closing
decades of the Tsarist period was quite rapid, possibly more so than in
several countries of western Europe, whose period of most rapid growth
was 50 years earlier, the late start and the low level of industrialisation
before 1860 meant that in 1913 the Russian Empire was lagging a long
way behind the leading capitalist powers (Table 8). Thus a good deal of
Soviet industrialisation represents a catching up with industrial powers
whose development began at a much earlier date, and data showing
relative rates of growth by various countries since 1917 should always
be viewed with this in mind.

Pre-revolutionary economic growth was not only limited in volume
but was also extremely uneven, both sectorally and regionally. Quite
apart from the slow development in agriculture, which in 1913 still
employed 70 per cent of the labour force and accounted for more than
half the national income, major branches of modern industry, notably
many forms of engineering, were very poorly represented. Another
outstanding feature of this period was the extent to which Russian
industry was dependent on foreign capital. The slow accumulation of
indigenous capital, due among other things to the backwardness of
agriculture, resulted in a lack of funds for industrial development,
which came increasingly from abroad. Thus large sections of modern
industry were in the hands of west European concerns and more than
half the industrial capital was foreign. Foreign interest was at its peak in
the mining industry, where it exceeded 90 per cent. It also represented

Table 8

RUSSIAN/SOVIET PRODUCTION OF SELECTED COMMODITIES
AS A PERCENTAGE OF US AND UK PRODUCTION, 1913, 1940, 1971

| | USA | | | UK | | |
	1913	1940	1971	1913	1940	1971
Coal	6	45	106	10	85	398
Oil	27	17	80	–	–	--
Natural gas	0. 1	4	33	–	–	1157
Electricity	8	26	44	49	121	316
Iron ore	15	40	242	57	166	1906
Pig iron	15	35	103	44	179	579
Steel	15	29	95	63	139	499
Mineral fertilisers	3	64	92	5	200	1143
Cement	13	25	143	69	77	561
Cotton textiles	41	36	114	32	130	1214
Woollen textiles	7	32	397	2	33	316

Source: *Narodnoye Khozyaystvo SSSR*, various years

50 per cent of investment in the chemical industry, 42 per cent in
metallurgy, 37 per cent in the timber industries and even 28 per cent in
textiles.[3] These industries were protected by high tariffs and 'throve
more on government orders than on satisfying the ordinary consumer',[4]
whose purchasing power was in any case very limited.

The nature of the Russian Empire's foreign trade bears witness to the
underdeveloped nature of the economy. Among her exports, primary
products predominated, foodstuffs accounting for about two-thirds,
minerals and other raw materials for a quarter and manufactures for a
mere 2 per cent. On the import side, manufactured goods made up about
one-third of the total (and accounted for two-thirds of consumption of
such goods) and raw materials 42 per cent. The latter included
commodities not available from within the Empire, but also involved
such items as cotton, where home production had not kept pace with the
demands of industry.

Not only was industrial development limited to a few sectors, it was
also heavily concentrated in half a dozen regions, which accounted for
well over 80 per cent of total output and contained a similar proportion
of the country's industrial labour force. Such 'early start' regions,
which had obvious advantages in the early stages of post-revolutionary
industrial expansion, were a natural choice for the location of new
industrial capacity.

The most important of these regions was that centred on Moscow,
which was responsible for nearly 30 per cent of all industrial

production. Here the leading activity was textile manufacture, an industry with a long history in the mixed forest zone, where domestic weaving of linen and woollen cloth was part of the traditional economy. After 1860, with the establishment of a mechanised factory industry, the making of cotton cloth became dominant. This was partially supported by raw cotton from the Empire's newly acquired Middle Asian territories but also needed large-scale imports, mainly from the United States, which continued until World War I. Textile industries were most highly developed in a zone to the north-east of Moscow, including the provinces of Kostroma, Vladimir, Ivanovo and Yaroslavl, which accounted for some 80 per cent of the Empire's textile production. The central region benefited greatly from its nodal position in the expanding railway network, from the role of Moscow as the country's leading commercial centre, from the plentiful labour force available in a zone of high population density and from the reservoir of skills built up in the past. Thus, in addition to its dominant role in textiles, the centre also took first place in the more limited growth of the engineering industries. Tula and Lipetsk were iron-smelting centres of long standing and there were important engineering plants in those towns as well as in Moscow, Kolomna, Nizhniy Novgorod (Gorkiy) and several smaller centres. The development of this region was assisted by the simultaneous growth of basic industries in the Ukraine, whence came coal and iron in increasing quantities.

About 15 per cent of total industrial production was derived from the Baltic provinces, mainly in and around St Petersburg and Riga. Here, too, textiles were a major activity, along with engineering (especially shipbuilding) and some chemical industries. In this zone there was a particularly heavy reliance on imported raw materials, which the two port cities were well placed to receive and process.

In a very different category was the eastern Ukraine, which by 1913 had emerged as the Russian Empire's main centre of coal-and iron-based heavy industry and her second most important industrial region, with some 18 per cent of total industrial production. The development of heavy industry in the Ukraine was a wholly nineteenth-century phenomenon. As late as 1870 practically all Russian pig iron was produced in charcoal-fired furnaces, two-thirds of which were in the Urals, but with the introduction of the coke-smelting process the centre of the iron industry shifted to the Donbass coalfield, where numerous plants were constructed between 1870 and 1900. In the early stages coal measure ironstones from the Donbass itself were the main source of ore, but these soon proved inadequate and, after the completion of the necessary rail link in 1884, large-scale production of iron ore began at Krivoy Rog, inside the Dnepr bend, where additional iron and steel plants were established. As a result of these developments, the eastern Ukraine was producing 70 per cent of the country's pig iron and 56 per cent of its steel by 1913, as well as nearly 90 per cent of its coal.

While the Ukrainian heavy industrial base expanded, that of the Ural region, operative since the early eighteenth century, declined in relative though not in absolute terms. The virtual absence of coking coal from the region, its remoteness from the chief manufacturing centres of European Russia and the strong competition of the better endowed and more favourably located Ukraine resulted in the Urals' share of iron and steel production falling to about 20 per cent in 1913. Nevertheless, the Ural region remained of considerable importance as a source not only of iron but also of copper, other non-ferrous metals and mineral salts, responsible for about 5 per cent of the Empire's industrial output.

A fifth industrial zone was to be found in the extreme west in the Empire's Polish territories, which had a thriving textile industry, together with small-scale coal and iron mining, metallurgy and engineering. About 11 per cent of total industrial production was derived from this region.

The only other industrial region of major significance, with about 5 per cent of total output, was the Caucasus which, as we have seen, was the main oil-producing district. It also provided a variety of other minerals.

Outside these half dozen regions industrial development was still in its very early stages. Some coal was mined in the Kuzbass and at various sites along the Trans-Siberian railway. There were ironworks in the Kuzbass and Transbaykalia and some textile manufacture was carried on in Middle Asia, but the Asian regions as a whole made a minimal contribution to the industrial economy. They were a good deal less important than, for example, the timber industries of Finland and Karelia or the food-processing industries of the Ukraine and North Caucasus.

The pattern outlined above formed the embryo from which present-day patterns of industrial location have grown during the Soviet period. While the latter saw the establishment of new sectors of industry and new industrial regions, areas which were of major importance before the Revolution are still important today, and the similarities between the patterns of 1913 and 1970 are at least as striking as the contrasts.

The Inter-war Period

World War I, the Revolution, and particularly the Civil War which followed, caused large-scale destruction of Russian industry and a massive decline in production. Gross industrial output in 1920 was down to one-fifth of the 1913 level,[5] a drop so great that, in a sense, industrialisation had to begin afresh in the 1920s, though pre-existing patterns of industry had a strong influence on the early stages of the process. The years 1917-20 constitute the period of 'War Communism' during which everything was subordinated to the overriding objective of establishing the new régime by the defeat of the counter-revolutionary forces and their foreign allies. Described by Nove as 'a siege economy with a Communist ideology',[6] War Communism involved the national-isation of nearly all forms of industry, the prohibition of private trading and the confiscation of agricultural 'surpluses' to feed the army and towns. The organisational and other strains imposed on the Soviet economy proving too great, it was replaced in 1921, and only after much debate, by Lenin's 'New Economic Policy' (NEP). This was envisaged as a tactical retreat, essentially temporary, from the advance towards full Communism, and involved the restoration of private enterprise in several sectors of the economy. The 'commanding heights' – banking, foreign trade and large-scale industry – remained in the hands of the State, but private entrepreneurs were permitted to operate small industrial enterprises and the bulk of retail trade. In agriculture, the confiscation of 'surplus' produce was replaced first by taxes in kind and then by a monetary tax.

By releasing some of the intolerable pressures imposed on the Soviet economy and society by War Communism, and under relatively peaceful conditions, the NEP permitted a fairly vigorous economic expansion, particularly in industry. By 1927 production in most sectors had returned at least to 1913 levels, and recovery from the ravages of war could be considered complete, though a full decade after the Revolution. The first 10 years of Soviet rule were thus a period of decline and recovery, the latter achieved almost entirely by the rebuilding or repair of destroyed and damaged plant in pre-war locations, so there was very little change in the distribution of individual industries or in the relative importance of the various regions. Furthermore, recovery was achieved by methods running counter to the ideological basis of the Bolshevik Revolution, in that large parts of the economy were beyond the direct control of the State and thus could not be fully within the orbit of any centralised system of economic planning.

Consequently, the middle 1920s saw much debate concerning the manner in which the economy should develop once the process of reconstruction was complete. It had already become apparent to the Soviet rulers that, if an economically and politically powerful USSR was to survive in a largely hostile world, industrialisation on a scale far beyond anything so far achieved was a prime necessity. Thus debate centred on the means by which industrialisation was to be carried out. Although the capitalist solution had been rejected, In Miller's words, 'it cannot be too greatly emphasised that the problem of industrialisation was not changed by the political revolution'.[7] The basic problem was that of 'gathering together from the resources of a poor country enough concentrations of wealth to establish a large fixed heavy industrial capital (factories, mines, railways, power stations) and to feed and clothe a labour force while it was learning to be a modern skilled working class'. Since the great mass of the population was still dependent on agriculture, the necessary wealth, or a large part of it, would have to come from the agricultural sector, as would the necessary labour force. How was this to be achieved?

Two opposing views emerged. One possibility, which could probably be achieved by the indefinite prolongation of the New Economic Policy, was a relatively slow evolutionary process whereby industry would be devoted mainly to satisfying the requirements of the consumer, thus providing a flow of goods that could be exchanged with the peasantry for their agricultural surplus. 'The peasantry, protected from arbitrariness in requisitions and more or less unmolested by the government, would gladly produce this surplus'.[8] Industrialisation would thus stimulate agricultural production, increases in which would provide additional raw materials for industry and food for the industrial labour force. As the demand for industrial goods increased and production expanded, unit costs in industry would be progressively reduced, thus generating profits that could be invested in further industrialisation, along with the savings of an increasingly prosperous peasantry. The development of agriculture would thus go hand in hand with industrial growth, providing raw materials, foodstuffs and a major source of exports.

Protagonists of the opposing view held in general terms that such an evolutionary process would be too slow and, more specifically, that it would not produce sufficient investment capital, would lead to the development of consumer-oriented rather than basic industries and would involve an excessive dependence on the world market. It would also invite such dangers as the strengthening of the *kulak* class by the revival of capitalism in agriculture and the influx of foreign capital and interests into the Soviet economy. In any case, what was needed, according to this view of the situation, was rapid industrialisation, concentrating first on the establishment of a large heavy industrial capacity to serve as a base on which the complex of consumer industries could be built up at a later stage. An important consideration was that, during the period of reconstruction, large returns had been obtained

Table 9

PERCENTAGE DISTRIBUTION OF CAPITAL INVESTMENT BY MAJOR SECTORS OF THE ECONOMY, 1918-70

	1918 -27	1928 -32	1933 -37	1938 -41*	1941† -45	1946 -50	1951 -55	1956 -60	1961 -65	1966 -70	Total 1918-70
Industry	17.2	38.3	37.6	34.7	43.4	39.0	41.4	36.2	36.9	35.7	36.9
group A	11.9	32.0	30.7	28.8	40.0	33.8	36.9	30.9	32.0	30.3	31.7
group B	5.3	6.3	6.9	5.9	3.4	5.2	4.5	5.3	4.9	5.4	5.2
Agriculture	3.1	15.5	11.8	10.7	9.3	11.7	14.1	14.2	15.4	16.9	15.1
Transport & communications	11.1	17.5	19.9	18.1	15.5	12.3	9.1	8.6	9.7	9.3	10.0
Railways	8.9	10.2	10.6	10.7	11.6	7.7	5.0	3.4	3.3	2.8	4.1
Housing	64.1	15.3	12.7	16.9	14.8	19.2	19.6	23.2	18.3	17.0	18.8
Others	4.5	13.4	18.0	19.6	17.0	17.8	15.8	17.8	19.7	21.1	19.2
000,000,000 rubles at 1967 prices	4.4	8.8	19.9	20.6	20.8	48.1	91.1	170.5	247.6	353.8	985.6

* up to 30 June 1941
† from 1 July 1941

Source: *Narodnoye Khozyaystvo SSSR v 1970 godu*, 482-3

Table 10

INDICES OF GROSS INDUSTRIAL PRODUCTION, 1928-73

		1928 = 100			1940 = 100			1960 = 100	
	All industry	Group A	Group B	All industry	Group A	Group B	All industry	Group A	Group B
1928	100	100	100						
1932	203	267	156						
1940	639	1000	406	100	100	100			
1945	611	1110	247	92	112	59			
1950	1138	2044	500	173	205	123			
1955	2083	3890	906	320	390	217			
1960	3417	6664	1375	524	666	326	100	100	100
1965	5167	10533	1844	791	1056	442	151	158	136
1966	5611	11489	1969	860	1153	475	164	173	146
1967	6167	12667	2188	946	1269	522	180	190	160
1968	6667	13711	2375	1024	1375	566	195	206	174
1969	7139	14667	2531	1097	1471	608	209	221	186
1970	7750	15890	2750	1190	1593	662	227	239	203
1971	8361	17110	2969	1282	1716	713	245	257	219
1972	8917	18267	3188	1370	1832	763	261	275	234
1973	9577	19765	3376	1471	1982	810	280	298	248

Source: *Narodnoye Khozyaystvo SSSR 1922-72*, 125-6; *Soviet News*, various dates

from a relatively low rate of capital investment, since the latter had gone mainly to the repair and restoration of existing capital stock. With reconstruction complete, further industrial investment would have to be devoted to the creation of new industrial capacity, and returns would thus inevitably be smaller. The peasantry would never willingly provide sufficient capital for industrial growth along these lines, so that a means had to be found of compelling them to do so, particularly if industry was to be developed with the long-term interests of the Soviet state rather than the immediate needs of the consumer in mind.

In the event, the latter view prevailed. Top priority was given to the capital goods industries and forced collectivisation of agriculture became a mechanism whereby wealth was channelled from the agricultural sector to support the industrialisation process. The interests of the peasants were sacrificed to the needs of industry and current living standards were sacrificed in the interest of future economic strength. All this was, of course, only possible under a system of highly centralised national economic planning.

As a result of these decisions, the period from the inception of the first Five Year Plan in 1928 until the early 1950s was one in which a particularly large share of capital investment went to the industrial sector and agriculture received very little (Table 9). In the industrial sector, more than 80 per cent of investment was in 'Group A' industries, that is in industries producing energy, raw materials and capital goods, as opposed to 'Group B' industries producing items for consumption.

Conflicting views have been expressed concerning the actual rates of economic growth achieved in the Soviet Union over the past 45 years of planned economic development. Soviet data on this topic (Table 10) have been widely criticised by western economists as exaggerating the progress made but there can be little doubt that the rate of industrial growth was more rapid than that of most other industrial powers, and akin to that achieved during the industrialisation of western Europe in the nineteenth century. Despite marked annual fluctuations, the rate of industrial expansion was extremely rapid from 1928 until the early 1950s (Fig 7). To a large degree this was a result of the low level of production before 1928 rather than an indicator of the efficacy of Soviet economic planning. So well endowed was the Soviet Union with both raw materials and labour that, once a determined effort was made to utilise these resources, rapid expansion was almost inevitable, particularly since the USSR could reap the benefit of technological innovations laboriously worked out elsewhere. As Lydolph has put it:

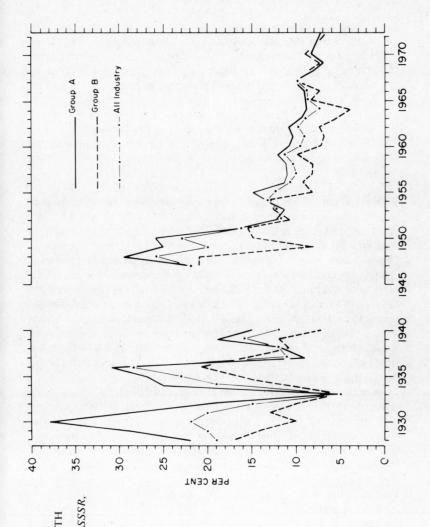

Fig 7.
ANNUAL RATES OF
INDUSTRIAL GROWTH
SOURCE: data from
Narodnoye Khozyaystvo SSSR,
various years

Group A
Group B
All Industry

PER CENT

During the 1930s as well as during the first decade after World War II, the Soviet industrial drive was of such an unsophisticated nature that it was neither hampered by the need for domestic development of new technology at the input end of the cycle, nor by delicate balances of supply and demand at the output end of the cycle. The Soviets merely had to plug in existent technologies in their simplest forms and produce and produce and produce in sectors that would show the fastest short-run gains, without much attention paid to balances between different sectors or to the danger of glutting the market, because everything was needed in as big quantities as possible.[9]

Over the past 20 years there has been an inevitable decline in the *rate* of industrial growth, though this is still well above that of most developed countries and continues large in absolute terms. As well as total growth, Table 10 and Fig 7 indicate the relative performances of Group A and Group B industries. Here, too, there has been a significant change. Before the 1950s growth in Group A industries was invariably more rapid than that in Group B, and over the whole period since 1928 the former have expanded about six times as much as the latter. For the period since 1940, however, the ratio is $2 \cdot 4 : 1$ and for the years since 1960 it has been about $1 \cdot 2 : 1$. Current plans envisage a more rapid growth for Group B than for Group A during the 1970s, though the latter will, of course, continue to represent by far the greater part of the Soviet Union's industrial capacity and production.

In addition to the drive for an ever-greater volume of production, industrial planning in the Soviet Union has also been deeply concerned with the regional distribution of industry. We have already seen that industry before the Revolution was not only limited in scale and variety but also restricted in its areal distribution. Immediately after the Revolution the latter feature was emphasised by the secession of Poland and the Baltic States, areas responsible for about one-sixth of the Empire's industrial production. This excessive concentration of the more advanced forms of economic activity in a few restricted sections of the national territory ran counter to the basic principles of Soviet economic planning, which involved the following premises. First and foremost was the insistence on rapid industrialisation, the economic and political reasons for which have already been discussed. Secondly it was held that industry should be much more widely dispersed throughout the country, implying the particularly rapid development of industry in areas outside the 'established European core'[10] and, incidentally, the modernisation of the more remote areas and less advanced peoples of the Union. At the same time it was considered

Table 11

REGIONAL SHARES OF PRODUCTION OF SELECTED INDUSTRIAL COMMODITIES, 1940-70 (per cent)

	W.	1940 Ural	E.	1960 W.	Ural	E.	1970 W.	Ural	E.
Coal	64.1	7.2	28.7	53.3	10.8	35.9	49.4	7.4	43.2
Oil	93.1	0.6	6.3	90.4	2.4	7.2	75.1	6.8	18.1
Gas	99.4	0.1	0.5	96.5	1.1	2.4	60.1	1.1	29.8
Electricity	78.3	12.5	9.2	61.6	16.8	21.6	62.0	12.0	26.0
Iron ore	71.7	26.6	1.7	63.5	25.4	11.1	70.7	13.4	15.9
Pig iron	71.9	17.8	10.3	60.3	32.0	7.7	62.7	26.8	10.5
Steel	68.6	20.8	10.6	57.6	33.1	9.3	58.5	31.2	10.3
Sulphuric acid	82.3	13.5	4.2	62.8	18.5	18.7	63.0	15.2	21.8
Mineral fertilisers	68.5	24.6	6.9	59.5	24.6	15.9	72.5	10.5	17.0
Synthetic fibres	100.0	0.0	0.0	79.6	1.9	18.5	83.7	0.9	15.4
Metal-cutting lathes	92.9	5.5	1.6	86.0	6.9	7.1	87.8	6.9	5.3
Sawn timber	64.0	11.5	24.5	62.0	12.1	25.9	59.4	11.4	29.2
Paper	80.6	19.1	0.3	70.6	21.7	7.7	72.1	19.7	8.2
Cement	80.5	6.0	13.5	65.6	13.0	21.4	65.5	10.7	23.8
Cotton textiles	96.2	0.0	3.8	91.7	0.2	8.1	90.9	0.2	8.9
Woollen textiles	97.3	1.4	1.3	86.2	3.6	9.2	71.9	9.6	18.5
Silk textiles	91.8	0.0	8.2	90.3	0.1	9.6	84.1	3.6	12.3

Eastern regions: West Siberia, East Siberia, Far East, Kazakhstan, Middle Asia

Source: *Narodnoye Khozyaystvo SSSR 1922-72*, **142**-6

desirable that industrial production should take place as close as possible to raw materials, power sources and markets, thus minimising the load on the transport system. Since vast undeveloped resources were to be found in areas far removed from existing centres of industry and population, this implied the creation of new population concentrations in thinly settled regions and thus a large-scale movement of population away from the main settled zone. It was also considered desirable that each region should produce as wide a range of industrial commodities as its resources would permit, and should achieve the highest possible degree of regional self-sufficiency. Here again, the need to minimise the burden on transport facilities was implicit and, in the inter-war period at least, there were major strategic implications as well. If all regions were to develop a wide range of industrial activities, there was a chance that the national economy could continue to function after the loss of some regions to an invader. The validity of the latter argument, at least, was amply demonstrated by the events of World War II, when, after the loss of a large part of the older industrial regions, the Soviet war machine was supported mainly by the new industrial regions which had been established since the Revolution. In addition, however, it was envisaged that each region should have its own specialism, concentrating much of its effort on the production for the all-Union market of a few items it was particularly suited to produce.

These last two concepts – regional self-sufficiency and regional specialisation – draw our attention to the great importance attached by Soviet economic planners to the matter of regionalisation – the identification or formulation of regional systems to serve as a framework for the economic development of the country (See Chapter 8).

In the inter-war period, and particularly during the first Five Year Plan (1928-32), a large share of investment was directed to the pre-existing industrial regions, which consequently experienced rapid industrial growth. This direction of investment was inevitable, partly because these were regions that already had sizeable reservoirs of skilled labour and industrial equipment and also because, in order to develop new industries in new areas, it was necessary first to strengthen the old industrial regions, which alone could supply the capital equipment necessary for the establishment of new ones. At the same time there were some important locational shifts, the most striking of which was the resuscitation of the Urals as the country's 'second metallurgical base', a process involving associated developments in Siberia and Kazakhstan. Nevertheless, even in the case of heavy industry, the predominance of the European sector remained strong. In the lighter branches, which anyway expanded much more slowly (Table

12) dispersal from the old European regions was very limited indeed
(Table 11).

World War II

Movement of heavy industry eastwards was greatly accelerated by
the events of 1941-5, which involved the loss of a number of major
industrial complexes, notably the first metallurgical base in the eastern
Ukraine, and the threatened loss of others such as the Moscow region
and the Caucasian oilfields. Wholesale evacuation of industrial plant
was undertaken in 1941 and 1942, when an estimated 1360 major
industrial enterprises were moved, 455 going to the Urals, 200 to the
Volga region, 210 to Western Siberia and 250 to Kazakhstan and
Middle Asia.[11] This evacuated capacity, together with new plant
established in the eastern regions during the 1930s, enabled those
regions to support the bulk of Soviet war production during the darkest
days of the war. Activity was greatest in the Urals and West Siberia,
which, at the height of the war, were producing three-quarters of the
country's coal, iron and steel. The war also stimulated a number of new
developments, notably the exploitation of the Volga-Ural oilfield as a
replacement for the threatened Caucasus.

Although, according to Soviet sources, gross industrial production in
1945 was 92 per cent of the 1940 level,[12] the industrial structure was
greatly distorted by war needs. While the output of Group A industries
in 1945 was 12 per cent up on 1940, production in Group B was only 60
per cent of the pre-war figure. A large part of industry was, of course,
converted to the production of war materials, and the output of many
items, including basic commodities, declined. Reconversion to peace-
time production resulted in very low output figures in 1946, when total
industrial production was only 77 per cent of pre-war. Malenkov
reported in 1952 that 'the war retarded our industrial development by
eight or nine years'.[13]

The Post-war Period

With the restoration of industrial output to its pre-war level in the late
1940s, expansion was resumed on lines very similar to those of the
inter-war period, with a continued heavy emphasis on the basic
industries. As long as Stalin remained in control there appeared to be
little change in the goals of Soviet economic planning or in the methods
used to achieve them, but after his death in 1953 all was thrown into
ferment and vigorous policy debates ensued. While some were of the
opinion that the time had come to relax the excessive emphasis on heavy
industry and to step up the growth of consumer goods industries, thus
ensuring a more rapid rise in the material living standards of the Soviet

people, others felt that the political and military threat from the capitalist world necessitated a continuation of development along Stalinist lines and that the time for relaxation had not yet arrived. The debate was not, of course, confined to economic affairs, and the clash of 'liberal' and 'Stalinist' views has been a major theme in the affairs of the Soviet Union and her Comecon neighbours throughout the past two decades. In the USSR the debate involved both the objectives and the methods of industrial development. Thus, in addition to the argument over the relative rates of growth to be achieved by Group A and Group B industries, there was also much discussion concerning the relative merits of centralised and decentralised control of industry. A large measure of decentralisation was achieved under Khrushchev, with the substitution of 'territorial management' for 'branch management' in most sectors of industry, and this heightened the importance attached to economic regionalisation. Khrushchev's successors have reverted to a highly centralised system of economic planning and control, but regional considerations remain of paramount importance in the 'optimal location of productive forces'.

Since 1950 industrial development has continued at a rapid pace. According to the figures given in Table 10, gross industrial output has risen more than sevenfold over the past two decades, with a nine-fold growth in Group A and a six-fold increase in the output of Group B industries. In purely quantitative terms, over 60 per cent of all industrial growth since the Revolution has occurred during the 1960s, despite the fact that percentage growth rates have been well below those of earlier decades.

Soviet industrialisation no longer benefits from the inbuilt advantages described in the earlier part of this chapter. Labour is becoming shorter, particularly in the eastern regions, and great emphasis is now laid on the need to increase labour productivity. In several instances exhaustion of more easily accessible industrial resources now necessitates the use of more expensive alternatives. At the same time the economy is becoming more sophisticated and more complex. During the 1960s the Soviet Union progressed beyond the relatively simple first phase of industrialisation, based primarily on coal, iron and steel, to a second phase involving new sources of energy, new raw materials and new products, and depending heavily on continuous technological advance. This had caused, among other things, a reassessment of the resources and future development of the various regions.

Regional Aspects of Industrial Development

Regional patterns of industry are considered in detail in Chapters 9-11, and at this stage attention will be confined to the broader aspects of this topic. The present pattern of industrial location includes elements from the various phases of development outlined above and, in Mellor's words, 'represents a product of the struggle between the centripetal tendencies to locate plant in the most favoured sites and the centrifugal tendencies of Soviet planners to spread industry as widely as possible throughout the country'.[14] Western writers[15] have distinguished four different types of region from the point of view of industrial development, and these largely reflect the phases of industrialisation already described. Using Hooson's terminology,[16] the four types are as follows.

Long-established Centres of Market-oriented Labour-intensive Industries

The most important region in this category is the industrial Centre, which accounts for some 20 per cent of Soviet industrial output.[17] Others include the Leningrad district and a number of major cities in the European USSR such as Kiev, Riga and Odessa. These areas all experienced considerable industrial development before the Revolution, particularly in the engineering and textile branches. Development occurred despite a relative poverty of natural resources, owing much to their central location with respect to European Russia or to their individual regions. Each is a major centre of transport and communications, and of commercial and political activity. During the Soviet period these areas, especially the Centre, have developed important concentrations of labour-intensive industry, and have become especially important in engineering, particularly the more advanced and highly skilled branches. Since World War II they have benefited from the establishment of oil and gas pipeline networks, which have helped to offset their chronic energy deficit, and have attracted a large share of the newer branches of industry, such as chemicals, synthetic textiles and a wide range of consumer goods production. Heavy metallurgical industries are rather poorly represented in these areas. Although there are several major iron and steel plants, these play a supporting rather than an initiating role in industrial development. During the 1960s there was a marked growth of modern light industry in many of the medium-sized cities of the European USSR, as well as in the larger regional centres. This has been particularly noticeable in regions suffering a certain pressure of population on limited land resources, such as Belorussia and the Baltic republics.

Centres of Heavy Industry

These areas, in contrast to those in the first category, have been favoured both by their rich resources of coal and/or iron and by the

Table 12

PRODUCTION OF SELECTED INDUSTRIAL COMMODITIES, 1928-73

	1928	1940	1950	1960	1970	1973
Coal (000,000 tons)	35.5	165.9	261.1	509.6	624.1	668
Oil (000,000 tons)	11.6	31.1	37.9	147.9	352.6	421
Gas (000,000,000 cu m)	0.3	3.4	6.2	47.2	199.6	236
Electricity (000,000,000 kWh)	5.0	48.3	91.2	292.3	740.4	915
Peat (000,000 tons)	5.3	33.2	36.0	53.6	57.5	n.a.
Iron ore (000,000 tons)	6.1	29.9	39.7	105.9	195.5	216
Pig iron (000,000 tons)	3.3	14.9	19.2	46.8	85.9	95.9
Steel (000,000 tons)	4.3	18.3	27.3	65.3	115.9	131.5
Sulphuric acid (000,000 tons)	0.2	1.6	2.1	5.4	12.1	14.8
Mineral fertilisers (000,000 tons)	0.1	3.2	5.5	13.9	55.4	72.3
Synthetic resins & Plastics (000 tons)	—	10.9	67.1	311.6	1673	2300
Synthetic fibres (000 tons)	0.2	11.1	24.2	211.2	623.0	830
Motor tyres (000,000)	0.1	3.0	7.4	17.2	34.6	42.3
Turbines (000,000 kW)	0.04	1.2	2.7	9.2	16.2	16.5
Electric motors (000,000 kW)	0.2	1.3	4.2	13.5	27.8	41.6
Metal-cutting lathes (000)	2.0	58.4	70.6	155.9	202.3	211
Main-line railway locomotives	479	928	1212	1699	1808	1754
steam	479	914	985	—	—	—
diesel	—	5	125	1303	1485	1400
electric	—	9	102	396	323	354
Railway freight wagons (000)	7.9	30.9	50.8	36.4	58.3	71.8
Railway passenger wagons (000)	0.4	1.1	0.9	1.7	1.8	n.a.
Motor vehicles (000)	0.84	145.4	362.9	523.6	916.1	1602
trucks (000)	0.74	136.0	294.4	362.0	524.5	629
cars (000)	0.05	5.5	64.6	138.8	344.2	917
buses (000)	0.05	3.9	3.9	22.8	47.4	56
Tractors (000)	1.3	31.6	116.7	238.5	458.5	500
Grain combines (000)	—	12.8	46.3	59.0	99.2	93.9
Excavators (000)	—	0.3	3.5	12.6	31.0	35.8
Sawn timber (000,000 cu m)	13.6	34.8	49.5	105.6	116.4	125
Cellulose (000,000 tons)	0.09	0.5	1.1	2.3	5.1	6.1
Paper (000,000 tons)	0.3	0.8	1.2	2.3	4.2	4.9
Cement (000,000 tons)	1.8	5.7	10.2	45.5	95.2	109.5
Textiles (000,000 m)	3010	4522	4522	8226	10134	11000
cotton (000,000 m)	2678	3954	3899	6387	7482	7997
woollen (000,000 m)	87	120	155	342	496	542
linen (000,000 m)	174	285	282	559	725	815
silk (000,000 m)	10	77	130	810	1241	1457
Leather footwear (000,000 pairs)	58	211	203	419	676	667
Radio receivers (000)	3	160	1072	4165	7815	8600
Television receivers (000)	—	0.3	11.9	1726	6682	6300
Domestic refrigerators (000)	—	3.5	1.2	529	4140	5400
Washing machines (000)	—	—	0.3	895	5243	3000
Vacuum cleaners (000)	—	—	6.1	501	1509	2700
Sewing machines (000)	286	175	502	3096	1400	n.a.

n.a. = not available   * = estimate

Source: *Narodnoye Khozyaystvo SSSR 1922-72*, 136-41. *Soviet News* No. 5726, Feb 19, 1974

Table 13

INDUSTRIAL FIXED CAPITAL AND VALUE ADDED IN INDUSTRY, BY MAJOR ECONOMIC REGIONS, 1968

	Population		Fixed industrial capital			Value added		
	000	per cent	000,000 rubles	per cent	per capita	000,000 rubles	per cent	per capita
North-west	11,855	5.0	13,220	7.3	1,115	19,350	8.1	873
Centre	26,763	11.3	21,300	11.7	796	24,680	19.4	922
Volga-Vyatka	8,288	3.5	5,180	2.9	625	6,320	5.0	763
Black Earth Centre	7,948	3.4	3,990	2.2	502	2,880	2.3	362
Volga	18,004	7.6	17.650	9.7	980	8,450	6.7	469
North Caucasus	13,867	5.9	8,380	4.6	604	5,420	4.3	391
Urals	15,262	6.4	18,120	10.0	1,187	11,210	8.8	735
West Siberia	12,201	5.2	10,260	5.7	841	7,300	5.7	598
East Siberia	7,321	3.1	8,840	4.9	1,207	3,870	3.1	529
Far East	5,709	2.4	7,050	3.9	1,235	3,950	3.0	692
Donets-Dnepr	19,922	8.4	24,660	13.6	1,238	12,880	10.2	646
South-west	20,389	8.6	7,270	4.0	357	7,940	6.3	389
South	6,070	2.6	3,500	1.9	577	2,730	2.2	450
Baltic	7,359	3.1	5,150	2.8	700	4,860	3.8	660
Belorussia	8,820	3.7	4,210	2.3	477	4,150	3.3	471
Transcaucasia	11,882	5.0	7,600	4.2	640	3,100	2.4	261
Middle Asia	18,867	7.9	6,400	3.5	341	3,420	2.7	181
Kazakhstan	12,678	5.4	8,680	4.8	685	3,370	2.7	266
Moldavia	3,484	1.5	nd	—	—	nd	—	—
Total	236,689	100.0	181,500*	100.0	778*	126,880*	100.0	545*

* In the absence of data for Moldavia, that republic is excluded from these totals.

Sources: Population: *Narodnoye Khozyaystvo v 1967 godu*
Fixed industrial capital: L. Dienes, 1972, Table 2, reproduced by permission from the *Annals of the Association of American Geographers*, Volume 62, 1972
Value added: L. Dienes, 1972, Table 4
Per cent and per capita data: author's calculations

emphasis of Soviet economic planning on the growth of metallurgy and the heavier branches of engineering. Light industry in general and consumer goods production in particular are poorly represented. The first and second metallurgical bases of the Ukraine and Urals are the major elements in this group, together accounting for nearly a fifth of Soviet industrial production. The two bases differ in their development chronology. In the Ukraine the basic patterns were established before the Revolution, and the region's relative importance has declined during the Soviet period, though the volume of output has continued to rise. The Urals, Russia's main source of iron in the eighteenth century, were eclipsed by the growth of the Ukraine in the late nineteenth century and then revitalised by developments during the 1930s and 1940s, when the energy supply problems were solved by the establishment of links with regions further east. In both the Ukraine and the Urals traditional sources of iron ore were nearing exhaustion during the 1960s, but their replacement by alternative supplies has meant that growth has continued. Both areas have a large fixed industrial capital in relation to the size of their industrial labour force. Another district that may be placed in this group is the Kuzbass, though it is responsible for only about 4 per cent of total production. Its status as a heavy industrial region was originally a by-product of its link with the Urals, but the region is now much more self-contained, though continuing to supply coking coal to the second metallurgical base.

Emerging, Mainly Power-based Regions

The most important of these are the Volga-Ural and Yenisey-Baykal zones. These regions were of little industrial significance before World War II and have developed mainly as a result of the post-war emphasis on oil, natural gas and electric power. Their rich power resources supply large quantities of energy to other regions, and have also attracted new industries, particularly chemicals and non-ferrous metallurgy. Industrial development began earlier and has progressed further in the Volga-Ural zone, where the Volga economic region now accounts for nearly 7 per cent of Soviet industrial production. The Yenisey-Baykal zone is at an earlier stage of development and is experiencing labour supply problems. It therefore continues to act mainly as a source of power and raw materials for more highly developed regions to the west. The Karaganda district of northern Kazakhstan may also be placed in this category. Like the Kuzbass, it was first developed as a supplier of coking coal to the Urals, but in the post-war years it has become the main organising centre of the varied industrial activities of northern and central Kazakhstan.

Outlying Areas of Small-scale, Mainly Resource-oriented Industries

These are to be found in the European north, northern Siberia, the Far East and Middle Asia. Important developments are now taking place in these regions, but they seem destined to remain peripheral to the main core area of the Soviet industrial economy, acting as suppliers of energy and industrial raw materials.

This broad classification may act as a link between our discussion of phases of industrial development in the earlier part of this chapter and the chapters immediately following, which deal with the growth of major sectors of the industrial economy. It will, however, be necessary to return to the topic of regionalisation before a concluding discussion of the industrial geography of the major regions of the USSR.

PART TWO

MAJOR SECTORS
OF SOVIET INDUSTRY

Table 14

EMPLOYMENT 1940-70. All totals are given in thousands. (Figures in brackets are percentages)

(a) All civilian employment

	1940		1950		1960		1970	
Industry	13,079	(16.8)	15,317	(19.2)	22,620	(23.8)	31,593	(26.8)
Agriculture	46,503	(59.8)	42,937	(53.7)	39.993	(42.0)	37,180	(31.4)
Others	18,144	(23.3)	21,666	(27.1)	32,619	(34.2)	49,313	(41.8)
Total	77,726	(100.0)	79,920	(100.0)	95,232	(100.0)	118,086	(100.0)

(b) Agricultural employment

	1940		1950		1960		1970	
State	2,703	(5.8)	3,437	(8.0)	6,793	(17.0)	9,180	(24.7)
Collective	29,000	(62.4)	27,600	(64.3)	22,300	(55.8)	17,000	(45.7)
Private[1]	14,800	(31.8)	11,900	(27.7)	10,900	(27.2)	11,000	(29.6)
Total[2]	46,503	(100.0)	42,937	(100.0)	39,993	(100.0)	37,180	(100.0)

(c) Non-Agricultural employment

	1940		1950		1960		1970	
Industry	13,079	(41.8)	15,317	(41.4)	22,620	(40.9)	31,593	(39.0)
Forestry	280	(0.9)	444	(1.2)	359	(0.6)	433	(0.5)
Transport	3,525	(11.3)	4,117	(11.1)	6,279	(11.4)	7,985	(9.9)
Communications	484	(1.6)	542	(1.5)	738	(1.3)	1,330	(1.6)
Construction	1,993	(6.4)	3,278	(8.9)	6,319	(11.4)	9,052	(11.2)
Trade	3,351	(10.6)	3,360	(9.1)	4,675	(8.5)	7,537	(9.3)
Housing and communal services	1,516	(4.9)	1,371	(3.7)	1,920	(3.5)	3,052	(3.8)
Public health services	1,512	(4.9)	2,051	(5.5)	3,461	(6.3)	5,080	(6.3)
Education and cultural services	2,678	(8.5)	3,315	(9.0)	4,803	(8.7)	8,025	(9.9)
Science and scientific services	362	(1.2)	714	(1.9)	1,763	(3.2)	3,238	(4.0)
Credit and insurance	267	(0.9)	264	(0.7)	265	(0.5)	388	(0.5)
State apparatus	1,837	(5.9)	1,831	(5.0)	1,245	(2.3)	1,883	(2.3)
Others	339	(1.1)	379	(1.0)	792	(1.4)	1,310	(1.7)
Total	31,223	(100.0)	36,983	(100.0)	55,239	(100.0)	80,906	(100.0)

(d) Industrial employment

	1940		1950		1960		1970	
Fuel and power	972	(7.4)	1,257	(8.2)	1,965	(8.7)	2,175	(6.9)
Ferrous metallurgy	526	(4.0)	743	(4.9)	1,047	(4.6)	1,359	(4.3)
Chemicals and petro-chemicals	414	(3.2)	469	(3.1)	792	(3.5)	1,568	(5.0)
Metal-working and machine-building	3,519	(26.9)	4,307	(28.1)	7,206	(31.8)	12,017	(38.0)
Timber industries	1,990	(15.2)	2,208	(14.4)	2,698	(11.9)	2,848	(9.0)
Building materials	368	(2.8)	699	(4.6)	1,575	(7.0)	1,996	(6.3)
Light industries	2,853	(21.8)	2,653	(17.3)	3,860	(17.1)	5,019	(15.9)
Food industries	1,568	(12.1)	1,683	(11.0)	2,164	(9.6)	2,901	(9.2)
Others	869	(6.6)	1,298	(8.5)	1,313	(5.8)	1,710	(5.4)
Total	13,079	(100.0)	15,317	(100.0)	22,620	(100.0)	31,593	(100.0)

1 Employment on private plots as estimated in Mickiewicz, 1973
2 Labour temporarily engaged in farming is not included (see Clarke, 1972, 25)

Sources: *Narodnoye Khozyaystvo SSSR 1922-72*, 147, 346-7. E. Mickiewicz, 1973, 55-7. R. A. Clarke, 1972, 23-5

Table 15

GROWTH OF INDUSTRIAL PRODUCTION, BY SECTORS, 1950-70

	1950 as percentage of 1940	1960 as percentage of 1950	1965 as percentage of 1960	1970 as percentage of 1965	1970 as percentage of 1950
All industry	173	304	151	150	689
Electricity generation	187	364	178	154	998
Fuel industries	145	243	137	132	439
Ferrous metallurgy	177	269	147	132	522
Chemical industries	196	398	195	178	1, 381
Metal-working and machine-building	215	428	179	174	1, 333
Timber industries	137	211	128	131	354
Building materials	217	366	153	150	840
Glass and ceramics	197	554	156	161	1, 391
All light industry	112	249	113	151	425
Textiles	113	232	115	142	379
Clothing	116	273	108	178	525
Footwear	107	255	120	144	441
Food industries	97	234	142	133	442

Source: *Narodnoye Khozyaystvo SSSR*, various years

Table 16

CAPITAL INVESTMENT IN INDUSTRY, BY SECTORS, 1966-70

	000 000 rubles	per cent
Electricity generation	14, 216	11. 5
Coal	7, 429	6. 0
Oil	11, 223	9. 1
Gas	4, 496	3. 6
Ferrous metallurgy	10, 232	8. 3
Chemicals	11, 077	9. 0
Metal-working and machine-building	22, 966	18. 6
Timber industries	4, 252	3. 4
Cellulose and paper industries	1, 796	1. 5
Building materials industries	6, 990	5. 7
Light industry	5, 487	4. 5
Food industries	10, 410	8. 5
Others	12, 677	10. 3
Total	123, 251	100. 0

Source: *Narodnoye Khozyaystvo SSSR v 1970 godu*, 484

4
Fuel and Power

IN THE FIRST PART of this book we were concerned with the broader aspects of the geography, resources and economic development of the Soviet Union. We turn now to a more detailed examination of the various sectors of industry, both extractive and manufacturing. In each case we shall attempt to assess the resources available, to discuss the main phases of development, to indicate the sequence of locational changes that have given rise to present distribution patterns and to suggest the most likely future trends.

Among the many factors that have favoured the industrial growth of the Soviet Union, none has been more important that that country's possession, within its own borders, of vast energy resources of all types. The exploitation of these resources has naturally received top priority in Soviet economic planning, and at no stage has any shortage of fuel and power supplies hindered development. This is not to say that the energy sector has presented no problems to Soviet economic planners, who have had to make numerous difficult decisions regarding the rate of growth of alternative energy sources – coal, lignite, peat, shale, oil, gas, hydro-electricity – and the regional distribution of production. Regional problems have been particularly severe. Some regions of major industrial importance, of which the Centre is the clearest example, have suffered from a chronic lack of energy resources and have thus required large-scale transfers of fuel and power from other, more favoured regions. This has increased the burden on transport facilities, a major problem in the general development of the Soviet economy and, to counter this, there has been vigorous development in energy-deficient regions of the poorer fuels like peat, lignite and shale. The regional problem is also apparent in the fact that many of the country's biggest energy reserves are to be found in remote

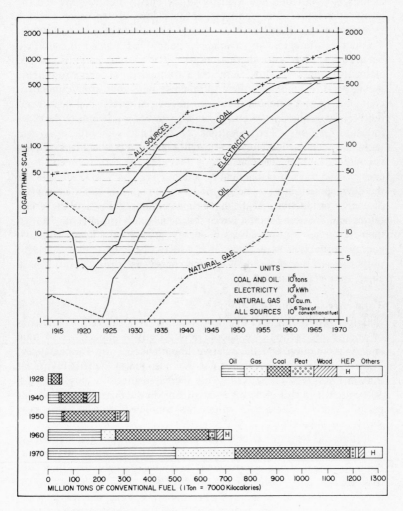

Fig 8. ENERGY PRODUCTION
SOURCE: data from *Narodnoye Khozyaystvo SSSR*, various years

and thinly populated areas, notably in Siberia. The development of such resources necessitates a choice between the establishment of major new centres of population and industry in the energy-rich regions and the costly transfer of fuels and power over long distances to existing industrial areas. Here, as in so many instances where very different alternative strategies are available, policy has tended to oscillate between the available alternatives, so that present patterns include elements from both. Thus, in the case of the Siberian energy resources, the clearest example of these problems, new industrial complexes containing power-oriented industries have been established near them, but very large amounts of energy are also moved westwards to the older industrial regions. The questions of regional self-sufficiency and regional specialisation already referred to are also relevant here. Soviet economic planning has consistently favoured the establishment of an energy base in each of the major economic regions, and this has led to the development of new energy-producing complexes and the dispersal of energy production. At the same time certain regions, like the Volga region and Western Siberia, have proved eminently suitable by virtue of their resources to specialise in energy production. Thus, although energy production as a whole is a widely dispersed activity, a large proportion of the total output of each energy source is derived from a small number of regions.

Total energy Production

Before proceeding to a detailed examination of the various branches of energy production, we should look briefly at the matter of total energy production and the relative importance of the various types. Table 17 and Fig 8 show that, since the inception of the first Five Year Plan in 1928, total energy output has increased almost twenty-five fold. Although the rate of growth has inevitably slowed down in the post-war period, a rapid increase in output has continued, with a 30 per cent growth between 1965 and 1970.

Before the Revolution coal was predominant in the national energy supply, accounting for nearly half the total. Oil constituted 30 per cent, but a good deal of this was exported, and it was probably less important than timber as a source of energy for the internal economy of the Russian Empire. Since the published data take no account of domestic woodcutting, the significance of wood, especially in areas remote from coal supplies, was probably even greater than the 20 per cent indicated in Table 17.

Throughout the inter-war period and also in the early post-war years the coal industry received the bulk of investment in the energy sector. Oil was relatively neglected, at least during the 1930s, when the output

Table 17

ENERGY PRODUCTION, 1913-70

(a) *Million tons of conventional fuel* (one ton = 7, 000 kilocalories)

	Oil	Natural gas	Coal	Peat	Shale	Wood	HEP*	Total
1913	14.7	n	23.1	0.7	n	9.7	n	48.2
1928	16.6	0.4	29.8	2.1	n	5.7	0.2	54.8
1940	44.5	4.4	140.5	13.6	0.6	34.1	3.1	240.8
1950	54.2	7.3	205.7	14.8	1.3	27.9	7.6	318.8
1955	101.2	11.4	310.8	20.8	3.3	32.4	13.9	493.8
1960	211.4	54.4	373.1	20.4	4.8	28.7	30.5	723.3
1965	346.4	149.8	412.5	17.0	7.4	33.5	48.9	1015.5
1970	504.2	235.6	451.2	21.4	8.5	27.7	74.6	1323.2

(b) *Percentage of total energy production*

	Oil	Natural gas	Coal	Peat	Shale	Wood	HEP
1913	30.5	n	47.9	1.4	n	20.1	n
1928	30.3	0.7	54.4	3.8	n	10.4	0.4
1940	18.5	1.8	58.3	5.6	0.2	14.2	1.3
1950	17.0	2.3	64.5	4.6	0.4	8.8	2.4
1955	20.5	2.3	62.9	4.2	0.7	6.6	2.8
1960	29.2	7.5	51.6	2.8	0.7	4.0	4.2
1965	34.1	14.8	40.6	1.7	0.7	3.3	4.8
1970	38.1	17.8	34.1	1.6	0.6	2.1	5.6

* Hydro-electric power is converted at 1000kWh = 0.6 tons; see
J. P. Cole and F. C. German, 1961, 111

Source: *Narodnoye Khozyaystvo SSSR*, various years

of coal increased nearly twice as rapidly as that of oil. As a result, by 1950 coal was contributing nearly two-thirds of total energy production compared with about one-fifth derived from oil and natural gas. Since 1950, however, these trends have been reversed: although the output of coal continues to increase quite rapidly, its share of total energy production is now barely one-third, while that of oil and gas is approaching 60 per cent. Production of oil and gas was scheduled to rise by 30 per cent between 1970 and 1975 but that of coal by only 10 per cent. This striking change denotes the somewhat belated recognition among Soviet planners of a number of economic and technological factors – oil and gas are a good deal cheaper than coal per unit of energy produced; they can be moved by pipeline, thus lessening the load on the railways; and, in addition to their role as sources of energy, they provide raw materials for a wide range of chemical industries.

Coal, oil and natural gas now constitute 90 per cent of all energy

Table 18

COAL PRODUCTION, 1913-74

Millions of metric tons (per cent)

	1913		1940		1950		1960		1970		1974 (est)	
Donbass	25.3	(86.9)	94	(56.6)	95	(36.4)	188	(36.9)	217	(34.8)	220	(32.2)
Kuzbass	0.8	(2.7)	22	(13.2)	39	(14.9)	84	(16.5)	113	(18.1)	128	(18.7)
Urals	1.2	(4.1)	12	(7.2)	32	(12.3)	62	(12.2)	47	(7.5)	39	(5.7)
Moscow	0.3	(1.0)	10	(6.0)	31	(11.9)	43	(8.4)	36	(5.8)	35	(5.1)
Karaganda	—	—	6	(3.6)	16	(6.1)	26	(5.1)	38	(6.1)	45	(6.6)
Ekibastuz	—	—	—	—	—	—	6	(1.2)	23	(3.7)	42	(6.1)
Pechora	—	—	0.3	(0.2)	9	(3.4)	18	(3.5)	22	(3.5)	23	(3.4)
Middle Asia	0.2	(0.7)	1.7	(1.0)	4	(1.5)	8	(1.6)	8	(1.3)	10	(1.5)
East Siberia	0.8	(2.7)	9	(5.4)	18	(6.9)	37	(7.3)	57	(9.1)	60	(8.8)
Far East	0.4	(1.4)	7	(4.2)	13	(5.0)	22	(4.3)	28	(4.5)	30	(4.4)
Georgia	0.1	(0.3)	0.6	(0.4)	2	(0.8)	3	(0.6)	2	(0.3)	2	(0.3)
Others	—	—	3.3	(2.0)	2	(0.8)	13	(2.5)	33	(5.3)	50	(7.3)
Total	29.1	(100.0)	165.9	(100.0)	261	(100.0)	510	(100.0)	624	(100.0)	684	(100.0)

Sources: 1913-60: *Narodnoye Khozyaystvo SSSR v 1961 godu*
1970: T. Shabad. 'News Notes', *Sov. Geog.* XIV (5), 1973, 337
1974: T. Shabad. 'News Notes', *Soviet Geog.* XVI (5), 1975, and author's estimates

produced in the Soviet Union. Despite this, the minor energy sources have by no means been neglected. The production of peat and shale has increased more than tenfold since 1928, and the use of timber for fuel is still about three times the 1913 level. In view of the vast existing potential and the great significance attached by Soviet publicists to major hydro-electric plant, it should be noted that, despite a rapid rise in production, hydro-electricity still accounts for less than 6 per cent of total energy output.

Energy production is, of course, a major sector of the industrial economy. In 1970 it employed nearly 7 per cent of the industrial labour force (Table 14), and it received between 1966 and 1970 some 30 per cent of all capital investment in industry (Table 16).

Coal

By any standard Soviet coal resources can only be described as vast. According to Hodgkins' interpretation of Soviet data,[1] total estimated reserves in the late 1950s amounted to 8,699,510 million metric tons, of which 941,890 million, about one-ninth, were classed as 'probable'. Less than 3 per cent of total reserves were actually 'proven', but even this small proportion represented 241,200 million tons, sufficient to support present output for close on 400 years. While the situation regarding total reserves is clearly very favourable, their distribution is less so, for under 10 per cent lie in the European part of the country and more than 60 per cent in the Tunguska, Lena and other north Siberian fields.[2] The great bulk of the 'proven' reserves, however, are to be found in coalfields already in use,[3] and such reserves could support present output for at least 3 centuries. Clearly, no major locational changes are likely to be imposed on the industry in the foreseeable future by exhaustion of fields currently producing most of Soviet output. Such changes might well occur as the result of changes in policy towards the resources of outlying regions, but it seems almost certain that some of the huge deposits in the Siberian north will remain untouched for a long time to come.

As already indicated, the Soviet period has seen a massive increase in coal production, which now stands at more than twenty times the 1913 level (Table 18). Rapid growth in output, checked only by World War II, continued until the late 1950s, since when there has been a perceptible slackening. Even so, annual production rose by 174 million tons (34 per cent) between 1960 and 1974. Within these general trends, there have been changes in the type of coal produced (Table 19). Between 1940 and 1950 there was a significant decline in the proportion of high-grade bituminous coals (anthracite and coking coal) and a corresponding increase in the proportion of lignite and other lower-

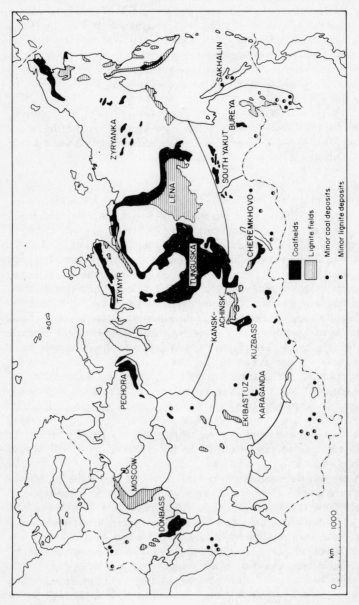

Fig 9. COAL AND LIGNITE BASINS AND DEPOSITS
Based on *Atlas SSSR* (Moscow, 1969), 76–7

Table 19

COAL PRODUCTION BY TYPES, 1940-70

Millions of metric tons (per cent)

	1940		1950		1960		1970	
Anthracite	35.7	(21.5)	40.2	(15.4)	74.1	(14.5)	75.8	(12.1)
Coking coal	35.3	(21.3)	51.7	(19.8)	110.2	(21.6)	164.8	(26.4)
Other bituminous coals	69.0	(41.6)	93.3	(35.7)	190.6	(37.4)	235.8	(37.8)
Lignite	25.9	(15.6)	75.9	(29.1)	134.7	(26.4)	147.7	(23.7)
Opencast	6.3	(3.8)	27.1	(10.4)	102.0	(20.0)	166.6	(26.7)
Deep-mined	159.6	(96.2)	234.0	(89.6)	407.6	(80.0)	457.5	(73.3)
Total	165.9	(100.0)	261.1	(100.0)	509.6	(100.0)	624.1	(100.0)

Source: *Narodnoye Khozyaystvo SSSR v 1970 godu*, 187-8

grade types. Since 1950, however, the proportion of lignite has fallen off again, while that of coking coal has increased. A more clearly marked trend of the past two decades has been the expansion of opencast mining. In 1940 this method was used only on a very small scale, but in 1974 it produced 202 million tons (more than the entire production of the United Kingdom) and was responsible for nearly 30 per cent of the Soviet output. The Soviet coalmining industry is increasingly becoming divided into two distinct sectors: opencast mining of low-grade bituminous coals and lignite, a growing proportion of which is fed to large thermal electricity generating plant close to the mining sites, and deep mining of higher quality coals, particularly anthracite and coking coal, which are tranported to consuming centres by rail. These two types of operation are to a large degree separated regionally as well as technologically.

Major changes have occurred in the location of coal production during the Soviet period. As already indicated, pre-Revolution production was heavily concentrated in the Donbass, which in 1913 accounted for well over 80 per cent of the total output. Production from all other fields was small at that time, and growth in output has involved the dispersion of the industry and the development of numerous other fields virtually from scratch. The distribution of output among the various fields and regions is indicated in Table 18. It should be noted that in some cases data are given for individual coal basins but in others production figures are only available for large regions, which may contain several widely separated producing districts (Fig 9). Of the areas listed, Donbass, Kuzbass, Karaganda and Pechora are considered

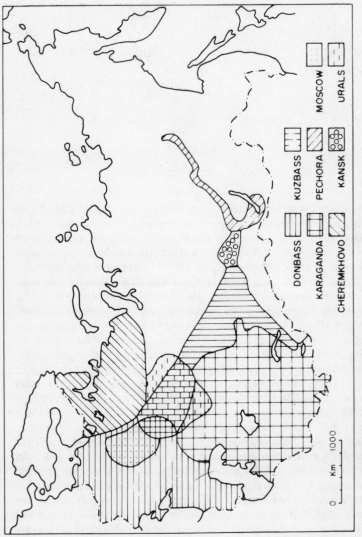

Fig 10. AREAS OF COAL DISTRIBUTION FROM MAJOR FIELDS
Based on *Atlas Razvitiya Khozyaystva i Kultury SSSR* (Moscow, 1967), 26

by Soviet economic geographers to have 'all-Union' importance, this term implying that, in addition to satisfying local or regional requirements, they produce large surpluses which are distributed over considerable distances to energy-deficit regions. These four also produce the great bulk of the country's coking coal. Most other fields are of local or regional significance only, but in recent years several of them have become the sites of large generating stations whence electricity is transmitted to other regions.

Donbass

Despite the fact that it has now been intensively exploited for more than 100 years, the Donbass still stands head and shoulders above all others, its 1974 production of 220 million tons, nearly nine times the 1913 level, representing about a third of the total Soviet output. This leading position has been maintained despite a somewhat unfavourable geological structure giving seams that are, by Soviet standards, both thin and distorted. These factors, together with the need for progressively deeper mining, result in production costs well above the national average. However, these disadvantages are offset by the high quality of the coal – most of the USSR's anthracite and more than half her coking coal – and the field's favourable location with respect to the main population concentrations and industrial centres. Donbass coal is widely distributed within the European USSR (Fig 10), supplying the needs of a zone extending from the Baltic to Transcaucasia and from the western frontier to the Volga. In particular it supplies most of the higher-grade coal requirements of the energy-deficient Central Industrial region.

Kuzbass

Of all the coalfields which have been developed mainly since the Revolution, the most important by far is the Kuzbass, which takes second place to and produces half as much coal as the Donbass. Like the latter, the Kuzbass has a large proportion of higher-grade coals, accounting for nearly a third of Soviet coking coal production. It has the additional advantage of thick seams, many of them quite close to the surface, and production costs are only about 60 per cent of those in the Donbass. Kuzbass coal was mined on a small scale in the closing years of the nineteenth century, mainly to supply the Trans-Siberian railway, but intensive development dates from the establishment of the Ural-Kuznetsk combine in the 1930s. Rapid growth continued during the war, when this was the biggest field remaining in Soviet hands, and has gone on throughout the post-war period; production rose by more than half between 1960 and 1974. Kuzbass coal still goes in very large

quantities to the Urals and some is used in areas further west. It supplies
the needs of the West Siberian region and is carried along the Turksib
railway to the Middle Asian republics.

Karaganda

This field now produces about 6 per cent of all Soviet coal and some
10 per cent of the country's coking coal. It is an indication of the scale
of the industry that Karaganda now produces some 50 per cent more
coal than the entire Russian Empire in 1913. Like the Kuzbass, the
Karaganda field was developed in the inter-war years to supply coking
coal to the Urals, a function it still performs, in addition to supplying
most of the needs of Kazakhstan and Middle Asia. A more recent
development in this part of the Kazakh republic was the opening up,
during the 1950s, of the Ekibastuz field, which has reserves as large as
those at Karaganda, though of poorer quality. Mining is mainly
opencast, and most of the coal is fed to large thermal generating plant
nearby.

Pechora

The Pechora basin lies in the far north-east of the European USSR,
much of it beyond the Arctic Circle. Small-scale production for local
use began in the 1930s, but the main phase of development was during
World War II, when a rail link was built from Kotlas to Vorkuta. The
field now produces more than 20 million tons a year, but production
costs are high owing to the difficult environment, and further expansion
is unlikely. Pechora coals are consumed entirely within the north-
western region, mainly at Leningrad and in the Cherepovets steel plant.

Other fields

The four fields discussed so far account for about two-thirds of total
Soviet coal production and an even higher proportion of the country's
output of coking coal. The remaining fields are of regional or local
significance, though some of the product is distributed over long
distances. These secondary sources are of various types. In terms of
production the most important is the Urals, with a 1974 output of 39
million tons. This comes from a number of relatively small fields, the
largest being at Kizel on the west flank. The region is, however, much
less rich than production figures would suggest. Most of the output is in
the form of lignite or low-grade bituminous types and coking coal is in
very short supply. The latter is produced mainly in the Kizel field, but
the quality is poor, and it has to be mixed with higher-grade coking
coals from the Kuzbass and Karaganda, on which the Ural steel industry

is still heavily dependent. Reserves are in any case limited, and output from the Ural region has declined by nearly 40 per cent since 1960.

The Moscow basin also ranks high in volume of production, but in this case only lignite is produced. This resource was pressed into service in the inter-war years and is consumed in thermal generating plant. Output continued to rise until the mid-1950s, but, with the development of the oil and gas pipeline networks, new supplies of energy are now available in the region, and the production of lignite has begun to decline.

Eastern Siberia and the Far East together produce some 90 million tons annually from a large number of scattered sources. The vast fields of northern Siberia, in the Tunguska and Lena basins, remain virtually untouched, and production is mainly from more southerly districts close to the Trans-Siberian railway. The most important of these is still the Cheremkhovo field, with an annual production of about 20 million tons. High quality coals have been mined here since the 1890s, and the field supplies the bulk of the requirements of the East Siberian region. Production costs are below the Soviet average, but distance from the main industrial centres prevents this field assuming all-Union importance. Other important Siberian producers are the Bukachacha, Bureya and Sakhalin fields.

As already mentioned, a major aspect of the recent growth of the Soviet coal industry has been the exploitation of large low-grade coal and lignite deposits and their use in thermal generating plant at sites remote from the main industrial areas. A major example is the Kansk-Achinsk field, straddling the Yenisey, which now produces more than 20 million tons a year. The Ekibastuz field is also in this category.

Finally, mention should be made of the small-scale coal production carried on in Middle Asia and Transcaucasia. In both cases output is insufficient to supply regional requirements, and there are sizeable 'imports', in the case of Middle Asia from Karaganda and the Kuzbass and in Transcaucasia from the Donbass.

Oil

No reliable figure can be given for the total oil reserves of the USSR, since prospecting is still going on, and fresh discoveries are constantly being made, not only in competely new regions but also in long-established oil-producing areas. Proven reserves in the mid-1950s were put at 9200 million tons,[4] and the present figure is probably close to 20,000 million tons, sufficient to maintain current output for more than 60 years. This is a very much shorter period than for coal, and proven oil reserves make up only a very small fraction of the Soviet

Table 20

OIL PRODUCTION, 1913-74
Millions of metric tons (per cent)

	1913	1940	1950	1960	1970	1974
Baku and N. Caucasus	9.0 (87.4)	26.8 (86.2)	20.8 (54.9)	29.9 (20.2)	55.4 (15.7)	51 (11.1)
Volga-Ural	—	1.8 (5.7)	11.0 (29.0)	104.0 (70.3)	207.3 (58.8)	212 (46.2)
West Siberia	—	—	—	—	31.4 (8.9)	116 (25.5)
Middle Asia	0.1 (1.0)	0.8 (2.6)	3.4 (9.0)	7.4 (5.0)	16.8 (4.8)	18 (3.9)
Kazakhstan	0.1 (1.0)	0.7 (2.3)	1.1 (2.9)	1.6 (1.1)	13.2 (3.7)	23 (5.0)
Ukraine	1.1 (10.6)	0.4 (1.3)	0.3 (0.8)	2.2 (1.5)	13.9 (3.9)	14 (3.1)
Belorussia	—	—	—	—	4.2 (1.2)	8 (1.7)
Sakhalin	—	0.5 (1.6)	0.6 (1.6)	1.6 (1.1)	2.6 (0.7)	3 (0.7)
Others	—	0.1 (0.3)	0.7 (1.8)	1.3 (0.9)	8.2 (2.3)	14 (2.8)
Total	10.3 (100.0)	31.1 (100.0)	37.9 (100.0)	148.0 (100.0)	353.0(100.0)	459(100.0)

Sources: 1913-1970: T. Shabad, 1969, and 'News Notes', *Sov. Geog.* various dates, *Narodnoye Khozyaystvo SSSR*, various years
1974: T. Shabad, and 'News Notes', *Soviet Geog.* XVI (5) 1975, and author's estimates

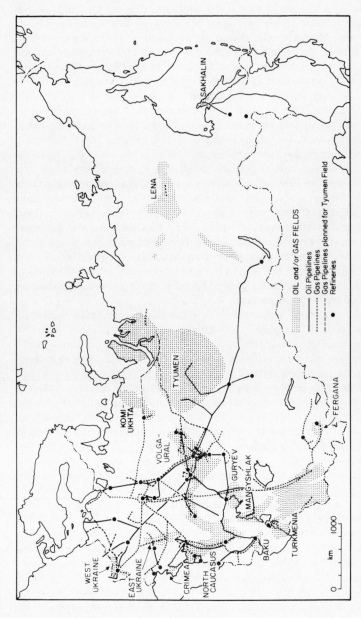

Fig 11. OIL AND GAS FIELDS AND PIPELINES
Based on *Atlas Razvitiya i Kultury SSSR* (Moscow, 1967), 105

Union's known energy reserves. Furthermore, during the 1960s, while output increased nearly two and a half times, reserves rose by only 70 per cent.[5] However, this should not be taken as indicating any likely shortage of oil resources in the near future, though there may be problems in matching growth to demand. The USSR possesses some 12 million sq km of territory underlain by sedimentary formations, and so far only one well has been drilled for every 100 sq km of such prospective oil-bearing land. The continental shelf areas, amounting to 2·5 million sq km are virtually untouched.[6] In short, vast potential oil-bearing areas are largely unexplored, and it seems likely that actual reserves are many times greater than those proven so far. This does mean, however, that large-scale investment in prospecting and in the development of new oilfields will be required if planned rates of growth are to be achieved. This situation results from the relatively late development of really large-scale oil production in the USSR, and the much greater attention paid to coal during the 1930s and 40s. Between 1938 and 1951 world petroleum production doubled, whereas that of the Soviet Union rose by only 50 per cent. Since then the position has been reversed: between 1950 and 1970, world production increased fourfold, but Soviet output rose eightfold and her share of world production climbed from 8 to 16 per cent.

The tremendous increase in oil production is an outstanding feature of Soviet economic development during the last two decades. In 1974 output stood at forty-five times the 1913 level: more significantly, 1974 production was nearly fifteen times that of 1940 and more than three times that of 1960 (Table 20). Output is scheduled to rise by a further 65-80 per cent during the 1970s, and this will almost certainly make the USSR the world's leading producer, a position occupied briefly by the Russian Empire at the beginning of the twentieth century. Output rose by 30 per cent between 1970 and 1974, reaching 459 million tons in latter year.

Changes in the volume and world significance of Soviet oil production have been accompanied by major shifts in the location of the main producing areas (Fig 11), changes which have been a good deal more striking than in the case of coal. Before the Revolution oil came almost entirely from the Baku-North Caucasus zone, which in 1913 accounted for well over four-fifths of the total output. Small-scale production had also begun in the Emba (Guryev) field near the mouth of the Ural river, on the Caspian shore of Turkestan and in the western Ukraine.[7] While output increased threefold between 1913 and 1940, there was remarkably little change in this pattern, the Maykop, Groznyy and Baku districts producing almost exactly the same proportion of the total at both dates. Small quantities were produced in 1940 from the

Emba, Ukrainian, Middle Asian and Sakhalin fields, and the Volga-Ural field had come into operation, though producing less than 2 million tons.

World War II, which caused the loss of Maykop and a serious threat to Groznyy and Baku, was one factor leading to the rapid development of the Volga-Ural or 'Second Baku' field, which by 1950 was producing nearly 30 per cent of Soviet oil. By this stage output from the Baku-North Caucasus zone had fallen below the pre-war peak and exhaustion was feared, stimulating further expansion in the Second Baku and elsewhere. This expansion, together with a much higher rate of investment in the oil industry from the mid-1950s, resulted in extremely rapid growth of output from the Volga-Ural field, which increased its production nearly tenfold between 1950 and 1960 to become by far the most important producer, responsible for 70 per cent of the total. The 1950s also saw rapid growth in most other oilfields. Even the North Caucasus-Baku zone increased its output by nearly 50 per cent, and production in 1960 was higher than in 1940. This area had been revivified by the discovery of additional oil pockets along the north flank of the main Caucasian range and beneath the waters of the Caspian.

The 1960s witnessed a third phase in the development and locational spread of the Soviet oil industry. While the combined output of the North Caucasus-Baku and Volga-Ural zones doubled, both passed their peak of production and their share of total output declined from 90 to 75 per cent as a result of the opening up of other regions. Among the latter, by far the most important was the West Siberian lowland, where a 'Third Baku' is undergoing rapid development in the sparsely populated swamp and forest lands of the Ob-Irtysh basin. Oil was first struck in this region in 1959, and commercial production began in 1964; in 1970 the West Siberian (Tyumen) field produced 31 million tons, some 9 per cent of the Soviet total and equivalent to the entire Soviet output in 1940. Production in 1974 was 116 million tons. The region is scheduled for rapid expansion throughout the 1970s, with a planned output of 146 million tons in 1975 and 230-60 million tons in 1980, by which date it will be responsible for some 40 per cent of total production and will be the most important oil field.[8] If this development occurs, as now appears almost certain, no further movement of oil eastwards from the Volga-Ural field will be necessary.[9] Meanwhile a number of promising finds have been made still further east, notably in Yakutia and in the Kamchatka-Chukotka zone of the far north-east. These are remote, thinly settled and environmentally hostile regions, to which the technological expertise gained during the development of the Tyumen field will be highly relevant. Thus the next decade is likely to see a

Table 21

NATURAL GAS PRODUCTION, 1940-74
Thousand million cubic metres (per cent)

	1940		1950		1960		1970		1974	
RSFSR	0.2	(6.3)	2.9	(49.8)	24.4	(53.9)	83.3	(42.1)	100.0	(38.4)
Europe	0.2	(6.3)	2.9	(49.8)	24.0	(52.9)	70.0	(35.0)	59.0	(22.6)
Urals	–		n		0.2	(0.5)	2.3	(1.6)	12.0	(4.6)
Siberia	–		n		0.2	(0.5)	11.0	(5.5)	29.0	(11.1)
Ukraine	0.5	(15.6)	1.5	(26.7)	14.3	(31.5)	60.9	(30.7)	68.3	(26.2)
Uzbekistan	n		n		0.4	(1.0)	32.1	(16.2)	37.2	(14.3)
Kazakhstan	n		n		n		2.1	(1.1)	5.4	(2.1)
Azerbaydzhan	2.5	(78.1)	1.2	(21.4)	5.8	(12.9)	5.5	(2.8)	9.2	(3.5)
Kirgizia	–		–		n		0.4	(0.2)	0.5	(0.2)
Tadzhikstan	n		n		n		0.4	(0.2)	0.6	(0.2)
Turkmenia	n		n		0.2	(0.5)	13.1	(6.6)	39.3	(15.1)
Total	3.2	(100.0)	5.8	(100.0)	45.3	(100.0)	197.9	(100.0)	260.5	(100.0)

Sources: 1940-1970: T. Shabad, 1969, and 'News Notes', *Sov. Geog*, various dates *Narodnoye Khozyaystvo SSSR*, various years
1974: T. Shabad, 'News Notes', *Soviet Geog*, XVI (5), 1975, and author's estimates

major shift in the centre of gravity of the Soviet oil industry: whereas in 1970 about 80 per cent of Soviet oil was produced west of the Urals, by 1980 the figure could be less than 50 per cent.

Output has also continued to rise in Kazakhstan and Middle Asia. Although these areas produce less than 10 per cent of the total, their output has trebled since 1960. Major developments include the opening up of the Mangyshlak field on the eastern side of the Caspian. In addition to these events in the east, intensive prospecting has revealed the presence of significant quantities of oil in regions previously considered negative, and production has begun at several new sites in the Ukraine and Belorussia.

Rapidly increasing oil output has necessitated a big increase in the number and capacity of oil refineries, but this has not always kept pace with the growth of output and changes in location. For several years in the 1950s Volga-Ural oil was sent to Baku for refining, and some commentators have seen increasing Soviet exports of crude oil as a result of inadequate refinery capacity. Such problems, however, are only temporary. The building of pipelines, too, has not always kept up with increases in oil output, and large quantities of petroleum products are still carried over long distances by rail. The growth of the pipeline network continues, however, and this has encouraged the building of refineries and petro-chemical complexes in the older industrial areas as well as on the oilfields.

Natural Gas

A recent estimate[10] places Soviet natural gas reserves at more than 26,000 million metric tons of coal equivalent, by far the largest in the world.[11] Natural gas is a very recent major addition to Soviet energy supplies. As late as 1955 it made up little more than 2 per cent of total energy production, with an output of only 10,300 million cu m. Since then it has increased more than twenty-fold, passing 260,000 million cu m in 1974, when it accounted for some 20 per cent. Continued very rapid growth is envisaged, with a 1975 target of 285,000 million cu m.

In the early stages of its development natural gas came mainly from operating oilfields, but more recently it has to an increasing extent been derived from separate gasfields, though these have often been in the same general regions as the oil wells. Thus, in the 1940s, the small output of natural gas came mainly from the Baku district of Azerbaydzhan, with minor production from Dashava in the West Ukrainian oilfield. Exploration of the Volga-Ural zone revealed numerous sources of natural gas in that region, and large-scale development also occurred along the north flank of the Caucasus in the 1950s. Rapid growth of output during the 1960s involved the

exploitation of major 'non-associated' gasfields, particularly at Shebelinka in the eastern Ukraine and in the Amu Darya valley of Middle Asia.
Since the majority of published data are given on the basis of republics
or economic regions (Table 21), it is difficult to be precise about the
contributions made by individual fields, particularly as the situation is a
rapidly changing one. In 1970 the proportions were roughly as follows:
Krasnodar and Stavropol districts of the North Caucasus 30 per cent,
Shebelinka 20 per cent, Volga-Ural oilfield 20 per cent, Uzbekistan 16
per cent, and Dashava 8 per cent. As with oil, production is at present
concentrated in the European part of the country, with about 70 per cent
coming from regions to the west of the Urals, but the situation is
changing with the rapid growth of production in the Middle Asian fields
and the recent discovery of very large reserves in the northern part of the
Tyumen oblast. There can be little doubt that further large deposits exist
still further east, notably in the middle Lena basin of the Yakut ASSR.

Pipelines
The rapid growth of oil and gas production has been accompanied by
the building of an extensive system of pipelines. The Soviet Union now
has 41,000km of oil pipeline and 71,000km of gas pipeline (Fig 11).
West of the Urals a complex network now links the main producing and
consuming districts and extends across the western frontier to the
Comecon countries and beyond. Among the most important elements in
the Asiatic regions are the Trans-Siberian pipeline, which carries oil as
far east as Irkutsk and is destined for eventual extension, possibly with
Japanese participation, to the Pacific coast, and the gas lines from the
Middle Asian fields to the Urals and the European centre. Long-
distance gas lines are now under construction from the Tyumen fields to
both these regions.

Electricity
Great importance is attached by Soviet economic planners to the
development of the electricity supply industry, not least as a result of
Lenin's dictum that 'Communism is Soviet power plus the electrification of the whole country'. At the same time it should be remembered
that a rapid rise in the output of electric power over the past 50 years is a
common characteristic of all advanced economies and the Soviet
achievement is in no way exceptional. The actual increase in electricity
production has of course been very great (Table 22). From the very low
level of 2 milliard kWh in 1913, it reached 740 milliard in 1970 and is
scheduled to rise by another 40 per cent to 1035 milliard in 1975.[12]
While this is certainly an impressive growth, it still leaves the Soviet
Union some distance behind the United States, which in 1970 produced

Table 22

POWER STATION CAPACITY AND ELECTRICITY PRODUCTION, 1913-70

	1913	1930	1940	1950	1960	1970
Total capacity 000, 000 kW	1.1	2.9	11.2	19.6	66.7	166.8
Total production 000,000,000 kWh	2.0	8.4	48.3	91.2	292.3	740.4
HEP capacity 000,000 kW	0.016	0.13	1.6	3.2	14.8	31.4
per cent	1.5	4.4	14.3	16.3	22.2	18.8
HEP production 000,000,000 kWh	0.035	0.56	5.1	12.7	50.9	124.4
per cent	1.8	6.6	10.6	13.9	17.4	16.8

Source: *Narodnoye Khozyaystvo SSSR,* various years

1638 milliard kWh of electricity. The relative position of the USSR can be seen more clearly if gross output figures are transformed to per capita production, a measure frequently used as an indicator of levels of economic development. In 1970 the Soviet Union produced 3059 kWh per head of the population, a figure exceeded by several major industrial powers (USA 7875, UK 4439, West Germany 4118) as well as by a number of smaller countries where hydro-electricity is the main source of power (Norway 14,700, Switzerland 5270).

Electric power in the USSR is generated from a great variety of sources – coal, lignite, oil, natural gas, shale, peat and even wood. A start has been made on the development of atomic power[13] and hydro-electric plants are a major element, but the mineral fuels remain overwhelmingly predominant. A great deal of emphasis is laid in Soviet publications, especially where these have a propagandist slant, on the development of hydro-electric power since the Revolution. Major hydro-electric plant are hailed as 'landmarks along the road to Communism' and feature prominently among the technological achievements of the Soviet period, which has seen the construction of several of the world's largest hydro-electric stations. There is indeed a very large hydro-electric potential, which has been assessed at 12 per cent of the world total,[14] but, as with so many Soviet resources, the geographical distribution of this potential hinders its development. An estimated 80 per cent lies in the Asiatic regions, mainly in the rivers of Siberia, and presents the usual problems of remoteness from consuming areas and a hostile physical environment. So far, only a minute fraction of the country's vast potential has been realised, and in recent years the pace of development appears to have slackened.

As a share of total electricity generated, hydro-electric power rose steadily from less than 2 per cent in 1913 to a peak just below 20 per cent in 1958. In the latter year it was announced that, in future, there would be a stronger emphasis on the construction of large thermal-generating plant, fired by oil, natural gas and low-grade coal, and this policy decision was reflected in a slight decline in the proportion of hydro-electric power during the 1960s. Several reasons were advanced for this change of emphasis, most of them concerned with relative costs. Construction costs per unit of installed capacity are significantly lower for thermal plant, which can also be built much more rapidly, thus tying up capital over a shorter period. Hydro-electric plants are obviously cheaper to operate, in that fuel costs are virtually nil, but the increasing use of oil and gas, together with the economies of scale that result from the increasing size of thermal plants, have reduced the significance of this factor. Thermal plants are far more flexible, in the sense that they can be built where the power is required, whereas potential sites for large hydro-electric stations are restricted by physical factors. The cost of bringing fuel to thermal stations has also been reduced by the use of oil and gas pipelines. Finally, in recent years at least, thermal plants in the USSR would appear to be a good deal more efficient, partly because they are less affected by the winter freeze and partly because some of the hydro-electric plants have worked below capacity. In 1970 thermal plant produced 4542 kWh per kilowatt of installed capacity, compared with a figure of 3961 kWh for hydro-electric plant.

The geographer, of course, has a unique interest in the location of hydro-electric plant, whose distribution reflects the often conflicting influences of physical feasibility and economic needs, but this should not lead us to lose sight of the very much greater importance of thermal generating plant in the Soviet electricity supply. The distribution of power stations of both types is shown in Fig 12 and regional production data are given in Table 23. Not surprisingly, given the dominance of 'market-oriented' thermal generating plant, the distribution of power stations shows a marked similarity to the general distribution of population and industry. About 70 per cent of total electricity generation occurs in the European section of the country, where the most striking features are the clusters of larger thermal plants in the Centre, Donbass and Urals, the strings of major hydro-electric stations along the Dnepr and Volga and the numerous small hydro plants in Karelia and the Caucasus, where local relief favours this type of development. East of the Urals the building of major plant, both thermal and hydro, has taken place mainly in the energy-rich zone extending from northern Kazakhstan to Lake Baykal.

Table 23 also indicates a wide range in per capita electricity production among the major economic regions. In general, the figures

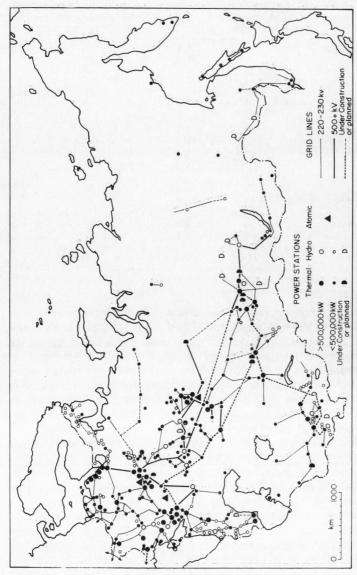

POWER STATIONS

Thermal	Hydro	Atomic

>500,000 kW ● ○ ▲

<500,000 kW ● ○

Under Construction
or planned D D D

GRID LINES

——— 220–230 kv

——— 500+ kV

------- Under Construction
or planned

km 1000

0

Fig 12. POWER STATIONS AND ELECTRIC TRANSMISSION LINES
Based on the 1 : 5,000,000 map *Elektrifikatsiya SSSR* (Moscow, 1973)

Table 23

PRODUCTION OF ELECTRICITY, BY MAJOR ECONOMIC REGIONS, 1970

| | Production | | Per capita production | |
	000, 000, 000 kWh	per cent	kWh	per cent of average
North-west	34. 4	4. 7	2820	92
Centre	81. 5	11. 0	2942	96
Volga-Vyatka	14. 9	2. 0	1795	59
Central Black Earth	8. 6	1. 2	1075	35
Volga	80. 6	10. 9	4380	143
North Caucasus	29. 8	4. 0	2084	68
Urals	87. 1	11. 8	5730	187
West Siberia	44. 2	6. 0	3653	119
East Siberia	74. 0	10. 0	9867	322
Far East	14. 1	1. 9	2431	79
Ukraine	138. 0	18. 6	2930	96
Belorussia	15. 1	2. 0	1678	55
Baltic	21. 7	2. 9	2855	93
Moldavia	7. 6	1. 0	2111	69
Transcaucasus	27. 1	3. 7	2203	72
Kazakhstan	34. 7	4. 7	2712	89
Middle Asia	26. 8	3. 6	1340	44
Total	740. 4	100. 0	3059	100

Sources: *Narodnoye Khozyaystvo SSSR v 1970 godu,* 180
          Narodnoye Khozyaystvo RSFSR v 1970 godu, 72

reflect regional variations in the level of industrial development so far
achieved. Thus such regions as Middle Asia, the Black Earth Centre
and Belorussia rank low in per capita electricity output. The
correspondence is, however by no means complete. Among major
industrial zones, the Centre and Ukraine record figures slightly below
the national average and 'import' electricity from other regions, while
the Volga and particularly East Siberia, where electricity generation is a
major regional specialisation, have very high per capita figures and
'export' a good deal of their electric power.

    Two other features of the development of the electricity supply
industry since the late 1950s are particularly noteworthy – the
progressive increase in the size of the producing units and the
organisation of a nationwide transmission system. Before 1950 the great
majority of thermal generating plants were quite small, usually wih
capacities of 100,000 to 200,000 kW, and based on local fuels.
Hydro-electric stations, though on average much bigger than thermal
plants, were of modest size, the largest being that at Zaporozhye, on the
Dnepr, with an installed capacity of 648,000 kW. Technological
developments over the past two decades have included the increasing
use of oil and natural gas, facilitating the long-distance movement of

fuel to support progressively larger thermal generating plants in the consuming areas. At the same time, a number of big thermal stations have been built near sources of low-grade opencast coal and lignite, and the power from these is transmitted over long distances to the consuming centres. New thermal plants built between 1955 and 1965 had capacities ranging from 600,000 to 1,200,000 kW and, over the past few years, plants with capacities up to 2,400,000 kW have been constructed. Individual generating units of 200,000 to 300,000 kW have become common and, more recently, units up to 800,000 kW have been brought into operation. Thus the newer thermal plants are a good deal bigger than the largest hydro-electric plants of 20 years ago. At the same time, the size of hydro-electric plant has also increased. As already indicated, in 1950 the biggest of these had a capacity of 648,000 kW; in 1960 this distinction was held by the 2,300,000 kW station at Kuybyshev, on the Volga, and today it belongs to the Krasnoyarsk station on the Yenisey, with a capacity of 6,000,000 kW. Note the eastward movement that has accompanied this increase in size. As Table 22 shows, these developments have supported an acceleration in the rate at which new capacity has been installed, from an average of 4,710,000 kW per annum in the 1950s to 10 million in the 1960s. The rate envisaged for the 1971-5 Plan is 13,200,000 kW per annum.

The same period has also seen major developments in the field of electricity transmission. Power losses involved in long-distance transmission from generating to consuming areas are a problem in the development of remote energy resources, and Soviet scientists have devoted much effort to the reduction of these losses. The layout of the main transmission lines is indicated in Fig 12. Before the 1950s transmission took place only over short distances, generally within the confines of a single economic region. In the late 1950s and early 1960s regional grids at 220-230 kV were established for the European USSR, Caucasia, north Kazakhstan, central Siberia and Middle Asia. These are now in the process of being linked together by 500-1500 kV lines, and there will soon be a single transmission system covering the whole of the USSR west of Lake Baykal.

5
The Metallurgical and Engineering Industries

Ferrous Metallurgy

BECAUSE OF ITS fundamental nature in industrial development of the Soviet type, the iron and steel industry has already received some attention in Chapter 3 and will be discussed in some detail in Part Three ot this volume. Consequently its treatment here will be relatively brief.

Soviet economic planners have consistently alloted high priority to the growth of steel production as a prerequisite for industrial growth in other sectors, and the establishment of the world's largest iron and steel industry has been one of the outstanding achievements of the period since the Revolution. While it may no longer be true that steel production is one of the best measures of a country's economic strength, there remains some value in international comparisons in this sphere. From less than five million tons in 1913, Soviet steel production reached 136 million tons in 1974, when the USSR was the world's leading producer. Her output was nearly twenty per cent greater than that of the United States and not far behind those of Japan, Germany and the United Kingdom combined. In terms of per capita output, however, the USSR, with a production equivalent to 544kg per head of the population, compares unfavourably with Japan (823kg) and West Germany (651kg).

The USSR is extremely well endowed with iron ore resources, and a recent estimate[1] places total 'recoverable' reserves at 109,700 million tons, sufficient to support the present level of production for more than 500 years. This marks a very big increase over estimates made in the 1950s[2], the difference being due largely to new discoveries in the Kursk Magnetic Anomaly area.[3] Soviet iron ore reserves are not only extremely large, they also include a high proportion of ores with a high metal content and, until recently, the USSR was able to support the growth of her steel industry by using only ores with a metal content above 50 per cent. This is no longer the case and there is an increasing use of lower-grade materials, often mined opencast and requiring concentration; nevertheless in 1970 the average iron content of ores used in the Soviet industry was still 54 per cent,[4] a figure well above that of many leading steel producers. Here, as in so many other instances, the main problem is that of choosing between the various sources of ore available for exploitation.

Ferrous metallurgy, which has a long history in the Soviet Union, displays an interesting sequence of major locational changes associated with the various phases of its development. In its growth over the past 50 years the industry, as the most basic of all manufacturing activities, provides a particularly good example of the problems, methods and achievements of Soviet economic planning. The optimal location of steel plant has been and remains a topic of lively debate, not only concerning the more obvious locational factors of raw materials, power, labour, transport and markets but also the whole problem of regional development policy.

The oldest tradition of ironworking is found in the forested zone of European Russia, where handicraft metal industries were an integral part of the economy of Slav agricultural communities from early times and where state-owned ironworks were opened at Tula in 1712. These used local high-grade iron ores and charcoal for smelting. In the early eighteenth century a charcoal-based iron smelting industry was established in the Urals and, for more than 100 years, this was Russia's leading iron-producing region, which for a time exported iron to other countries of Europe.

The late nineteenth century witnessed a new phase in the evolution of the industry. Developments that had occurred several decades earlier in western Europe – the mechanisation of industry, the building of a railway network, and the establishment of plant using the coke-smelting process to deal with a rapid increase in the demand for iron and steel – affected the Russian Empire only from about 1860 onwards. The presence of rich supplies of coking coal and iron ore in the eastern Ukraine, together with that region's favourable location with respect to the main centres of population and industry, ensured its rapid rise to a dominant position in the industry. New iron and steel plants were built in the Donbass and Dnepr bend, linked by the exchange of coking coal and iron ore along railways built to connect the two districts. The Urals, relatively remote and lacking coking coal, could not compete and, although the region's output continued to rise, it was soon outstripped

Table 24

PRODUCTION OF IRON ORE, PIG IRON AND STEEL, 1913-74
Millions of metric tons (per cent)

(a) Iron Ore

	1913		1940		1950		1960		1970		1974	
European RSFSR	0.6	(6.5)	1.1	(3.7)	0.9	(2.3)	6.4	(6.0)	25.7	(13.1)	40	(17.8)
Urals	1.8	(19.6)	8.1	(27.1)	15.5	(39.0)	27.3	(25.8)	26.2	(13.4)	26	(11.6)
Siberia	–		0.5	(1.7)	2.2	(5.5)	6.0	(5.7)	12.8	(6.5)	15	(6.7)
Ukraine	6.7	(72.8)	20.2	(67.6)	21.0	(52.9)	59.1	(55.8)	111.0	(56.8)	122	(54.2)
Kazakhstan	–		–		–		5.8	(5.5)	18.2	(9.3)	20	(8.9)
Transcaucasus	–		–		–		1.3	(1.2)	1.4	(0.7)	2	(0.8)
Total	9.2	(100.0)	29.9	(100.0)	39.7	(100.0)	105.9	(100.0)	195.5	(100.0)	225	(100.0)

(b) Pig iron

	1913		1940		1950		1960		1970		1974	
European RSFSR	0.4	(9.5)	1.0	(6.8)	0.9	(4.7)	3.1	(6.6)	11.8	(13.7)	16	(16.0)
Urals	0.9	(21.4)	2.7	(18.2)	7.2	(37.5)	15.1	(32.3)	22.9	(26.7)	26	(26.0)
Siberia	–		1.5	(10.1)	1.9	(9.9)	3.3	(7.1)	7.3	(8.5)	9	(9.0)
Ukraine	2.9	(69.1)	9.6	(64.9)	9.2	(47.9)	24.2	(51.7)	41.4	(48.2)	45	(45.0)
Kazakhstan	–		–		–		0.3	(0.6)	1.8	(2.1)	3	(3.0)
Transcaucasus	–		–		–		0.7	(1.5)	0.8	(0.9)	1	(1.0)
Total	4.2	(100.0)	14.9	(100.0)	19.2	(100.0)	46.8	(100.0)	85.9	(100.0)	100	(100.0)

(c) *Steel*

	1913		1940		1950		1960		1970		1974	
European RSFSR	0.9	(20.9)	3.4	(18.6)	4.4	(16.1)	9.2	(14.1)	18.5	(15.9)	21	(15.4)
Urals	0.9	(20.9)	4.0	(21.9)	10.7	(39.2)	21.9	(33.5)	36.0	(31.0)	42	(30.9)
Siberia	—		1.9	(10.4)	3.4	(12.5)	5.5	(8.4)	9.4	(8.1)	13	(9.6)
Ukraine	2.4	(55.8)	8.9	(48.6)	8.4	(30.7)	26.2	(40.1)	46.6	(40.2)	52	(38.2)
Kazakhstan	—		—		0.1	(0.4)	0.3	(0.5)	2.2	(1.9)	5	(3.7)
Transcaucasus	—		n	n	0.1	(0.4)	1.7	(2.6)	2.1	(1.8)	2.2	(1.6)
Latvia	0.1	(2.3)	n		n	n	0.1	(0.2)	0.4	(0.3)	0.5	(0.4)
Uzbekistan	—		—		0.1	(0.4)	0.3	(0.5)	0.4	(0.3)	0.4	(0.3)
Total	4.3	(100.0)	18.3	(100.0)	27.3	(100.0)	65.3	(100.0)	116.0	(100.0)	136.1	(100.0)

Sources: T. Shabad, 1969 and 'News Notes', *Soviet Geog*, various dates
Narodnoye Khozyaystvo SSSR, various years

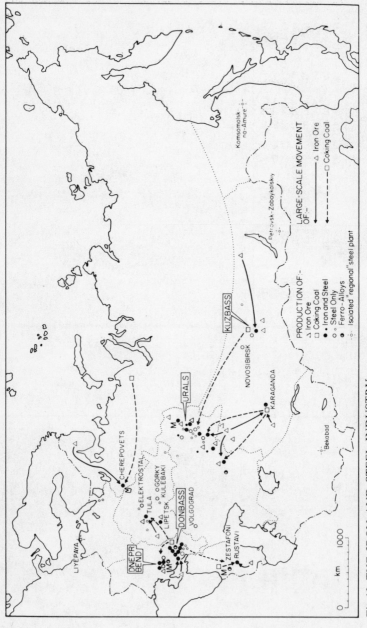

Fig 13. THE IRON AND STEEL INDUSTRY
For details, see regional maps, Figs 22-30

by the Ukraine. In 1913 the latter was producing more than half the country's steel (Table 24). About a fifth came from the Urals and a similar amount from a number of European districts that relied on the Ukraine for much of their pig iron.

The inter-war period saw the building of iron and steel plant in several new areas, but the most important development was the establishment of the 'second metallurgical base', founded on the interchange of Urals iron ore and Kuzbass coking coal. This link permitted the modernisation of existing plant in the Urals and the building of many new ones, and steel production rose rapidly. However, there was also rapid growth in other regions and the Urals' share of steel production in 1940 was much the same as in 1913. Indeed the contribution made by the two metallurgical bases combined declined somewhat between 1913 and 1940 owing to the establishment of additional capacity in other districts, notably the Kuzbass, which in 1940 produced one-tenth of Soviet steel.

Particularly rapid growth occurred in the more easterly steel-producing districts during World War II. Whereas Ukrainian steel production in 1950 was slightly below the 1940 level, output from the Urals and Siberia had doubled and now accounted for more than half the total.

During the 1950s grandiose schemes were proposed for the establishment of a 'third metallurgical base' in the area between the Urals and Lake Baykal, a zone with massive reserves of coking coal and iron ore. In the event this has not materialised: although some new capacity has been built, Siberia's share of total steel production actually declined between 1950 and 1970, as did that of the Urals, while the contribution made by the western regions, notably the Ukraine, increased.

Somewhat paradoxically, the Soviet iron and steel industry today is more widely dispersed than ever before, yet remains highly concentrated in the sense that the great bulk of the output is derived from a small number of major producing districts. Steel is made in no fewer than fifteen of the nineteen major economic regions[5] but now, as in 1913 and 1950, some 70 per cent comes from the two metallurgical bases in the Urals and the Ukraine.

Soviet steel-producing districts (Fig 13) thus fall into a number of fairly distinctive categories. Dominant in terms of production are the eastern Ukraine and the Urals, both of which owe much of their prominence to the local resource base. There are, however, contrasts between the two. The Ukraine remains largely self-contained and still has large reserves of both coking coal and iron ore; the latter could, if necessary, be supplemented from the nearby Kursk Magnetic Anomaly.

The Ural district, on the other hand, has for nearly 40 years relied on coking coal from the Kuzbass and Karaganda and is no longer self-sufficient in iron ore, increasing quantities of which are brought from adjacent areas of the Kazakh republic.

Among the secondary steel-producing areas, the Kuzbass and Karaganda owe their initial development to their links with the Urals, to which they still send coking coal, while now obtaining the bulk of their iron ore from local sources. During the 1960s both developed new long-distance links, Karaganda receiving some of its iron ore from north-western Kazakhstan and the Kuzbass from the Ust-Ilim district of eastern Siberia.

The European Centre is quite different. Here, although iron ore has been mined in the Tula district for some time, there is no coking coal, and the iron and steel industry has been developed as a support for the region's manufacturing activities, not as a result of the local resource base. Until recently the Centre relied on the Ukraine for both coal and pig iron but it is now developing its own iron ore resources in the Kursk Magnetic Anomaly, as a result of which the Black Earth Centre is destined to become a major steel-producing district.

Small steelworks have been established in a number of regions as support for their metal-using industries, reflecting the idea that each economic region should have its own metallurgical base. In this category we may place the works at Komsomolsk-na-Amure in the Far East, at Petrovsk-Zabaykalskiy in eastern Siberia, at Bekabad in Middle Asia and at Liyepaya on the Baltic. All these depend on scrap metal supplemented by long-haul pig iron from other regions, and are only small-scale producers. A more recent manifestation of the idea of regional steelworks is the large integrated plant at Cherepovets on the Rybinsk reservoir. Designed to supply the needs of the north-western economic region, this draws its coking coal from the Pechora field and its iron ore from the Kola peninsula.

Mention should also be made of the small iron and steel industry of the Transcaucasus. This uses local coal, manganese and iron ore, but requires additional coking coal shipments from the Donbass.

The most likely short-term trend in the future location of the Soviet iron and steel industry is an increase in the importance of the western part of the country. While official views still favour the installation of added capacity in Siberia, progress is slow, and there is a growing body of opinion that favours a concentration of effort in the west, where the Kursk Magnetic Anomaly ores offer tremendous possibilities for the future.[6]

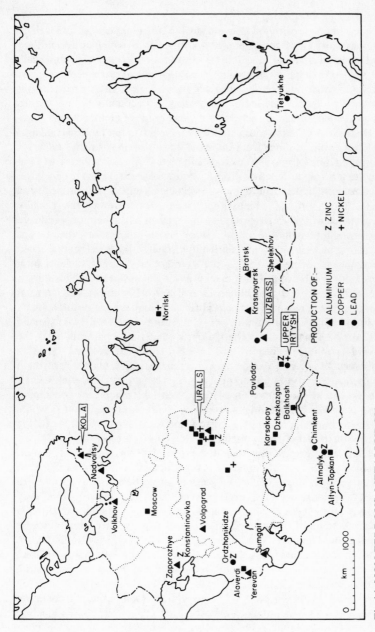

Fig 14. NON-FERROUS METALLURGY
For details, see regional maps, Figs 22–30

Z ZINC   + NICKEL

PRODUCTION OF:-
▲ ALUMINIUM
■ COPPER
● LEAD

Norilsk
Bratsk
Krasnoyarsk
Shelekhov
KUZBASS
UPPER IRTYSH
URALS
KOLA
Nadvoitsy
Volkhov
Moscow
Konstantinovka
Volgograd
Zaporozhye
Ordzhonikidze
Sumgait
Aloverdi
Yerevan
Pavlodar
Karsakpay
Dzhezkazgan
Balkhash
Chimkent
Almalyk
Altyn-Topkan
Tetyukhe

0   km   1000

Non-ferrous Metallurgy

In comparison with the iron and steel industry, which consumes huge quantities of raw materials and power to produce more than 130 million tons of metal annually, non-ferrous metallurgy is a relatively small scale activity, producing in all perhaps 4 million tons of metal each year. At the same time, non-ferrous metals are a vital element in any industrial economy; they become increasingly so as that economy becomes more sophisticated, producing an ever-widening range of commodities.

Discussion of this sector of Soviet industry is rendered particularly difficult by the absence from the standard statistical abstracts of data on the production of non-ferrous ores and metals. While estimates of total production can be obtained from a variety of sources, and the location of most producing centres can be obtained from Soviet atlases[7] and texts, it is virtually impossible to be precise about the relative importance of the various regions. Secrecy in this sphere may indicate an obsession with 'security', since most non-ferrous metals are 'strategic materials', or that, until quite recently, the USSR experienced shortages of some of these vital commodities[8]. The Soviet Union appeared to achieve self-sufficiency in most non-ferrous metals during the 1960s, though, as the only source of several items for her Comecon partners, the maintenance of self-sufficiency may present problems.

Non-ferrous metal-mining and metallurgy are widely dispersed activities owing to the variety of raw materials concerned and the several possible stages of processing before the finished metal is produced. It is very common to find the earlier stages of treatment, such as smelting or concentration of the ores, near the raw material source, while refining and metal production often take place near consuming centres and/or major sources of energy. Fully integrated works, which have become dominant in the iron and steel industry, are still the exception in non-ferrous metallurgy.

Most non-ferrous metal ores are abundant in the Soviet Union. Problems occur mainly in their location, and in the cost of exploitation and transport. Many of the ore sources are to be found in remote and empty regions, and the urge towards self-sufficiency, particularly marked in the case of non-ferrous metals, has led to their exploitation under extremely difficult physical conditions, adding greatly to the costs of production.

A fairly detailed discussion of the location of resources and producing centres will be found in the sections of this chapter dealing with individual metals and in Part Three. Many of the ores are found in association with igneous and metamorphic rocks, and are therefore extracted where such rocks are at or close to the surface. Consequently the major sources are such regions as the Urals, the Kazakh Uplands, the Kola peninsula and the mountains of Caucasia, Middle Asia, southern Siberia and the Far East, and a noteworthy feature is the virtual absence of economically accessible non-ferrous metal ores from most of the sedimentary-covered European plain. This has meant that the exploitation and processing of these materials has been a major element in the industrial development of outlying regions and, except in the Urals, is poorly represented in the main settled zone of the country (Fig 14).

Despite its considerable resources, the Russian Empire in the course of its nineteenth-century industrialisation made little progress in the non-ferrous sector. Although demand for these metals was small, they constituted the Empire's main mineral imports.

The early Five Year Plans thus paid considerable attention to non-ferrous metallurgy as an essential element in the industrialisation programme in general and the electricity generation, engineering and defence industries in particular. Considerable advances were made in the inter-war years, and by 1940 the basis of all the main branches of non-ferrous metallurgy had been laid. Despite this, the country was far from self-sufficient, and sizeable imports of several items were necessary during World War II. The continuing drive towards self-sufficiency, the needs of the industrialisation programmes of the Comecon countries, and the growing sophistication of Soviet industry have all contributed to an accelerated growth of non-ferrous metallurgy during the post-war period.

Thus the various branches of the industry have several features in common. Their locational patterns and sequence of development, however, differ a good deal, and the major metals will now be discussed individually.

Copper

Copper is one of the few metals in this group whose history of exploitation extends back earlier than the second half of the nineteenth century. Mining in the Urals is believed to have begun in the seventeenth century, and there was a sizeable export trade in the mid-eighteenth. By the eve of World War I the Russian Empire was producing over 30,000 tons of copper annually and importing a further 7000 or 8000 tons. The bulk of the output still came from the Urals, where, in 1913, there was mining at Kirovgrad, Karabash and Baymak and an electrolytic refinery at Kyshtym. Small-scale copper production was also carried on at Alaverdi and Kafan in the Transcaucasus.

Major developments in the inter-war years led to a fourfold increase in output, which reached 146,000 tons in 1940. Effort was again concentrated in the Urals, where mining and smelting centres were established at Krasnouralsk, Revda and Mednogorsk, and a second refinery was built at Verkhnyaya Pyshma. This period also saw the first stages of exploitation of the rich copper resources of Kazakhstan. A smelter was opened in 1938 at Balkhash, using ores from the nearby Kounradskiy deposit, and mining also began at Dzhezkazgan. Production from the latter source soon exceeded the capacity of the small smelter at Karsakpay, and ores and concentrates were sent in increasing quantities to the Urals for processing.

Since 1950, output has again increased more than fourfold, reaching an estimated 900,000 tons (smelter production) in 1970. The Urals and Kazakhstan have remain dominant, but the balance has changed in favour of the latter. In the Urals new sources of copper ore have been opened up at Sibay, Uchaley and Gay, and smelter capacity at older centres has been much increased. A decline in ore production from the older mines, however, has meant that Urals smelters have been increasingly concerned with Kazakh ores. During the 1960s the Urals continued to produce a good deal more finished metal than any other region, but the lead is now passing to Kazakhstan, where metal production has increased rapidly in the last few years. New sources of ore at Sayak and Bozshakul supplement supplies to the Balkhash refinery, but the biggest growth has been at Dzhezkazgan, which is now the largest single source of copper in the USSR and supports a large smelter and refinery opened in 1971.

While the Urals and Kazakhstan seem destined to supply the great bulk of the country's copper ore and metal in the foreseeable future, there have been significant developments in other regions. Potentially the most important of these has been at Almalyk, in the Uzbek republic, where mining began in the early 1960s and a concentrator, smelter and refinery were opened in 1964. Armenia continues to be of some importance, with mines at Kafan, Kadzharan and Alaverdi, where there is also a smelter. Copper is also produced in association with other metals, at Monchegorsk and Pechenga in the Kola peninsula, at Norilsk in northern Siberia and in the upper Irtysh basin of eastern Kazakhstan. Additional major sources of copper ore, which may become important producers in the near future, are Urup in the Caucasus and Udokan in the Chita oblast.

These developments have enabled the Soviet Union to achieve self-sufficiency in copper. Large imports, chiefly from Zambia, continued until the mid-1960s, but have now virtually ceased, and trade with her Comecon partners makes the USSR a net exporter. She now produces about 15 per cent of world output of both copper ore and metal, a figure exceeded only by the United States. Production is scheduled to rise by 35-40 per cent during the 1971-5 Plan.

Lead and Zinc

These two metals are derived from 'polymetallic' ores, where they occur in conjunction with other metals, including copper, silver and gold. Concentration is carried out in the mining districts, but smelters and refineries are more widely dispersed. Production began on a very small scale in the late nineteenth century and has risen steeply during the Soviet period. It increased roughly twenty-fold during the inter-war years and fourfold during the post-war period. An estimated 450,000 tons of lead and 610,000 tons of zinc were produced in 1970, and output is scheduled to rise by a further 20 per cent between 1971 and 1975.

The oldest producing site is near Ordzhonikidze (formerly Vladikavkaz) on the north flank of the Caucasus, where lead and silver were first mined in the 1850s and a zinc refinery was opened in 1904. Output continues to expand, a new mine and concentrator being opened in the late 1960s, but this area has been overshadowed by developments further east. The most important mining centre is now in the upper Irtysh valley of eastern Kazakhstan. Other major centres are at Chimkent and Tekeli, in southern Kazakhstan, at Almalyk in the Angren valley of Uzbekistan, at Salair in the Altay and at Tetkyukhe in the Sikhote Alin range of the Far East.

The biggest lead smelters are found near the mining districts, at Chimkent, Tetyukhe, and in the upper Irtysh valley, but zinc refining, an operation that now requires large quantities of electric power, is more widely dispersed. The earliest Soviet zinc refineries, using coal and coke distillation processes, were built in the 1930s at Konstantinovka in the Donbass and Belovo in the Kuzbass. The first electrolytic refineries were opened in the same decade at Ordzhonikidze and Chelyabinsk. Post-war expansion of zinc output has been assisted by the construction of four more large electrolytic refineries at Ust-Kamenogorsk, Leninogorsk, Konstantinovka and Almalyk.

Although some zinc is still imported from Poland and North Korea, this is outweighed by exports, which go mainly to East Germany, Hungary and Czechoslovakia.

Aluminium

Of all the non-ferrous metallurgical industries, the largest and most widespread is the production of aluminium, and this branch displays a particularly interesting sequence of locational changes in association with technological developments and a rapid increase in production. Output was negligible before World War I and still insufficient for the country's needs in 1940, necessitating large imports from the west during World War II. Production in 1950 was still only 155,000 tons of metal, but since then it has increased nearly tenfold to an estimated 1,500,000 tons in 1970. The slow development of the industry in the inter-war years may be ascribed to the apparently rather limited size of the Soviet Union's bauxite resources,[9] and its rapid growth since 1950 has necessitated the development of new processes making use of alternative raw materials such as nephelite, alunite and kaolinite. Considerable quantities of bauxite are imported from Greece, and Hungarian alumina is also processed in the USSR.

The making of aluminium includes three main processes – the mining of the various raw materials, the production of alumina and the conversion of alumina to aluminium (the last requiring large quantities of electric power). Each of these activities has its own location pattern, and, given the wide variety of raw materials, processes and markets, it is not surprising that the aluminium industry is widely dispersed, with some very long inter-regional links.

The earliest major developments in the Soviet aluminium industry, using the traditional bauxite-alumina-aluminium chain of processes, took place in the early 1930s. Bauxite from deposits at Boksitogorsk, about 200km south-east of Leningrad, was transformed into alumina nearby, and the alumina was taken to the hydro-electric station at Volkhov, opened in 1926, for conversion to aluminium. In 1932 the first of the Dnepr hydro-electric plants came into operation at Zaporozhye, and Boksitogorsk alumina was taken there as well. Meanwhile intensive mineral prospecting in the Urals had revealed several sources of bauxite, the largest of which proved to be those near Severouralsk, in the northern part of the region. Severouralsk bauxite was the main support of a combined alumina-aluminium plant opened at Kamensk-Uralskiy in 1939. Unlike those further west, which depended on hydro-electric power, this plant drew its electricity from thermal stations powered by the low-grade coals of the Chelyabinsk district.

The destruction of the Volkhov and Zaporozhye plants during World War II, preceded by the eastward evacuation of much of their equipment, led to accelerated growth in the eastern regions. A second alumina-aluminium complex was opened at Krasnoturinsk, only 50km from the Severouralsk bauxites, and a large aluminium plant using Urals alumina and powered by thermally generated electricity was built at Novokuznetsk in the Kuzbass. These developments enabled the USSR to increase her production of aluminium from 60,000 to 85,000 tons during the war years, despite the loss of the western plant, but the latter total was far from adequate for her needs.

Rapid growth of the aluminium industry in the post-war period has meant the exploitation of new sources of ore, the introduction of new processes and the building of massive additional plant. The

Boksitogorsk-Volkhov complex continues to produce both alumina and aluminium, but local bauxite deposits are nearing exhaustion and the main raw material is now nephelite, a by-product of apatite production at Kirovsk in the Kola peninsula. This is converted to alumina in a works that was opened at Pikalevo, near Boksitogorsk, in 1959. Pikalevo alumina is converted to aluminium not only at Volkhov but also in electrolytic refineries using locally generated hydro-electric power that were built during the 1950s at Nadvoitsy and Kandalaksha in Karelia. The resource base of this part of the country has recently been strengthened by the discovery of a major source of bauxite at Plesetsk in the Onega valley. The first ore was produced here in 1970 and it is envisaged that this will replace Boksitogorsk ore by 1975.

Other early European centres continue to produce, though with new regional linkages. The Zaporozhye plant is now one of the few in the Soviet Union to make use of imported raw materials, for here the Boksitogorsk ores have been replaced by Greek bauxite, some 500,000 tons of which are shipped annually via the Black Sea-Dnepr waterway. In the Volga region the availability of large amounts of hydro-electric power at Volgograd has led to the establishment there of a large aluminium plant dependent almost entirely on Hungarian alumina, and there are plans for additional works at Mikhaylovka, north-west of Volgograd, and at Ulyanovsk, which would probably use alumina from Pikalevo.[10]

A somewhat isolated aluminium-producing complex has developed in Transcaucasia, where aluminium reduction plants were opened in the 1950s at Yerevan and Sumgait, near Baku. It was intended that both these works should use alumina from ores mined in the Transcaucasus, and plans included a nephelite-based alumina works at Razdan and another, using alunite, at Kirovabad. Both these projects were subject to long delays as a result of difficulties experienced in developing the appropriate technology.[11] The Kirovabad plant was finally opened in 1966 and that at Razdan is scheduled for completion during the current 1971-5 plan period. In the interim the Yerevan and Sumgait aluminium works have relied on alumina brought more than 2000km from the Urals.

These four relatively long-established regions – the North-west, the Ukraine, the Urals and the Transcaucasus – continue to increase their output and play an important role in the Soviet aluminium industry, but the most striking developments of the post-war period have occurred further east. A major feature has been the construction of very large aluminium reduction plants at the sites of the major hydro-electric projects of southern Siberia. The works opened at Shelekhov in 1962, Krasnoyarsk in 1964 and Bratsk in 1966, together with the older plant at

Novokuznetsk, are believed to produce nearly half the Soviet Union's aluminium. Siberian production of alumina, however, has not kept up with the large capacity of these aluminium plants, and at least a million tons of alumina are moved eastwards each year from the Urals. To correct this imbalance, new raw material sources are being developed east of the Urals. A major deposit was opened up in 1963 at Arkalyk in the Turgay oblast of northern Kazakhstan, and an aluminium plant using this ore began production at Pavlodar in 1964. More recently the Pavlodar works has also been supplied with bauxite from Krasnooktya-brskiy in the Kustanay oblast. At present Pavlodar alumina goes to the Novokuznetsk and Shelekhov aluminium plants, but it is envisaged that, in the near future, aluminium will also be produced at Pavlodar. Until very recently Pavlodar was the only source of alumina east of the Urals, but in 1969 a large plant came into operation at Achinsk, deriving its power from thermal stations based on the low-grade coals of the Kansk-Achinsk field. The completion of the Achinsk plant, begun in the 1950s, was long delayed by technological problems resulting from the nature of the ore, but it now produces a million tons of alumina annually from nephelite mined at Belogorsk, 100km to the south-west. Achinsk alumina now goes to the Krasnoyarsk and Bratsk aluminium works.

Finally, a number of important developments are under way in Middle Asia. Kaolin clay, which occurs as overburden in the Angren coalmining district, is to be used in an alumina plant under construction nearby, and this alumina will eventually be reduced to aluminium at Regar, near Dushanbe, using electric power from the Nurek project. Technological difficulties in obtaining alumina from kaolin have again caused delays, and there may well be a phase during which the Regar plant will depend on alumina from the Urals or Transcaucasus.

Others

Among the non-ferrous metals not mentioned so far, tin is one of the few essential commodities in which the USSR is still not self-sufficient. About half her requirements come from her own resources, which necessitates mining in remote districts of north-eastern Siberia as well as in the more accessible parts of the Chita oblast and the Far East, and the rest mainly from Indonesia and Malaysia.

Of great importance to Soviet industry are the various metals used in the production of alloy steels, notably manganese, chrome, molybden-um and tungsten. The Soviet Union is the world's leading producer of manganese ores, with a 1970 output in the region of 8 million tons; 90 per cent of this come from two major sources, at Nikopol in the Ukraine and Chiatura in Georgia, with minor production at Polunochnoye in the northern Urals and Dzhezdy in Kazakhstan. There is a large annual export, mainly to the Comecon countries but also to western Europe. The USSR also takes first place in the production of chrome ore, her output of more than 1·5 million tons representing about a third of the world total. Chrome ores are mined mainly at Khromtau in northern Kazakhstan and at Sarany in the Urals, and about half the output is exported. Nickel ores come mainly from three areas: Orsk in the southern Urals and Batamshinskiy in northern Kazakhstan, Pechenga and Monchegorsk in the Kola peninsula and Norilsk near the mouth of the Yenisey. With an estimated annual production of 110,000 tons (metal content), the USSR is responsible for one-sixth of world output and takes third place after Canada and New Caledonia. Molybdenum and tungsten are mined in several districts of the Caucasus, Middle Asia and southern Siberia.

Engineering

Engineering in all its forms constitutes the largest single branch of Soviet industry. In 1970 it employed about 12 million people, some 38 per cent of the industrial labour force and more than a tenth of the entire working population. Both the numbers employed and the proportion of the workforce engaged in engineering activities have rapidly increased during the past two decades, and gross output has risen faster than in any other sector except chemicals.

Geographical analysis of this sector of manufacturing industry, however, presents considerable difficulties, particularly in the case of the USSR. In the first place it is somewhat unrealistic to think of engineering as a single economic activity. It is true that engineering can be defined as the transformation of materials, chiefly but not exclusively metallic, into equipment, machinery and consumer goods, but here the common nature of its multitudinous branches ceases and the industry can be split into a host of sub-sectors, with an almost endless variety of products. Some of these, like machine tools, are used within the engineering industry itself; some, like mining equipment or textile machinery, are the means of production in other industries, both extractive and manufacturing; while others, like motor vehicles, go direct to the consumer. Thus the markets for engineering products are extremely diverse and the market factor in location operates differently in the various branches.

Another important influence on location is the fact that labour is a major element in total costs, and such matters as tradition and accumulated skills play a major role. There are, of course, pronounced contrasts between the various branches of engineering as regards the relative importance of labour costs on the one hand and the cost of raw materials, power and transport on the other. In the heavier branches labour costs are relatively low and large quantities of raw materials and energy are consumed to produce goods of unit value, but in the lighter industries raw materials may constitute only a small proportion of total costs, the bulk of which are derived from the employment of skilled labour. On the other hand, transport costs will form a much higher proportion of total costs in the heavier than in the lighter branches. Finally, the engineering activities have a complex set of economic linkages with both the metallurgical industries, which provide their materials, and the manufacturing industries, which use their products.

In the case of the USSR a number of more specific factors enter the picture. In the first place, there has been a marked concentration of effort on the heavier branches of engineering, and many of the lighter branches, particularly those engaged in the production of consumer goods, have begun a rapid expansion only in the last two decades. Another special factor has been the avowed policy of industrial dispersal, inspired by both ideological and strategic considerations, which has had a pronounced effect on the distribution of industry as a whole and the engineering industry in particular. Soviet writers frequently draw attention to the establishment of machine-building complexes as the main form of industrialisation in regions that formerly lacked modern industry of any kind.[12]

Several practical problems also add to the difficulty of any systematic discussion of Soviet engineering activity. Engineering of one kind or another may be assumed to occur in the vast majority of urban settlements – indeed it may often be the only form of industry present – but it is virtually impossible from the published data available to assess the importance of engineering in individual centres, either as a proportion of total employment in each centre or in terms of each centre's contribution to the engineering industry as a whole. To map all centres in which engineering takes place would be to map the great majority of urban settlements. Some sort of selection is inevitable, therefore, and it is here that difficulties arise.

Major sources of information are the excellent economic maps contained in recent Soviet atlases.[13] These maps are of two kinds – larger-scale (1 : 3 or 4 million) of each economic region and smaller-scale (1 : 15 or 20 million) of the country as a whole. The regional maps show engineering centres by size-graded symbols, but there is no precise indication of the significance of symbol size, which seems to be related primarily to the settlement's population. Such maps also indicate the speciality of many towns, but the majority of centres, particularly the smaller ones, are not differentiated. Maps of the entire country show a selection of the centres appearing on the regional maps,

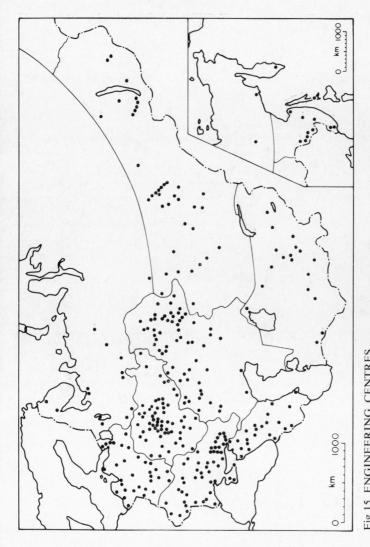

Fig 15. ENGINEERING CENTRES.
This map shows all engineering centres marked on small-scale maps in *Atlas Razvitiya Khozyaystva i Kultury SSSR* (Moscow, 1967) and/or *Atlas SSSR* (Moscow, 1969)

Fig 16.
ENGINEERING
CENTRES BY TYPE
These maps show
all centres whose
engineering speciality
is indicated on
small-scale maps in
*Atlas Razvitiya
Khozyaystva i Kultury
SSSR* (Moscow, 1967)
and/or *Atlas SSSR*
(Moscow, 1969)

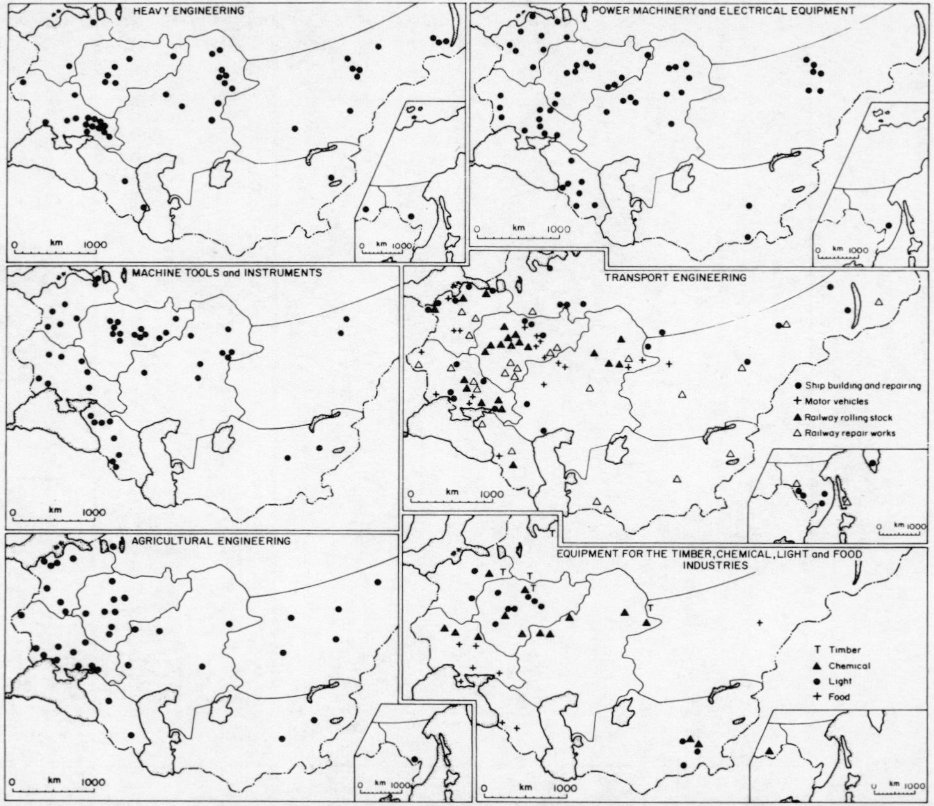

HEAVY ENGINEERING

POWER MACHINERY and ELECTRICAL EQUIPMENT

MACHINE TOOLS and INSTRUMENTS

TRANSPORT ENGINEERING

● Ship building and repairing
+ Motor vehicles
▲ Railway rolling stock
△ Railway repair works

AGRICULTURAL ENGINEERING

EQUIPMENT FOR THE TIMBER, CHEMICAL, LIGHT and FOOD INDUSTRIES

T Timber
▲ Chemical
◆ Light
+ Food

km 1000

and it can be assumed that these are the more important ones. However, they often differ from maps and lists of places defined as major engineering centres in recent Soviet textbooks, which in turn differ from each other in this respect. Neither these texts nor the various published statistical compilations give precise data on levels of employment or production in individual towns or regions on the basis of which precise factual statements can be made.[14] Consequently the following account is inevitably brief and impressionistic, since it is compiled from a variety of incomplete sources. The distributions shown in Figs 15 and 16 are based on the smaller-scale national maps in recent atlases.

Total engineering (Fig 15), as indicated by all the engineering centres shown on small-scale atlas maps, shows a wide distribution throughout the entire settled zone of the USSR, with pronounced clusters in the Moscow-Gorkiy area, the eastern Ukraine, the Urals and the Kuzbass. In Fig 16 these centres are classified into six major groups:

1 Heavy engineering
2 Power machinery and electrical equipment
3 Production of machine tools and instruments
4 Transport engineering
5 Agricultural engineering
6 Production of equipment for the timber, chemical and food industries, and for light industry.

All these major branches of engineering are quite widely dispersed in the sense that each is represented in most of the economic regions. They differ only in the degree of dispersion and their main areas of concentration.

Heavy Engineering

The most highly concentrated of the six branches distinguished in Fig 16, and primarily concerned with the manufacture of equipment for the mining and metallurgical industries, heavy engineering has a close affinity with the main steel-producing districts and about half the centres shown are in the eastern Ukraine, Urals and Kuzbass. Heavy engineering is also quite important in the Centre. Among the most important towns for the production of mining machinery are Kramatorsk, Gorlovka and Voroshilovgrad in the Donbass, Votkinsk and Kopeysk in the Urals, Prokopyevsk in the Kuzbass and Anzhero-Sudzhensk. Major centres for the production of metallurgical equipment are Kramatorsk, Sverdlovsk, Elektrostal and Alma-Ata.

Power Machinery and Electrical Equipment

The production of power machinery and electrical equipment is a good deal more widely dispersed, though with a marked concentration in the European part of the country. The items produced include boilers, turbines, diesel engines and electric motors of all kinds. The earlier works were established in the old centres of skilled engineering in the European regions, but more recently there has been some development in Siberia, Kazakhstan, Middle Asia and Caucasia. Boilers are built mainly at Podolsk, Taganrog, Belgorod, Biysk and Barnaul; turbines and generators at Leningrad, Kaluga, Kharkov, Kaunas and Novosibirsk; and diesel motors at Leningrad, Riga, Gorkiy and Kharkov.

Production of Machine Tools and Instruments

The manufacture of machine tools and instruments is also heavily concentrated in the European USSR, and there are only four important centres east of the Urals. This highly skilled branch is especially well developed in the Centre, with its tradition of skilled manufacturing, but in recent years 'the rise in the cultural and technical standards of the population. . . provided facilities for the manufacture of machine tools in new areas'.[15] The largest plants in operation today are at Moscow, Gorkiy, Kolomna, Leningrad, Kramatorsk, Kharkov, Kiev, Odessa, Minsk and Novosibirsk.

Transport Engineering

This is a particularly widely dispersed activity, largely because of the differing location patterns of its three main branches – shipbuilding, railway engineering and the production of motor vehicles.

Shipbuilding. Ocean-going vessels are still built entirely in the European part of the country, where there are important yards at Arkhangelsk on the White Sea, Leningrad, Tallin, Riga and Kaliningrad on the Baltic and Nikolayev on the Black Sea. Vessels for the Caspian trade are built at Astrakhan. A large number of shipbuilding centres, however, are at inland sites and are concerned with building river vessels for the country's extensive system of inland waterways. Among the more important of such centres are Rybinsk, Kostroma, Gorkiy and Volgograd on the Volga; Rostov-on-Don, Kiev and Kherson on the Dnepr; Kotlas and Syktyvkar on tributaries of the northern Dvina; Tyumen and Tobolsk on the Irtysh; Barnaul on the Ob, Krasnoyarsk on the Yenisey; Ust-Kut on the upper Lena; and Blagoveshchensk and Khabarovsk on the Amur. Numerous other centres have ship-repair facilities.

Railway engineering was one of the few branches at all well developed before the Revolution and is now a widely dispersed activity carried on in most regions. At the same time it is concentrated in a relatively small number of large works. The construction of steam locomotives ceased in the early 1960s and there has been a rapid increase in the number of plants building diesel and electric types. Diesel locomotives are now built at Kharkov and Voroshilovgrad in the Ukraine and at Kolomna, Murom, Kaluga, Bryansk and Lyudinovo in the Centre. Electric locomotives are built mainly at Novocherkassk and Tbilisi. Railway wagon construction is more widely dispersed – at Moscow, Kolomna, Mytishchi, Orekhovo-Zuyevo and Bryansk in the Centre; Kremenchug, Dneprodzerzhinsk and Zhdanov in the Ukraine; and at Nizhniy Tagil (Urals), Engels (Volga) and Novoaltaysk (West Siberia). Railway repair works are found in all regions at nodal points on the railway network.

The Soviet *motor vehicle* industry dates only from the 1920s and, until recently, remained very small. Annual production of all types of motor vehicle reached only 145,000 in 1940 and 523,600 (one to every 2500 people) in 1960. The great bulk of this output was in the form of lorries and buses. Output of motor cars was a mere 5500 in 1940 and 138,800 in 1960. Over the last decade, however, there has been a great expansion of the industry and in 1973 the USSR produced 1,602,000 motor vehicles, including 629,000 lorries, 56,000 buses and 917,000 cars. Despite this recent rapid growth, output of motor cars still remains well below that of such other leading industrial powers as the United States ($8 \cdot 2$ million), West Germany ($3 \cdot 2$ million), France ($2 \cdot 2$ million) and the United Kingdom ($1 \cdot 7$ million). With nearly 7 per cent of the world's population, the USSR produces 8 per cent of the world's commercial vehicles but only about 4 per cent of its passenger cars.

For much of its existence the Soviet motor vehicle industry remained heavily concentrated in the Moscow-Gorkiy region, with plant at Moscow, Yaroslavl, Likino-Dudyevo, Gorkiy, Zavolzhye, Pavlovo and Saransk. During the war additional works were built at Ulyanovsk on the Volga and Miass in the Urals. In the post-war period the industry became much more dispersed, new plant being opened at Riga, Minsk, Zhodino (Belorussia), Lvov, Odessa, Kremenchug, Zaporozhye, Melitopol, Engels, Tolyatti (on the Volga near Kuybyshev), Kutaisi (Georgia) and Petropavlovsk (northern Kazakhstan), the last two being the only automobile works outside the European USSR.

Aerospace Industries. Ideally this section would include a discussion of the Soviet aerospace industry as a branch of transport engineering in which the Soviet Union stands head and shoulders above all other powers except the United States, both in the size of the industry and its level of technology. Published Soviet sources, however, give little or no information on the scale or location of production in this field. The state airline, *Aeroflot*, operates one of the world's most extensive networks, carrying about one-fifth of the world's airline passengers,[16] and depends entirely on the Soviet industry for its supply of aircraft. This alone suggests an aircraft industry second in size only to that of the United States, which has produced a group of aircraft designers – Antonov, Ilyushin, Mikoyan, Tupolev, Yakovlev – of outstanding quality. It seems likely that the bulk of the industry, particularly the manufacture of engines and components, is concentrated in the European part of the country, especially in the Moscow and Leningrad regions, with their long tradition of skilled manufacturing and concentrations of skilled labour and scientific expertise. Partly for strategic reasons, however, it may well be that airframe and assembly plants, possibly backed up by local component and engine manufacture, are more widely dispersed, and it would be surprising if a sizeable section of the industry were not to be found to the east of the Urals.

Soviet achievements in space exploration, which include the world's first artificial satellite, launched in 1957, the first manned spaceflight (Gagarin, 1961) and numerous other 'firsts', are now well known and indicate a high level of technology. Among other things they show that, given a decision to devote the necessary funds and scientific resources to a particular project, Soviet industry is capable of advances in no way inferior to those of the capitalist world.

Agricultural Engineering

The production of *agricultural machinery*, including tractors and combines, is an activity found in every economic region. Before World War II there were only four tractor plants in operation, at Leningrad, Stalingrad, Kharkov and Chelyabinsk, and these produced about 100,000 units annually. Output is now close to 500,000, and additional works have been opened in western Siberia (Rubtsovsk), the Centre (Vladimir), the Black Earth Centre (Lipetsk), Belorussia (Minsk), the North-west (Petrozavodsk), Moldavia (Kishinev) and Georgia (Kutaisi), with the clear objective of making each region independent in this respect. The manufacture of grain combines, which are difficult to transport owing to their bulk, is also dispersed, being conducted at Riga, Gomel (Belorussia), Bezhetsk, Lyubertsy and Ryazan (Centre), Rostov, Taganorog, Kurgan, Tashkent, Krasnoyarsk and Birobidzhan (Far East).

Production of Equipment for the Timber, Chemical and Food Industries, and Light Industry

Fig 16 indicates some forty centres which are important in the manufacture of equipment for the timber, chemical and food sectors of industry, and for light industry. Not surprisingly, the location of each group is clearly related to that of the manufacturing industry that consumes its products. Thus equipment for the timber industry is produced largely in the forested north, notably at Arkhangelsk, Vologda and Tyumen; and production of chemical equipment takes place in major centres of the chemical industry, often near oil refineries. Equipment for light industry, in which textile machinery is the main element, tends to concentrate in the Centre (eg at Ivanovo, Moscow, Orel and Penza), but is also made in Middle Asia (Tashkent, Kokand, Dushanbe); while the main centres for the manufacture of machinery used in the food industries are to be found in the Ukraine (Kiev, Odessa, Kharkov, Simferopol, Poltava) and Transcaucasus (Batumi, Tbilisi).

6

The Chemical Industries

DURING THE PAST two decades, the chemical industry has been the most rapidly expanding major sector of the Soviet economy. Between 1950 and 1970 employment in this sector nearly doubled and gross output increased by a factor of fourteen. At the latter date some 1·6 million workers (5 per cent of the industrial labour force) were employed in the chemical industries, and they absorbed 9 per cent of capital investment in industry during the 1966-70 plan.

Geographical analysis of the chemical industry of a modern industrial economy presents many of the problems already discussed with respect to engineering. These include the great variety of raw materials consumed, the many and rapidly changing technological processes within the industry, the wide range of intermediate and final products and the varied markets to which these are supplied. Primary chemical raw materials, for example, include as a major element naturally occurring minerals of many kinds (Fig 3), and the extraction and processing of these are affected by the same location factors as other types of mining and mineral-processing. At the same time agricultural commodities, notably grain and potatoes, are major sources of chemical raw materials, so that there is a relationship between the distribution of the chemical industry and the agricultural background In addition, the industry both produces and consumes large quantities of chemical compounds that are not readily available in nature: these may be derived from minerals, from agricultural commodities or in the form of 'feedstocks' from oil refineries, gas-processing plant, coke ovens and smelters. With feedstocks, other sectors of industry – oil, gas coal and coke production, ferrous and non-ferrous metallurgy – become sources of chemical raw materials, and chemical products are made by industries that would not normally be considered part of the chemical sector. Indeed it has been estimated that at least a quarter of all Soviet chemicals are produced outside the chemical industry proper. The position is further complicated by the fact that, between the input of raw materials and the output of chemical products, there are often several stages of processing, each with a different set of locating factors and a different location pattern. Finally it should be remembered that, while some chemical products are of direct use to the individual consumer, such as cosmetics or pharmaceuticals, the majority are intended for use in other industries, as, for example, synthetic rubber, artificial and synthetic fibres or plastics. Thus, while it may be possible to discuss the chemical industry as a whole with respect to its role and importance in the Soviet economy, matters of location are best examined on the basis of individual branches. Here problems of classification abound. The following discussion starts with a brief examination of the growth of the industry as a whole, and proceeds to a more detailed geographical analysis of the main branches, which constitute a group of interrelated but extremely complex and varied industrial activities.

Pre-Revolutionary Russia was by no means devoid of chemical industries, which were established in a number of European cities, notably Leningrad, Moscow and other towns of the industrial Centre, Riga, the Donbass and the Urals. There was considerable expansion during the last 25 years of the Tsarist period, and by 1913 the home industry supplied more than 80 per cent of the country's limited consumption of chemical products. However, the industry lagged even further behind those of other European powers, notably Germany, than did some of Russia's other industries. Development before World War I relied heavily on foreign enterprise, and a large proportion of capital investment came from abroad. Consequently the chemical industry was accorded high priority in the early stages of the Soviet industrialisation programme, receiving in the first two Five Year Plans about 8 per cent of all the capital invested in industry. In the 1940s and early 1950s this proportion was much reduced, but renewed emphasis on the expansion of the chemical industry was a striking feature of the Seven Year Plan for 1959-65, during which it was allocated nearly 12 per cent of industrial investment. Since then the proportion has again declined, though it remains at a higher level than in the inter-war or early post-war periods.

This recent phase of unprecedented growth has been accompanied and made possible by major techological innovations. By far the most important of these have been in the field of petro-chemicals, whose development has permitted a rapid expansion in the manufacture of all types of synthetic materials. While chemical processes based on mineral raw materials, coal, coke and agricultural commodities remain important, their relative significance *vis-a-vis*, processes based on oil and natural gas has declined. The 1971-75 plan, for example, envisages that all expansion in the output of organic synthetics will be derived from oil and gas. The 1960s have witnessed particularly rapid growth in such branches as synthetic fibres and plastics, which were previously little developed, and this has brought the structure of the Soviet chemical industry closer to those of other advanced industrial powers, as well as causing considerable changes in its location. Such changes have formed part of wider movements in Soviet industry whereby, in Dienes' words:

> The middle and late fifties saw a significant change in industrial priorities. In a series of drastic efforts, the post-Stalin leadership exerted itself to shift the coal-and metal-bound economy onto a new track, more in line with mid-century conditions. The process started with strong measures to modernize the obsolete fuel mix and continued in the chemical and agricultural drives.[1]

Some indication of the scale of expansion in the chemical industry and its various branches is given in Table 25.

Table 25

PRODUCTION OF MAJOR CHEMICAL COMMODITIES, 1913-70

000 tons	1913	1940	1950	1960	1970
Sulphuric acid	121	1, 587	2, 125	5, 398	12, 059
Soda ash	160	536	749	1, 887	3, 668
Mineral fertilisers	89	3, 238	5, 497	13, 867	55, 400
nitrogenous		972	1, 913	4, 892	26, 442
phosphatic		1, 352	2, 551	4, 878	13, 370
ground phosphate rock		382	483	1, 473	5, 709
potassic		532	750	2, 606	9, 824
Synthetic resins and plastics	—	11	67	312	1, 673
Chemical fibres	—	11	24	211	623
Synthetic dyes	—	34	47	84	95
All chemicals (1940=100)	—	100	196	770	2, 683

Source: *Narodnoye Khozyaystvo SSSR*, various years

In turning to a consideration of the individual branches of chemical manufacture we are faced with the problem of classification. Chemical

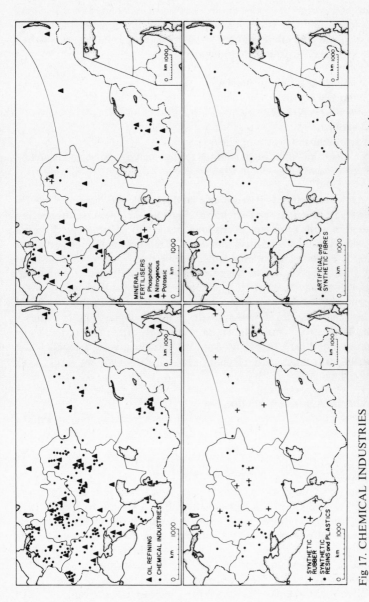

Fig 17. CHEMICAL INDUSTRIES
These maps show all centres whose chemical industries are indicated on small-scale maps in *Atlas Razvitiya Khozyaystva i Kultury SSSR* (Moscow, 1967) and/or *Atlas SSSR* (Moscow, 1969)

industries may be classified in a variety of ways – the raw materials used, the processes involved, the product manufactured or the market supplied – and any single classification is a compromise among these alternatives. The one used here is intended to focus on the end product and comprises the following categories:

1 industrial acids and alkalis
2 mineral fertilisers
3 synthetic rubber
4 synthetic resins and plastics
5 artificial and synthetic fibres
6 others, including such items as synthetic dyes, paints and lacquers, pharmaceuticals and photochemicals.

Of the six categories, five are end-products, though most of these are consumed in other, non-chemical, branches of manufacturing. The exception is the acids and alkalis branch, the bulk of whose products are consumed in other chemical industries. Each branch has its own set of location factors and patterns which, while overlapping, are also to be sub-divided according to the raw materials and processes employed. The accompanying maps (Fig 17), which show the distribution of the chemical industries as a whole and groups 2-5 individually, are based on assumptions already used for the maps of engineering activities – that the selected centres shown on small-scale atlas maps of the whole country are likely to be the more important among a much larger number of centres with chemical industries shown on larger-scale regional maps.

Industrial Acids and Alkalis

These are intermediate rather than final products. They are used in a variety of later-stage chemical manufactures, particularly in the production of mineral fertilisers.

Sulphuric acid

This is the most important item in this group and the rise in output of sulphuric acid from 2 million tons in 1950 to 12 million tons in 1970 took place mainly in response to the demands of the fertiliser industry. The mineral raw materials for sulphuric acid production include iron pyrites, native sulphur and gypsum. Throughout most of the Soviet period, the most important of these has been iron pyrites, mined at several sites in the Urals. Owing to the problem of transporting sulphuric acid in bulk, the iron pyrites is moved to consuming areas and the acid is manufactured close to the superphosphate plant in which a large proportion of it is used. The most important sulphuric acid works in this category were established at Leningrad, in the Centre (Voskresensk, Shchelkovo, Novomoskovsk) and in the Ukraine (Konstantinovka, Vinnitsa, Odessa). Until the mid-1950s at least three-quarters of Soviet sulphuric acid production was of this type, but the proportion has since fallen with the growing importance of other methods. In particular, the output of native sulphur, mined chiefly in the Volga valley near Kuybyshev, at Gaurdak in Middle Asia, and in the Carpathian foothills, has rapidly increased. The sulphur is shipped to sulphuric acid plant in the European USSR, and this form of production now accounts for about a third of Soviet output. The third main source of sulphur is the gases produced in non-ferrous metal smelting and the process-chain metal sulphides – sulphuric acid – superphosphates has been established at Alaverdi in the Transcaucasus, at Almalyk in Middle Asia and at Krasnouralsk and Revda in the Urals. About a quarter of all sulphuric acid is now produced by this method. An additional small amount is obtained from the hydrogen sulphide produced in oil refining.

Soda

A second major item is soda, the basic raw materials for which are common salt (sodium chloride) and limestone, and the main products soda ash and caustic soda. Since it takes about $1 \cdot 7$ tons of salt, $1 \cdot 6$ tons of limestone and $0 \cdot 2$ tons of coal to produce a ton of *soda ash*[2], the works tend to be placed near their raw materials, and the great bulk of Soviet production comes from the Ukraine and the Urals, where salt and coal are readily available. The salt deposits at Artemovsk, in the Donbass, supply soda ash plant at Donetsk and Slavyansk. In the Urals the Berezniki and Sterlitamak[3] works are based on the salt of Solikamsk and Sol-Iletsk respectively. Soda ash is produced from salt at Mikhailovskiy in the Altay Kray and in the northern Crimea. In addition, considerable quantities are derived as a by-product from the aluminium industry.

Caustic soda in the USSR is derived largely from soda ash, mainly in the Donbass and the Urals, but an increasing proportion is obtained by the electrolysis of salt, which also produces chlorine. This process tends to be attracted to sites with a large output of electric power, such as that near Kuybyshev, using salt from Lakes Elton and Baskunchak in the lower Volga valley; that near Irkutsk, using salt from Usolye Sibirskoye; and that at Pavlodar, where salt is obtained from Tavolzhan and other small lakes in northern Kazakhstan.

Sodium Sulphate

Glauber salts are a source of sodium sulphate. The main producing sites lie on the shores of the Kara Bogaz Gol (the world's largest source), at Aralsulfat on the north shore of the Aral Sea, and in the lake-strewn Kalunda district of the Altay Kray.

Mineral Fertilisers

Low output and consumption of mineral fertilisers have long been major contraints upon efforts to raise the productivity of Soviet agriculture. Particular attention was drawn to this deficiency by Khrushchev and others in the years immediately following the death of Stalin, and the need to produce vastly increased quantities as a major element in the planned development of the agricultural sector was one of the main reasons for the high priority accorded to the chemical industry during the 1960s. As Table 25 indicates, production has multiplied fourfold during the past decade. Despite this, the quantity of mineral fertilisers available per hectare of arable land (240kg in 1970) is still well below that of most developed countries, and the 1971-75 plan envisages a further massive increase to 90 million tons per annum.

There are three main classes of fertiliser, derived respectively from nitrogen, phosphates and potash, though these may be combined in various ways in the fertilisers that are actually applied to the land. Soviet statistics on fertiliser production, such as those displayed in Table 25, are given in standard units based on their mineral content. Standard nitrogenous fertiliser has $20 \cdot 5$ per cent nitrogen, phosphatic fertiliser $18 \cdot 7$ per cent P_2O_5 and potash fertiliser $46 \cdot 1$ per cent K_2O.

Nitrogenous Fertilisers

These used to be in short supply, probably because of the rather complex chemical processes necessary to their manufacture, but they are now the leading type. The basic raw material used in their production is ammonia, which is obtained when atmospheric nitrogen is combined with hydrogen (the synthetic ammonia process). Thus the availability of hydrogen is a major locating factor. At the same time, in common with other types of fertiliser, the bulky nature of the end-product favours a wide dispersal of production, and it will be observed from Fig 17 that works are scattered throughout the agriculturally productive parts of the country.

Hydrogen is obtained by a variety of methods. Until the late 1950s at least 80 per cent of the hydrogen used for ammonia synthesis in the USSR was derived either from coal (by the water-gas reaction process) or from coke-oven gases. As a result, nitrogenous fertilisers were produced mainly in coalmining and metallurgical districts, where several ammonia-synthesis plants supplied each fertiliser factory. Among the latter the most important were at Gorlovka and Dneprodzerzhinsk in the Ukraine, Novomoskovsk and Shchekino in the Moscow basin, Berezniki in the Urals, Rustavi in the Transcaucasus and Kemerovo in the Kuzbass. One major plant using a different method was built at Chirchik, near Tashkent. There hydrogen was obtained by the electrolysis of water, a process requiring large quantities of electric power.

These long-established processes remain important, but have been overshadowed by the production of hydrogen from natural gas. Today nearly 60 per cent of Soviet ammonia synthesis is based on natural gas, less than 40 per cent on coal and coke and only a small fraction on water electrolysis.[4] The increasing use of the natural gas – hydrogen – ammonia chain has resulted in major changes in the location of the nitrogenous fertiliser industry. Several of the older plants, including those at Gorlovka, Novomoskovsk, Shchekino and Chirchik, have been converted to the new process, but the most striking development has been the building of more than a dozen completely new works. Relying on natural gas brought by pipeline, these are widely dispersed, at Kohtla-Jarve (Estonia), Jonava (Lithuania), Grodno (Belorussia), Novgorod, Dorogobuzh (near Smolensk), Rovno, Cherkassy and Severodonetsk (in the Ukraine), Nevinnomyssk (near Stavropol), Tolyatti, Salavat, Fergana, Navoi and Kalininabad. The emphasis has clearly shifted from coal-metallurgical sites to sites on gasfields and pipelines.

Phosphatic Fertilisers

These fertilisers, in the form of superphosphates and double superphosphates, are made by treating phosphatic raw materials with sulphuric acid. Because sulphuric acid is difficult to transport in bulk, and because about 40 per cent of the sulphuric acid produced in the Soviet Union is consumed in fertiliser plants, the locations of superphosphate works and sulphuric acid plants are closely connected.

Superphosphate plant built before the Revolution, which relied mainly on imported phosphates, were situated mainly in ports, notably Leningrad, Riga and Odessa. In addition, a number of inland plants combined imported phosphates with local supplies of phosphatic rock, as at Vinnitsa, Perm and Dzerzhinsk (near Gorkiy). Since the late 1920s, however, the main source of phosphates has been the apatite deposit near Kirovsk, in the Kola peninsula. Apatite concentrate from Kirovsk is supplied to phosphate plants in the European part of the country, the most important of which have already been listed as sites of sulphuric acid production. An additional source of phosphates is ground phosphatic rock, which is extracted at numerous places, mainly in the European regions, and either applied direct to the land or mixed with apatite in the superphosphate plant.

In the post-war period a major additional phosphorite source was developed at Karatau, near Dzhambul, and this has supported the establishment of superphosphate works in the Middle Asian republics. For technical reasons it is uneconomic to process Karatau phosphorite by the sulphuric acid process,[5] and a new thermal reduction method is used in plant at Dzhambul and Chimkent. The large quantities of electric power required are provided by gas-fired thermal generating plants. Karatau phosphorite is also processed at Tolyatti on the Volga.

Potash Fertilisers

These constitute less than one-fifth of the total fertiliser output, and are produced at a relatively small number of sites close to deposits of suitable potassium salts. Until the early 1960s about 80 per cent of Soviet potash fertilisers were produced at Solikamsk and Berezniki, on the west flank of the northern Urals, and there was smaller-scale production at Stebnik and Kalush, in the Lvov oblast. A major potash deposit at Soligorsk, in Belorussia, which came into use in 1963, is expected eventually to supply 40 per cent of the country's requirements.

Synthetic Rubber

In view of the Soviet Union's physical environment and her drive towards economic self-sufficiency, it is not surprising that she has played a leading role in the development of the synthetic rubber industry. While natural rubber is still imported in considerable quantities,[6] synthetic rubber now supplies about two-thirds of the country's requirements. Early experiments in the production of rubber from various latex-bearing plants grown mainly in Middle Asia showed that it was uneconomic, if not physically impossible, to supply the country's needs in this way. Attention was therefore concentrated on the production of synthetic rubber, which has formed a major branch of the Soviet chemical industry since the 1930s.

Production on a commercial scale began in the 1930s, when plants were built at Leningrad, Yaroslavl, Voronezh, Yefremov (Tula oblast) and Kazan. These early plants all produced butadiene-sodium rubber (Buna), the chief raw material for which was alcohol obtained from agricultural produce, particularly potatoes. Buna rubber was used mainly for automobile tyres and footwear.

In 1940 a new process was established at Yerevan, in Armenia. This produced chloroprene (or neoprene) rubber, a type particularly suitable for use in the oil industry and in the manufacture of conveyor belts and cable casings.[7] The raw material was acetylene, produced from limestone by the calcium carbide process, which required large quantities of electric power. During World War II a tyre plant was opened at Yerevan to replace some of the capacity lost in the European regions.

In the post-war period, particularly since the mid-1950s, major changes have occurred in the technology and, consequently, in the location of the Soviet synthetic rubber industry. On the raw material side, alcohol derived from agricultural produce has been almost entirely replaced by alcohol from ethylene, a by-product of oil refining. The first such plant, producing butadiene rubber, was opened at Sumgait in 1957. Since then butadiene-sodium rubber has been replaced by the more advanced butadiene-styrene and butadiene-methelstyrene types.[8]

In the early 1960s the alcohol stage was eliminated from the manufacture of butadiene rubbers, which were then produced direct from the oil-refinery gases butane and butylene. Subsequently, still more advanced types of synthetic rubber, such as polyisoprene, polybutadiene and ethylene-propylene terpolymer, came into production.[9] These are made both at new plants (eg Sterlitamak, Tolyatti and Volzhskiy) and at some of the older ones (eg Yefremov, Voronezh and Yerevan) which have been converted to the new processes. As a result, the majority of synthetic rubber works today are to be found in oil-refining districts, most of them producing rubber from oil-refinery gases or natural gas derivatives. However, the calcium carbide process is still used at Usolye Sibirskoye, and alcohol derived from wood hydrolysis is used at Krasnoyarsk.

Synthetic Resins and Plastics

In contrast to her early start in the production of synthetic rubber, the Soviet Union was slow to establish a large-scale synthetic resins and plastics industry, for as late as 1950 her total output was only 67,000 tons, and the great bulk of this was in the form of thermo-setting resins (bakelite and the like). This is yet another branch of the chemical industry in which the oil and gas era has stimulated rapid growth, though the 1970 production of 1·7 million tons was still well behind that of other leading industrial powers. The considerable variety of raw materials and processes in the plastics industry, and the relatively low cost of transporting the final products, makes it a widely dispersed activity. Urea resins, being derived from ammonia, are produced near nitrogenous fertiliser plants in several regions. The thermoplastics side grew rapidly during the 1960s. Polyvinyl chloride (PVC) is associated with the production of chlorine at Novomoskovsk, Sterlitamak, Usolye and Yerevan, and plastics based on oil-refinery gases, such as polyethylene and polypropylene, are made in a number of oil-refining centres, both on the oilfields (Groznyy, Novokuybyshevsk, Guryev) and elsewhere (Novopolotsk). Regions possessing both a tradition of chemical manufacture and a high level of technology have proved particularly successful in attracting the more advanced plastics industries, the Centre being of particular significance in this respect.

Artificial and Synthetic Fibres

The man-made fibres industry displays a similar picture of late development and recent rapid growth. This branch includes the production of both cellulosic fibres, derived from timber and cotton linters, and wholly synthetic fibres, made by chemical processes. Before World War II the Soviet Union's small output of man-made fibres was almost wholly confined to the first of these two categories. Some 90 per cent of total production came in the form of viscose rayon, most of which was made at factories in Klin, Mogilev and Leningrad. The remainder was produced by the cuprammonium process at Kalinin and Shuya (near Ivanovo). It is significant that these works all lay in a zone with a long tradition of linen, woollen and cotton textile manufacture. In 1970 cellulosic fibres were still dominant, accounting for 73 per cent of all man-made fibres. The five pre-war plants were still in operation, together with numerous others built since 1940. Some of the latter, like the viscose rayon plants at Aramil in the Urals and Namangan in Middle Asia, where cotton linters were the raw material, together with the cuprammonium plant at Kustanay, were the result of war-time evacuation from the European regions. In the post-war years additional viscose rayon plants were opened at Lesogorskiy (near Leningrad), Svetlogorsk (Belorussia), Kamensk-Shakhtinskiy, Balak-ovo on the Volga, Barnaul and Krasnoyarsk. Important technological developments have affected rayon production during the past decade. In particular there has been a marked increase in the output of acetate rayon, which uses raw materials derived from acetylene. So long as the latter was derived mainly from the calcium carbide process, acetate rayon was expensive, but, with the production of acetylene from natural gas, it became much cheaper to make acetate rayon and new plants were built for this purpose at Kaunas, Serpukhov, Engels and Kirovakan.[10]

The production of wholly synthetic fibres has developed almost entirely since 1950. In that year synthetic fibres made up only 5 per cent of all man-made fibres and in 1960 only 7 per cent. By 1970 the proportion had reached 27 per cent and was rapidly increasing. Several products are made, of which the most important so far has been the polyamide fibre kapron, produced from caprolactam, a material associated with ammonia synthesis. Caprolactam plants are associated either with coal-based chemical complexes, as in the Moscow basin and the Kuzbass, or with natural gas. The kapron plants, which are also quite widely scattered, are situated at Daugavpils (Lithuania), Chernigov and Zhitomir (Ukraine), Volzhskiy, Rustavi (Georgia) and, in association with viscose or acetate rayon manufacture, at Klin, Serpukhov, Engels and Barnaul. Links with other forms of textile manufacture would appear to be more important than links with raw materials. Other synthetic fibres, produced on a relatively small scale at present but scheduled for rapid development, are the polyester fibre lavsan (the Soviet equivalent of dacron) and the acrylic fibre nitron (orlon). Both are based on natural gas derivatives. Lavsan is produced at Kursk and nitron at Polotsk, Saratov and Navoi (Middle Asia). Though individual man-made fibre plants are widely scattered, output is concentrated in the European part of the country, which accounts for three-quarters of total production, the Centre being by far the most important region. There is a clear association with the distribution of the textile industry.

Other Chemical Industries

The remaining branches of the chemical industry, including the production of paints, lacquers, dyes, photochemicals and pharmaceuticals, tend to be associated mainly with their markets, especially now that the all-important oil and gas are available at a large number of sites. Representatives of these branches are now found in the majority of regional centres[11], though there is a marked concentration of activity in the older industrial areas or 'centres of skill and research',[12] such as the Moscow region and Leningrad.

7
The Timber Industries, Light Industries and Food Industries

THE INDUSTRIES DESCRIBED in the last three chapters – fuel and power, metallurgy, engineering and chemicals – employ more than half the industrial labour force and, during the 1966-70 plan period, received more than two-thirds of all the capital invested in industry. The group of industries discussed in this chapter employ about a third of the Soviet Union's industrial workers but received less than a fifth of industrial capital between 1966 and 1970.[1] There is a contrast also in the two group's rates of growth. Over the past two decades those in the first group have generally expanded at rates well above the average for Soviet industry as a whole, whereas the second group has experienced a much less rapid increase of output. These contrasts are now less marked than in the inter-war or early post-war years but are still a major feature of the Soviet industrial economy.

Timber Industries

These are a major element in the industrial structure of the USSR and employ a surprisingly large number of workers. In 1970 no fewer than 2·8 million worked in this sector, representing 9 per cent of the industrial labour force and nearly as many as in ferrous metallurgy and chemicals combined. A further 433,000 were employed in forestry. These activities are labour-intensive and inputs of capital are relatively small – only 3·5 per cent of total investment in industry went to this sector during the 1966-70 plan period.

The Soviet Union has vast timber resources, far in excess of those of any other country. Forested areas exceed 700 million hectares, roughly

Table 26

OUTPUT OF TIMBER PRODUCTS, 1913-70

	1913	1940	1950	1960	1970
All timber (000, 000m^3)	67.0	246.1	266.0	369.5	385.1
Commercial timber (000, 000m^3)	30.5	117.9	161.0	261.5	298.6
Firewood (000, 000m^3)	36.5	128.2	105.0	108.0	86.5
Sawn timber (000, 000m^3)	14.2	34.8	49.5	105.6	116.4
Cellulose (000, 000 tons)	0.3	0.5	1.1	2.3	5.1
Paper and cardboard (000, 000 tons)	0.3	1.0	1.5	3.2	6.7

Source: *Narodnoye Khozyaystvo SSSR*, various years

one-third of the total land area, and the USSR is believed to contain at least 20 per cent of the world's timber reserves. After a rapid increase during the 1950s, timber production averaged some 370 million cu m a year during the 1960s, about a sixth of world output (Table 26). Some 80 per cent of Soviet production is softwood, and this represents one-third of world softwood production; her hardwood output is only 6 per cent of the world total. Commercial use accounts for 78 per cent of production, and firewood for the remaining 22 per cent, a proportion that has declined from about 50 per cent in 1940. Although only a small proportion, less than 5 per cent, of this vast output is exported, this represents about 20 per cent of the world trade in softwoods, and the USSR is second only to Canada in this respect. Timber and timber products constitute about 7 per cent of Soviet exports by value.

Although the country's resources are immense, there is a growing imbalance between the location of timber reserves and the main consuming areas. While Siberia and the Far East contain an estimated 80 per cent of total reserves, about two-thirds of Soviet timber production and three-quarters of consumption take place in the European regions, where only the Urals and parts of the Volga-Vyatka and north-western regions are classed as 'heavily forested'.[2] Intensive exploitation of the forest resources has been in progress for a long time and, in many of the more accessible areas, has reached the stage where the annual rate of cutting is far in excess of natural regeneration, necessitating reafforestation programmes. This is particularly evident in the European regions, whereas in Siberia the annual cut does not exceed 10 per cent of annual growth. As a result, in the European part of the

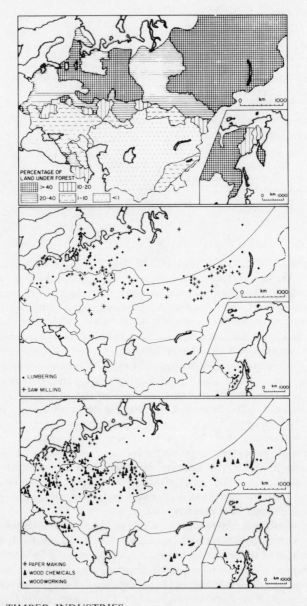

Fig 18. TIMBER INDUSTRIES

A. Based on *Atlas Razvitiya Khozyaystva i Kultury* (Moscow, 1967), 14

B and C. These maps show all centres marked on small-scale maps in *Atlas Razvitiya Khozyaystva i Kultury SSSR* (Moscow, 1967) and/or *Atlas SSSR* (Moscow, 1969)

Table 27

TIMBER PRODUCTION, BY REGIONS, 1950 and 1970
Millions of tons (per cent)

	1950		1970	
North-west	49.8	(18.7)	95.2	(24.7)
Centre, Volga-Vyatka and Black				
Earth Centre	61.2	(23.0)	60.3	(15.6)
Baltic republics and Belorussia	18.6	(7.0)	19.1	(4.9)
Ukraine and Moldavia	15.4	(5.8)	9.5	(2.5)
Volga and Urals	52.8	(19.8)	71.1	(18.5)
Siberia and Far East	60.8	(22.9)	122.9	(31.9)
North Caucasus and Transcaucasia	5.2	(2.0)	5.0	(1.3)
Kazakhstan and Middle Asia	2.2	(0.8)	2.0	(0.5)
Total	266.0	(100.0)	385.1	(100.0)

Source: *Narodnoye Khozyaystvo SSSR v 1970 godu*
Narodnoye Khozyaystvo RSFSR v 1970 godu

country there has been a progressive movement of lumbering into more remote parts of the tayga outside the main settled zone and, at the same time, a marked increase in the proportion of the timber supply coming from regions east of the Urals (Table 27). These trends have been reflected in a rapid rise in the volume of timber traffic on Soviet railways and waterways, which in ton-kilometre terms has increased nearly fourfold since 1950. Over the same period, while the average length of haul for all types of freight has risen by less than 20 per cent, that of timber has doubled (see Table 7).

Lumbering

In the European part of the country (Fig 18) lumbering now takes place almost entirely north of latitude 56°N. About a quarter of total production (Table 27) is now taken from the North-western region and a further 15 per cent from the Urals, the most important districts being in the Arkhangelsk, Vologda, Perm and Sverdlovsk oblasts and the Karelian and Komi ASSRs. These regions, together with the Centre and Volga-Vyatka, now produce about 55 per cent of Soviet timber, much the same proportion as in 1950. In the intervening period, however, while output has nearly doubled in the North-west and risen by about a third in the Urals, it has slightly declined in the Centre and Volga-Vyatka regions. Meanwhile output in Siberia and the Far East has more than doubled, rising from less than a quarter to nearly one-third of the total. Development has been most intensive along the southern fringes of the forest zone in the Tyumen and Irkutsk oblasts and in the Krasnoyarsk, Khabarovsk and Maritime Krays.

Saw-milling

The next stage of timber processing, saw-milling, also occurs mainly in the forested zone, though there are outlying centres much further south, notably along the Volga river. Major saw-milling centres are a good deal less numerous than lumbering sites, and there is large-scale movement of raw timber between the two, both by rail and water. Milling centres are situated mainly at transport nodes, especially at the junction of rail and water routes, and are a good deal more strongly represented in consuming areas. During the rapid expansion of timber production that occurred in the 1950s milling capacity fell substantially behind the growth of lumbering in many of the heavily forested districts, and the 1960s saw the establishment of many new milling centres in such areas, notably in Siberia, to restore the balance.

Pulp and paper

Table 28

PAPER PRODUCTION, BY REGIONS, 1950 and 1970
Thousands of metric tons

	1950		1970	
North-west	352.7	(29.9)	1,395.0	(33.3)
Centre, Volga-Vyatka and Black Earth Centre	257.5	(21.8)	712.2	(17.0)
Baltic republics and Belorussia	174.2	(14.8)	583.9	(14.0)
Ukraine and Moldavia	35.9	(3.0)	187.4	(4.5)
Volga and Urals	263.6	(22.3)	896.8	(21.4)
Siberia and Far East	60.9	(5.2)	318.6	(7.6)
North Caucasus and Transcaucasia	30.5	(2.6)	68.1	(1.6)
Kazakhstan and Middle Asia	5.0	(0.4)	23.3	(0.6)
Total	1,180.3	(100.0)	4,185.3	(100.0)

Sources: *Narodnoye Khozyaystvo SSSR v 1970 godu*
Narodnoye Khozyaystvo RSFSR v 1970 godu

Production has expanded rapidly in recent years (Table 28). These activities consume large quantities of timber, power and water and are thus rather less widely dispersed than other timber industries. About a third of total paper production takes place in the North-west, where Karelia is especially important, and about 20 per cent in the Urals, mainly in Perm oblast. Current plans envisage a big increase in pulp and paper production east of the Urals, where timber, power and water are

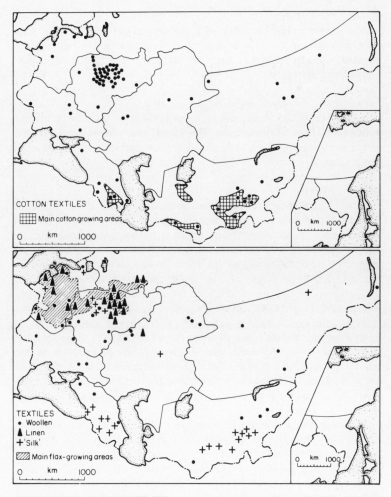

Fig 19. TEXTILE INDUSTRIES
These maps show all centres marked on small-scale maps in *Atlas Razvitiya Khozyaystva i Kultury SSSR* (Moscow, 1967) and/or *Atlas SSSR* (Moscow, 1969)

all available in very large quantities. Although paper production in Siberia and the Far East is still less than 8 per cent of the total, it has increased fivefold since 1950.

Woodworking Industries

Also shown in Fig 18, these are essentially market-oriented and thus very widely dispersed, with numerous important centres outside the forested zone. Nevertheless, the latter still has a pronounced concentration of these activities.

Timber-based Chemical Industries

Largely confined to the forested zone, they are usually associated with other chemical industries. The Urals, the Volga-Vyatka region and, more recently, Belorussia, have become particularly important in this respect.

Light Industries

In 1970 light industries employed about 16 per cent of the industrial labour force, a proportion that has changed very little over the past 20 years, though the number at work in this sector has nearly doubled. The rate of capital investment remains low – less than 5 per cent of all investment in industry during the 1966–70 plan period. Unfortunately the detailed breakdown of the light industrial sector in Soviet publications is far from satisfactory. While a considerable amount of information is provided concerning textiles, clothing and footwear, there is little about the production of other types of consumer goods apart from bald statements of total output. Similarly, maps entitled 'light industry' in Soviet atlases show only the distribution of the textile, clothing and footwear branches, and most texts confine their attention to these items. It is clear from the available data that these have constituted the great bulk of the light or consumer goods industries throughout most of the Soviet period. It is also clear that, during the past decade, the production of other types of consumer goods has risen rapidly, but precise data on location or numbers employed are lacking. Nor is it wholly clear to what extent the production of consumer durables is included in the engineering sector.

Given these difficulties, it is inevitable that in this section discussion will be concentrated on the textile industries (Fig 19). These are, of course, among the oldest industrial activities, since domestic textile manufactures based on local raw materials – flax and wool in the European forest zone, cotton and silk in Middle Asia and the Caucasus – were an integral part of the economies of those areas in the pre-industrial phase. In the industrialisation of the Russian Empire in

Table 29

TEXTILE PRODUCTION, 1913-70
Millions of sq m

	1913	1940	1950	1960	1970
Cotton	1, 817	2, 704	2, 745	4, 838	6, 152
Woollen	138	152	193	439	643
Linen	121	268	257	516	707
Hemp and jute	81	111	73	168	126
Silk and artificial	35	64	106	675	1, 146
Total	2, 192	3, 299	3, 374	6, 636	8, 774

Source: *Narodnoye Khozyaystvo SSSR*, various years

the second half of the nineteenth century the manufacture of linen, woollen and cotton cloth played a leading role in the European regions, as we have seen, though there was little development elsewhere. Over most of the Soviet period, in common with the majority of consumer goods industries, the growth of textile manufacture was slow in comparison with progress in heavy industry (Table 15). Between 1913 and 1950 the output of all types of cloth increased by little more than 50 per cent. Over the past two decades, however, there has been a pronounced acceleration, and output in 1970 was more than two and a half times the 1950 level (Table 29).

Cotton Textiles

The leading branch of the textile industry, they account for about 70 per cent of all Soviet cloth production, though this proportion has declined recently with the rapid expansion of the artificials. The location of cotton textile manufacture (Fig 19) still bears little relation to the sources of raw cotton, which comes wholly from Middle Asia (90 per cent) and the Transcaucasus; 87 per cent of Soviet cotton cloth is produced in the European regions (Table 30), 70 per cent in the Centre alone, where most of more than thirty cotton towns lie north-east of Moscow in the zone between the Volga and Oka rivers. This represents a degree of concentration greater than in any other major branch of Soviet industry. Although, during the Soviet period, large cotton mills have been built in Middle Asia and the Transcaucasus, notably at Tashkent, Fergana, Ashkhabad, Dushanbe, Leninakan, Kirovabad and Baku, these regions still produce only 10 per cent of the total. It is true that, in the post-war period, the predominance of the Centre has become

Table 30

TEXTILE PRODUCTION, BY REGIONS, 1970
Millions of linear metres (per cent)

	Cotton	Woollen	Linen	Silk*
Centre, Volga-Vyatka and Black Earth Centre	5,396 (72.1)	272 (54.8)	485 (66.7)	734 (59.1)
North-west, Baltic republics and Belorussia	602 (8.0)	68 (13.7)	152 (20.9)	117 (9.4)
Volga and Urals	218 (2.9)	55 (11.2)	30 (4.2)	44 (3.5)
Siberia and Far East	271 (3.7)	3 (0.6)	4 (0.6)	46 (3.7)
Ukraine and Moldavia	252 (3.3)	50 (10.1)	54 (7.6)	101 (8.2)
North Caucasus and Transcaucasus	349 (4.7)	34 (6.8)	—	69 (5.6)
Kazakhstan and Middle Asia	395 (5.3)	14 (2.8)	—	130 (10.5)
Total	7,483 (100.0)	496 (100.0)	725 (100.0)	1,241 (100.0)

* including artificials

Sources: *Narodnoye Khozyaystvo SSSR v 1970 godu*
Narodnoye Khozyaystvo RSFSR v 1970 godu

somewhat less pronounced,[3] but this change has been in favour of other European areas – the Ukraine, the Baltic republics and the Volga region – which, together with western Siberia, produce more cotton cloth than do the cotton-growing regions. This situation draws unfavourable comment from Soviet geographers and economists, but there has been relatively little change to a location pattern established at least a century ago. Not only is the industry poorly represented in the cotton growing areas, where it could provide a valuable source of employment for the rapidly increasing local populations, but it is also virtually absent from the heavy industrial zones, where it could provide a welcome element of diversity. In the last few years there have been some signs of change and it has been suggested that, in the future, the industry will become much more widely dispersed and that, eventually, each economic region will have a cotton-textile industry supplying the bulk of its requirements.[4]

Woollen Textiles

The production of woollen cloth is even more concentrated than cotton in the European regions, which account for some 90 per cent of total output, though the dominance of the Centre (50 per cent) is less marked (Fig 19). The Ukraine, the Volga region and the Baltic and Belorussian regions each produce about 10 per cent.

Linen Textiles

Also heavily concentrated in the European forest zone are linen textiles, for domestic linen manufacture was for centuries an integral part of the local economy and flax was the main industrial crop. Thus, in contrast to cotton, linen is produced close to the raw material source (Fig 19). The Centre is responsible for nearly two-thirds of total output, most of the remainder coming from the North-west, Baltic and Belorussian regions.

Silk Textiles

In Soviet data these include not only natural silk but also 'artificial silk' (rayon) and cloth made from the various synthetic fibres. This branch has grown particularly rapidly over the past two decades, almost wholly as a result of the growth of the artificial and synthetic textile sectors. The group now contributes about 12 per cent of total textile production, but only a very small proportion of this is natural silk produced wholly in Middle Asia and Transcaucasia, where the rearing of silkworms is a traditional activity. The synthetic textile industry is concentrated in a small number of large modern plants, mainly in traditional textile areas, notably the Centre, which is responsible for nearly 60 per cent of Soviet 'silk' production, most of it in the form of rayon. Another 10 per cent comes from the North-west and Belorussia and a large plant has recently been opened at Krasnoyarsk, the first such development to the east of the Urals. It should be realised that a large proportion of the synthetic fibres produced in the chemical industry is consumed by the cotton, linen and woollen industries in the production of mixed types of cloth, hence the small number of centres shown in Fig 19 as engaged in synthetic textile production.

Food Industries

The alimentary industries employ nearly 3 million people, some 9 per cent of the industrial labour force. Over the past 20 years this proportion has declined somewhat, and the volume of production in most food-processing industries (Table 31) has risen much more rapidly than the numbers employed. These trends suggest a considerable degree of modernisation and increased efficiency in this sector of Soviet industry industry.

Table 31

PRODUCTION IN MAJOR BRANCHES OF ALIMENTARY INDUSTRY, 1913-70
Millions of tons

	1913	1940	1950	1960	1970
Sugar	1.3	2.2	2.5	6.4	10.2
Meat products	nd	1.5	1.6	4.4	7.1
Fish products	1.1	1.4	1.8	3.5	7.9
Butter	0.1	0.2	0.3	0.7	1.0
Vegetable oils	0.5	0.8	0.8	1.6	2.8
Canned food (000, 000, 000 cans)	0.1	1.1	1.5	4.9	10.7

Source: *Narodnoye Khozyaystvo SSSR*, various years

Alimentary industries as a whole are very widely dispersed and there are few urban centres of any importance without a representative of this group, which displays a strong market orientation. At the same time the location of each branch is strongly influenced by the availability of the agricultural commodity on which it is based. Thus some forms of production – flour milling and meat processing for example – are widely scattered throughout the main agricultural zone while others – sugar refining, fruit and vegetable canning, the production of vegetable oils, wine-making – are much more localised. In addition, there has been a tendency in recent years to establish new processing plant in rural areas, not only in the smaller towns but also on the farms themselves, as a source of employment for surplus rural populations.

Fishing and Fish Processing

Landings of fish have more than doubled during the last decade and the Soviet catch is now about one-eighth of the world total, placing the USSR third after Peru and Japan. This recent rapid growth reflects the aim of increasing the protein consumption of the Soviet population, and fish now constitutes at least a quarter of the total 'meat' supply. The period since the Revolution, and the last 20 years in particular, have witnessed major changes in the Soviet fishing industry. Before the Revolution at least 80 per cent of the catch was derived from inland waters, about two-thirds of it from the Caspian Sea. By 1950 this proportion had fallen to half and today it is less than 20 per cent. These changes have been associated with a progressive increase in the size and efficiency of the Soviet fishing fleet. Today at least half the catch comes from the Atlantic and Arctic Oceans, where the Barents and White Seas are especially important, and about a third from the Pacific, mainly from the Sea of Okhotsk. While areas within a few hundred miles of the Soviet coastline are still the main source, Soviet fishing fleets are reaching further and further afield and are regular visitors to the coasts of north and south America. Internal sources remain important, and increasing attention is being paid to fish farming in lakes and ponds, and in reservoirs along the major rivers. Owing to the great distances it has to be transported to the main centres of population, the bulk of the catch is processed in one way or another before it is passed on to the consumer. The most important processing centres include Murmansk and Arkhangelsk in the Arctic, Zhdanov on the Sea of Azov, Astrakhan and Guryev on the Caspian and Khabarovsk and Vladivostok in the Far East.

Meat Processing

Plants are very widely dispersed, and are situated in both livestock farming areas and consuming centres. Not surprisingly, the most important region is the Ukraine, which supplies 22 per cent of the country's meat products. Other regions important in this respect are the Centre, Volga, North Caucasus and Kazakhstan.

Dairy Products

The dairy products industry shows a similar wide dispersion, with milk products plants in consuming centres and butter and cheese making in rural areas. The output of butter now exceeds a million tons a year, of which about a quarter is produced in the Ukraine and nearly a fifth in the three central regions.

Sugar Refining

With a total output in excess of 10 million tons, the Soviet Union is now the world's leading sugar producer. In contrast to the widely dispersed meat and dairy sectors, sugar refining is heavily concentrated in beet-growing areas. Nearly 60 per cent of Soviet refined sugar is made in the Ukraine, and more than 20 per cent in the adjoining Central Black Earth and North Caucasus regions.

Flour Milling

This takes place in all regions, mainly in consuming centres, since grain is more easily transported than flour.

Vegetable Oils

The output of vegetable oils has increased rapidly during the past decade. Production takes place in all regions but is most important in the more southerly parts of the country, with 70 per cent in the Ukraine, Moldavia, the North Caucasus and the Black Earth Centre, and a further 15 per cent in the Middle Asian republics.

Fruit and Vegetable Canning, Wine Making and Tobacco Processing

These industries are also specialities of the more southerly regions. The output of canned food has increased sixfold since 1950. Half is produced in the Ukraine, Moldavia and the North Caucasus, and a further 12 per cent in the Transcaucasus and Middle Asia.

PART THREE

REGIONAL CONTRASTS
IN SOVIET INDUSTRY

8

Regionalisation

SINCE THE REVOLUTION much effort has been expended by Soviet planners, economists and geographers on the process of regionalisation (*rayonirovaniye*) – the division of their vast homeland into smaller regional units. The regional patterns that have emerged at various times have included hierarchical structures designed to cope with such diverse yet interlinked functions as local administration, economic planning and industrial management. Regions have also been used as accounting units, particularly in the allocation of investment capital, and as units for the publication of a wide range of economic, demographic and other statistical data.

The powers and responsibilities of the various types of region have varied a great deal, not only with respect to their positions in the hierarchy, but also in response to changes in official policy towards their roles and functions. Policy has swung between the extremes of centralisation, with the various branches of the economy directed individually and centrally from the Soviet capital (the branch-management system), and decentralisation, with integrated planning and management of most forms of economic activity in the hands of local bodies (the territorial-management system). Over most of the Soviet period the former system has been favoured and regional bodies, where they have existed at all, have had very limited powers. A major exception was the Khrushchev period of the late 1950s and early 1960s, when a large measure of decentralisation was achieved, only to be reversed by Khrushchev's successors from 1965 onwards.

Whether management of the economy has been centralised or decentralised, however, certain basic ideas have persisted, and one of these has been the desirability of a logical system of economic regionalisation. In the USSR, with its planned economy and enormous territory, some sort of regional framework is necessary, if only in the realm of economic planning. The political division of the country into its fifteen constituent republics, though frequently used for this purpose, is highly unsatisfactory in view of the republics' greatly differing sizes, populations, levels of development and now somewhat anachronistic boundaries, based as they are on the ethnic distributions of 40 or 50 years ago.

Table 32

ADMINSTRATIVE-TERRITORIAL DIVISIONS OF THE USSR AT THE BEGINNING OF 1971

Republic	i	ii	iii	iv	v	vi	vii	viii	ix	x
RSFSR	16	5	10	6	49	1,750	22,587	1,882	458	513
Ukraine	—	—	—	—	25	476	8,598	861	275	112
Belorussia	-	—	—	—	6	117	1,544	120	52	33
Uzbekistan	1	—	—	—	10	115	916	85	12	32
Kazakhstan	—	—	—	—	17*	188	1,901	168	32	45
Georgia	2	1	—	—	—	67	922	57	39	12
Azerbaydzhan	1	1	—	—	—	60	963	119	47	10
Lithuania	—	—	—	—	—	44	648	22	83	9
Moldavia	—	—	—	—	—	32	700	33	12	8
Latvia	—	—	—	—	—	26	539	35	49	7
Kirgizia	—	—	—	—	3	32	355	35	2	13
Tadzhikstan	—	1	—	—	1	40	274	40	6	11
Armenia	—	—	—	—	—	34	460	28	4	19
Turkmenia	—	—	—	—	3	34	224	67	6	9
Estonia	—	—	—	—	—	15	235	24	27	6
USSR	20	8	10	6	114*	3,030	40,866	3,576	1,104	839

(i)	Autonomous republics (ASSRs)	(vi)	Rayons
(ii)	Autonomous oblasts (AOs)	(vii)	Village soviets
(iii)	National okrugs (NOs)	(viii)	Settlements of urban type
(iv)	Krays	(ix)	Cities under rayon jurisdiction
(v)	Oblasts	(x)	Cities under republic, kray, oblast or okrug jurisdiction

* In 1973 two additional oblasts were created in Kazakhstan - Mangyshlak, formerly the southern part of Guryev oblast, and Dzhezkazgan, formerly the southern part of Karaganda oblast.

Source: *Narodnoye Khozyaystvo SSSR v 1970 godu*, 52

Soviet writers are careful to distinguish two types of regionalisation: administrative-territorial regionalisation (*administrativno-territorialnoye rayonirovaniye*) and economic regionalisation (*economicheskoye rayonirovaniye*), with which we are here chiefly concerned. These two systems are, of course, closely linked, since 'there is an unseverable connection between economic regionalisation and the administrative-territorial division of the country (because) administration is based on the principle of the unity of political and economic leadership'.[1] In practice this has meant that economic regions have always been formed by aggregating administrative divisions, and it is an accepted rule that no administrative unit may be split by a boundary between economic regions. Another restraint on regionalisation is the inviolability of the boundaries between republics, most of which were established in the early 1930s. While an economic region may be a sub-division of a republic, or may combine several republics, it cannot be formed by amalgamating part of one republic with another.[2] This has led to a number of anomalies, the most obvious being the division of the Donbass coalfield by the boundary between Russia and the Ukraine, which splits the coalfield between the Donets-Dnepr and North Caucasus economic regions.

Administrative Divisions

Before considering the pattern of economic regions it is necessary to look at that of the administrative divisions. The full range of administrative units is shown in Table 32. These form a multi-level hierarchy, at the top of which are the fifteen full Union republics, theoretically equal partners in the federation constituting the USSR. Union republics vary greatly in their size and population, ranging from the RSFSR (17·1 million sq km, population 130 million) to Moldavia (33,700 sq km, population 3·6 million) or Estonia (45,100 sq km, population 1·4 million). Subordinate to the Union Republics are the Autonomous Republics (ASSRs) of which there are at present twenty, sixteen of them in the RSFSR. Those parts of Union Republics without ASSR status are mostly divided into the administrative units known as *krays* and *oblasts*, though this level of division does not obtain in some of the smaller SSRs. Autonomous Oblasts and National Okrugs are lower political units, subordinate for administrative purposes to the krays and oblasts in which they are situated.

Of the units mentioned so far, SSRs, ASSRs, AOs and NOs (Fig 20A) are political as well as administrative divisions in that they are directly represented in the Supreme Soviet of the USSR. Their boundaries reflect, though in a very imperfect manner, the distribution of the various ethnic groups after which they are named. Krays and oblasts, on the other hand, are purely administrative divisions. Since all these units except AOs and NOs have economic as well as administrative functions, they are often referred to by Soviet writers as economic-administrative areas. The current economic-administrative divisions are mapped in Fig 20B, the units shown being oblasts, krays, ASSRs, and the smaller SSRs in which these sub-divisions do not

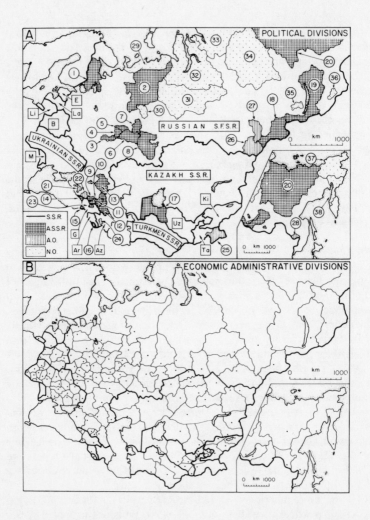

Fig 20. REGIONS

A. POLITICAL DIVISIONS. *Soviet Socialist Republics (SSRs) abbreviated*: Ar, Armenian SSR; Az, Azerbaydzhan SSR; B, Belorussian SSR; E, Estonian SSR; G, Georgian SSR; Ki, Kirgiz SSR; La, Latvian SSR; Li, Lithuanian SSR; M, Moldavian SSR; Ta, Tadzhik SSR; Uz, Uzbek SSR. *Autonomous Soviet Socialist Republics (ASSRs)*: 1, Karelian; 2, Komi; 3, Mordov; 4, Chuvash; 5, Mariy; 6, Tatar; 7, Udmurt; 8, Bashkir; 9, Kabardino-Balkar; 10, Severo-Osetin; 11, Chechen-Ingush; 12, Dagestan; 13, Kalmyk; 14, Abkhaz; 15, Adzhar; 16, Nakhichevan; 17, Kara-Kalpak; 18, Tuvinian; 19, Buryat-Mongol; 20, Yakut. *Autonomous Oblasts (AOs)*: 21, Adygey; 22, Karachayevo-Cherkess; 23, Yugo-Osetin; 24, Nagorno-Karabakh;

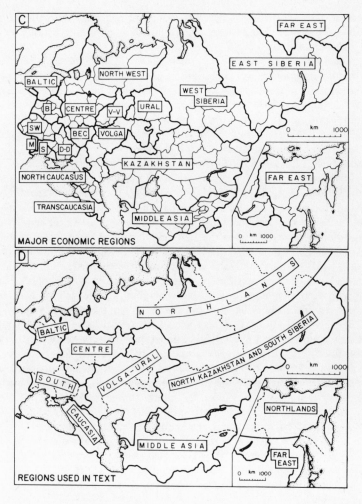

25, Gorno-Badakhshan; 26, Gorno-Altay; 27, Khakass; 28, Jewish (Yev-reysk). *National Okrugs (NOs)*: 29, Nenets; 30, Komi-Permyak; 31, Khanty-Mansiy; 32, Yamalo-Nenets; 33, Taymyr; 34, Evenki; 35, Ust-Orda Buryat-Mongol; 36, Aga Buryat-Mongol; 37, Chukot; 38, Koryak

B. ECONOMIC-ADMINISTRATIVE DIVISIONS – Krays, Oblasts, ASSRs and small SSRs

C. OFFICIAL MAJOR ECONOMIC REGIONS in 1973. Abbreviations: B, Belorussia; BEC, Black Earth Centre; D-D, Donets-Dnepr; S, South; SW, South-west; V-V, Volga-Vyatka

D. Regional scheme used in Chapters 9–11. Broken lines indicate the boundaries of the official Major Economic Regions

occur. Data on a limited range of topics are published at this level in
Soviet statistical handbooks, mainly in those relating to individual
Union republics.

Brief mention should also be made of the sub-divisions of
economic-administrative areas shown in Table 32. Oblasts, krays and
the various autonomous political units are divided into *rayons*, which in
1971 numbered 3030. These in turn are composed of subordinate rural
and urban areas. The former are administered by 40,866 Village
Soviets, while the latter are of various grades, the lowest being the
'settlement of urban type', of which there were 3576 in 1971. To
qualify for this status, a settlement must have a certain minimum size
and the majority of its labour force be engaged in non-agricultural
activities – the precise requirements, which vary between republics,
have been revised on a number of occasions. To be raised to 'city' rank,
the settlement's size must be at least 5000, and at least 85 per cent of its
population must belong to the families of manual or office workers.[3]
1943 centres had reached this level by 1971. Settlements of urban type
and small cities are under the jurisdiction of the rayon in which they lie,
but when a city reaches a certain population, usually 50,000 but less if it
is considered to be of particular economic significance, it may be
removed from rayon control and placed under the jurisdiction of its
kray, oblast, AO or NO. There were 839 such cities in 1971. Among
these, a number of major cities are under the direct control of the Union
Republic in which they are situated; these include the republican
capitals and, in the RSFSR, other cities with populations over 300,000.
Such cities are themselves divided into urban rayons, somewhat akin to
English metropolitan boroughs, for administrative purposes.

Although the full range of territorial divisions is summarised in Table
32, it must be emphasised that published data are rarely, if ever,
available below the level of the economic-administrative areas shown in
Fig 20B. It is the latter 150-odd units that form the building blocks for
the construction of the economic regions with which we are chiefly
concerned, and which feature so prominently in Soviet economic
geography.

Economic Regions

A number of general points should be made before any consideration
of the pattern of economic regions is undertaken, particularly as regards
their functions. Throughout the Soviet period, schemes of economic
regionalisation have involved two major considerations – 'the achievement of a geographical division of labour within the country which
would result in each region acquiring a specialisation in one or more of
the main branches of the economy'[4] and the creation within each region

of a diverse and largely self-sufficient economy. While these objectives are not necessarily contradictory, and it is possible to envisage an economic region with a highly diversified economy, self-sufficient in a wide range of commodities yet specialising in a few products which it supplies to other regions, the apparently conflicting concepts of heterogeneity and homogeneity as the bases for economic regionalisation have provided a major source of debate within the USSR, as elsewhere. Furthermore, the relative importance attached by Soviet economic planners to regional self-sufficiency and regional specialisation has varied with time.

A second area of debate has already been referred to, namely the relative merits of the branch-management and territorial-management systems. The former implies strong central direction of each sector of the economy and thus very limited devolution of control to regional bodies, and the latter a large measure of decentralisation of economic power and strong regional organisation.

Thirdly, there is the question of the optimum size, in terms of territory, resources and population, of economic regions, and here there is a conflict between the needs of local economic management, which requires relatively small units, and those of long-term planning, which require the division of the country into a relatively small number of large units. This is one reason why systems of economic regionalisation in the Soviet Union, like those of administrative regionalisation, have usually involved some kind of hierarchical structure.

Finally, the whole matter of economic regionalisation has been the subject of much theoretical debate. Soviet writers are of the opinion that economic regionalisation is 'especially important in the economic geography of socialist countries, where economic regions are used as territorial units in the planning and organisation of the national economy'.[5] In contrast to capitalist countries, where most if not all economic enterprises are in private hands, in the Soviet Union, state agencies, be they local or national, are responsible for day-to-day management as well as for medium and long-term economic planning. Given this situation, the philosophy behind economic regionalisation assumes a particular significance. According to many Soviet authors, economic regions are not a pattern imposed on the economic landscape for managerial and administrative convenience, but 'objective, existing realities' which it is the economic geographer's task to identify and define. Hence arises the idea that economic regions should in some way reflect the pattern of 'territorial production complexes', identifying areas in which there are strong economic links between the various sectors of the economy operating within each region. There would appear to be a conceptual difficulty here if the pattern of economic

Fig 21. ECONOMIC
REGIONALISATION
A. *The Gosplan proposals of
1921:* 1, North-western;
2, North-eastern; 3, Western;
4, Central Industrial;
5, Vyatka-Vetluga; 6, Ural;
7, Central Volga; 8, South-
western; 9, Southern Mining
and Industrial; 10, Lower
Volga; 11, Central Black
Earth; 12, Caucasus; 13, West
Kazakh; 14, East Kazakh;
15, Middle Asian; 16, West
Siberian; 17, Kuznetsk-Altay;
18, Yenisey; 19, Lena-Angara;
20, Yakut; 21, Far Eastern
B. *Major Economic Regions
in use from 1940 to 1960:*
1, North-western; 2, Northern;
3, Central; 4, Volga; 5, North
Caucasus; 6, Ural; 7, West
Siberian; 8, East Siberian;
9, Far Eastern; 10, Western;
11, Southern; 12, Trans-
caucasus; 13, Middle Asian
C. *Sovnarkhoz regions
established in 1957*
D. *Industrial management
regions established in 1963*
E. *Major Economic Regions
established in 1961*, with
subsequent amendments. For
key, see Fig 20C
F. *Hooson's scheme* (D. J. M.
Hooson, *The Soviet Union*,
University of London Press,
1966, Fig 17, p 120, reproduced by permission of the
author and publisher):
1, Moscow region; 2, Ukrainia;
3, Volga-Ural; 4, Ural-Ob;
5, Central Siberia; 6, Far
East; 7, North; 8, Baltic;
9, Caucasus-Caspian;
10, Central Asia

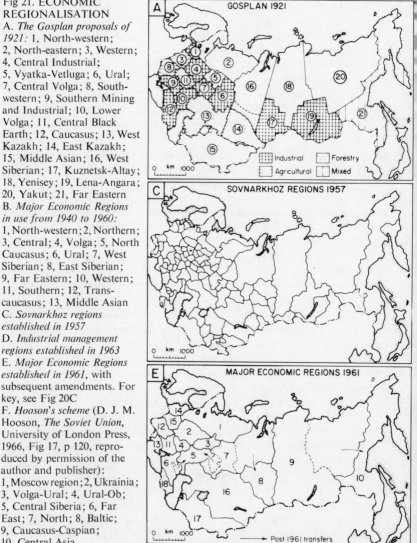

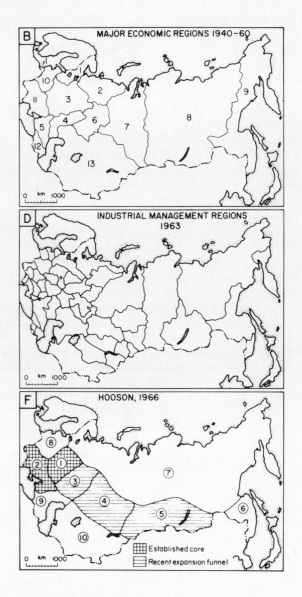

B MAJOR ECONOMIC REGIONS 1940-60

10
11
3   2
5   4   6   7
12
13
9
8

0   km   1000

D INDUSTRIAL MANAGEMENT REGIONS
1963

0   km   1000

F HOOSON, 1966

⑧
② ①
③
⑨   ④   ⑤   ⑦   ⑥
⑩

▦ Established core
▤ Recent expansion funnel

0   km   1000

regions reflects the present situation but is, at the same time, used as the basis for planning future development. 'Objective, existing reality' can presumably include an assessment of potential for future development, yet the very existence of a set of regions used as planning units is likely to influence the nature and location of such development. The idea that the boundaries of economic regions should reflect an existing situation implies that the boundaries should change with time. In practice boundary change frequently lags behind the realities of economic development and is slow to respond to changes in the economic characteristics and linkages of individual regions. Is the regional division to be used as a means of shaping the pattern of future economic development or should patterns of development, determined nationally, shape the pattern of regions? This is a question to which no definitive answer has yet been given.

A resumé of the history of economic regionalisation in the USSR will serve to illustrate the effects of the various considerations discussed so far. The earliest attempt at regional division occurred in 1920 when GOELRO (the State Commission for the Electrification of Russia) put forward a plan for the development of the electric power industry based on a system of regions 'whose main determining factor was the presence of one or more centrally situated sources of electric power'.[6] This scheme had a considerable influence on the first set of economic regions proposed by GOSPLAN (the State Planning Committee of the USSR) in 1921. This specified twenty-one large economic regions (Fig 21A). That a degree of broad regional specialisation was implicit in this scheme is shown by the fact that regions were classified as being 'predominantly industrial', 'predominantly agricultural' or 'forestry regions'. The straight-line boundaries on the Gosplan map indicate that at this stage administrative boundaries were still in a state of flux and could not yet be used in the precise delimitation of economic regions. The Gosplan scheme was, in fact, rejected, mainly on the grounds that it violated the integrity of the ethnically determined political divisions by, *inter alia*, uniting the Ukrainian and Russian sections of the Donbass in a Southern Mining and Industrial region.

During the 1920s the country was divided into large administrative areas – oblasts and krays – which for a time also functioned as economic regions. In the 1930s, however, administrative divisions increased in number while diminishing in size, and a need arose for larger regions to facilitate long-range economic planning. 'The division into administrative regions and territories was done chiefly to ensure concrete guidance of agriculture. At the same time, large-scale industry was centrally directed, its guidance concentrated in ministries and departments. . . .

There were so many regions that it became difficult to plan the development of the national economy by regions from the centre.'[7]

The result of this situation was the rise of what is sometimes referred to as the *Makrorayon* concept, that is the division of the country into a number of large economic regions, each the aggregate of several economic-administrative areas. Thus, in 1940-41, after the addition of large areas of territory in the west, the USSR was divided into thirteen Major Economic Regions (Fig 21B), which remained in existence, with only minor boundary changes, for some 20 years. With these large units, there was strong emphasis on the attainment of the highest possible degree of regional self-sufficiency. The most commonly stated practical reason was the need to lessen the load on the transport system by restricting the volume of inter-regional freight movement, but a general desire for industrial dispersion, motivated partly by strategic considerations and partly by the wish to lessen regional disparities in levels of development, was another motive. The Major Economic Regions were formed mainly as units for the planning of economic development, including the allocation of capital funds, while the subordinate economic-administrative areas were to be concerned with the management of agriculture and industry within the framework of national and regional plans.

A number of specific industrial developments may be attributed to the makrorayon idea, notably the establishment of steel plant in localities remote from the main centres of industry and designed to provide a metallurgical base for their regions, as at Begovat (Bekabad) in Middle Asia and Komsomolsk-na-Amure in the Far East. In theory it was intended to 'combine the vertical centralism of the trusts with the horizontal co-subordination of enterprises in the economic regions',[8] in other words to give regional bodies responsibility for the integrated development of regional economies. In practice, however, little movement in this direction took place during Stalin's rule. As one western observer has put it, 'until 1957, the economy was planned and managed by vertically centralised sectors and the large economic planning regions had no planning or administrative bodies of their own'. These regions were used only for 'purposes of internal statistics and accounting by Gosplan, whose regional department used (them) as a device for mechanical compilation of production data in an *a posteriori* fashion'.[9] The powers of industrial management allocated to the economic-administrative areas were confined to the control of enterprises deemed to be of local importance only. Major enterprises of national significance remained under the control of the various industrial ministries in Moscow.

The Khrushchev period was characterised by numerous modifications and outright reversals of Stalin's policies, including a strong movement towards decentralised economic control. In 1957 the great majority of the industrial ministries were disbanded and the powers of the economic-administrative areas were greatly increased by the establishment of 105 *Sovnarkhoz* regions (Fig 21c). Most of these new units corresponded with a single economic-administrative area at the level of the oblast, kray, ASSR, or small SSR, though in a few instances several such units were amalgamated to form a single Sovnarkhoz region. Each Sovnarkhoz was given full planning, managerial and budgetary responsibility for practically all forms of economic activity within its territory, only a few major activities, notably the construction of hydro-electric plant and the defence industries, remaining under centralised control. The introduction of the Sovnarkhoz system brought renewed emphasis on regional specialisation at that level, but the retention of a framework of major economic regions, each containing a number of Sovnarkhoz units, showed that the principle of integrated and diversified development within each of the larger sub-divisions of the country had not been abandoned. For a few years the boundaries of the major regions remained as established in 1940-41, but in 1961 reorganisation (Fig 21E) increased their number from thirteen to nineteen.[10] Here again some emphasis on regional specialisation could be seen, in the separation of the industrial Centre from the mainly agricultural Black Earth Centre, for example, and the division of the Ukraine into a predominantly industrial Donets-Dnepr and mainly agricultural South-western and Southern regions.

It was not long, however, before this system in turn came under attack as leading to excessive fragmentation of economic control. The best results had been achieved by the larger Sovnarkhoz units operating 'in areas with a larger economy and a bigger economic potential. . . . The larger areas have greater resources, it is easier for them to manoeuvre with their funds, and they can better organize co-operation among their enterprises. They have a bigger share of highly skilled personnel and can establish the necessary research establishments and design organizations. They solve new economic problems faster and more easily.'[11] By a series of decrees published in 1962 and 1963 the 105 Sovnarkhoz regions were consolidated into forty-seven larger units designated Industrial Management Regions (Fig 21D); at the same time the Major Economic Regions were modified to accommodate these new units. There was also a step back towards centralisation with the establishment of State Production Committees (later to become Ministries) responsible for individual branches of industry throughout the country.

By 1963 the systems of economic management and control, together with the regional frameworks through which they operated, had become extremely complex, with a variety of councils and committees at all-Union, republican, major economic region, industrial management region and economic-administrative area levels, and there was undoubtedly a great deal of overlap among the various controlling bodies. Several writers at this time saw hopes of the evolution of a single set of economic regions and a reorganisation of administrative divisions to coincide with these, giving a multi-purpose set of regions which would achieve that unity of economic and administrative control considered so desirable. Suggestions along these lines even included the idea of federation among groups of republics, for example in the Baltic, Transcaucasian and Middle Asian regions. The 1962 programme of the CPSU[12] stated that 'the boundaries between union republics within the USSR are gradually losing their former importance. The creation of the material and technical basis of communism requires increasingly close inter-relationships and mutual assistance between Soviet republics'. This statement was said to

> open up great prospects for economic geography, especially for the theory of territorial production complexes. In the past, the boundaries of oblasts, autonomous republics and especially union republics could never be violated in defining these complexes, even when it was clear that such boundaries had lost their previous significance and were cutting across economically integral territorial production complexes of a regional scale. Now life itself points the need for investigating territorial production complexes irrespective of oblast and republic boundaries. The main criterion for delimiting these complexes will be their effectiveness of economic development within the USSR as a whole.[13]

Acceptance of this view would imply that the most satisfactory set of regional units would be one based on territorial production complexes, 'historically formed' and 'objectively existing'. Much research effort was devoted by Soviet geographers and economists between 1963 and 1965 to the identification and delimitation of territorial production complexes, and many schemes were put forward for the division of the USSR into economic regions on such a basis.

A complete reversal of policy occurred towards the end of 1965, when the branch-management system was reinstated as the officially favoured policy. In a speech to the Central Committee of the CPSU in September 1965, Brezhnev stressed the inefficiency of existing regional bodies and the great advantages to be derived from a return to the branch-management system. This was followed by a law establishing twenty-eight industrial ministries 'to ensure the branch management of industry and to give effect to a far-reaching economic reform'. At the same time regional economic councils at all levels except that of the Union republics were abolished. Thus there are now no planning or managerial bodies between the republics and the individual enterprises, and the economic regions have been relegated to a role of little importance. Despite this, the major economic regions are still used for planning purposes; they continue to feature in Soviet textbooks and statistical handbooks, where they are used as units for regional description and for the tabulation of data respectively, and are subjects of study in Soviet journals.

That the existing Major Economic Regions are by no means wholly satisfactory is implicit in much Soviet writing and has been emphasised by several western authors, some of whom have devised their own system of regions for description and analysis. Among the latter, the most valuable is that used by Hooson[14], (Fig 21F). In arriving at his set of regions Hooson took account of six factors: contribution to the Soviet economy, population (especially urban) growth, accessible resources, economic specialisation, 'community of historical associations' and ethnic considerations (where these are an important element of regional identity). As the author himself admits, several of these criteria are subjective to a considerable degree, but such a scheme is in many ways more meaningful than the 'official' one. A further valuable concept was Hooson's allocation of each region to one of three zones:

1 *The established European core*, embracing a zone centred on Moscow, together with the Ukraine and certain adjacent areas. With at least 40 per cent of the population and industrial capacity of the USSR, this zone plays a leading role in nearly every branch of the Soviet economy and has been of outstanding importance since long before the Revolution.

2 *The Volga-Baykal zone*, described as the 'recent expansion funnel', which has been the zone of most rapid industrial growth throughout much of the Soviet period. It developed little before 1917, and the industrial geography of the area is almost entirely a product of the last 50 years.

3 *The marginal zones*, which include the European north and west, northern Siberia, the Far East, Middle Asia and the Transcaucasus. Most of these areas have considerable resources and have been the scene of major developments during the Soviet period, but they remain 'outside the main stream of Soviet industrial activity' and are 'largely marginal in the economic as well as in the purely locational sense'.

The regional scheme used in Chapters 9-11 of this book uses elements both from the official set of major economic regions and from the ideas of Hooson and other western writers. With the exception of that between the northern and southern sections of Siberia, which lies along the fifty-eighth parallel of latitude, the boundaries used are those of either the Major Economic Regions or the subordinate economic-administrative areas (Figs 20-21). This permits a fairly precise use of published statistics. At the same time an attempt has been made to link together territories with a similar history of industrial development and a common significance to the Soviet economy as a whole. Clearly each region has a great deal of internal diversity, but this is subordinate to those common features from which its unity and uniqueness are derived.

The nine regions and their relation to the official set of economic regions are as set out below. They are mapped in Fig 20D and data on their size and population characteristics have already been given in Table 3.

THE NINE REGIONS USED IN CHAPTERS 9–11

1 *Centre:* the Centre, Volga-Vyatka and Black Earth Centre, which are now three of the official Major Economic Regions but formed a single unit before the reorganisation of the early 1960s.

2 *South:* the three economic regions of the Ukraine – Donets-Dnepr, South-west, South – together with Moldavia and the Rostov oblast (officially in the North Caucasus region of the RSFSR.)

3 *Volga-Ural:* the Volga and Ural Major Economic Regions, together with the three western oblasts of Kazakhstan – Aktyubinsk, Guryev[15] and Uralsk.

4 *North Kazakhstan and South Siberia:* the nine northern oblasts of Kazakhstan – East Kazakh, Karaganda,[16] Kokchetav, Kustanay, North Kazakh, Pavlodar, Semipalatinsk, Tselinograd and Turgay – together with those parts of the West Siberian and East Siberian economic regions south of the fifty-eighth parallel.

5 *Far East:* The Far Eastern economic region south of the fifty-eighth parallel.

6 *Baltic:* the Baltic republics of Estonia, Latvia and Lithuania which, together with the detached Kaliningrad oblast of the RSFSR, constitute the official Baltic region, Belorussia and the three most westerly oblasts of the North-western region – Leningrad, Novgorod and Pskov.

7 *Northlands:* the remainder of the North-western region, together with Siberia and the Far East north of the fifty-eighth parallel.

8 *Middle Asia:* the Kirgiz, Tadzhik, Turkmen and Uzbek republics, which constitute the official Middle Asian region, together with the five southern oblasts of Kazakhstan – Alma-Ata, Chimkent, Dzhambul, Kzyl Orda and Taldy-Kurgan.[17]

9 *Caucasia:* the North Caucasus region, excluding Rostov oblast, plus the Transcaucasus, which comprises the republics of Georgia, Armenia and Azerbaydzhan.

In terms of Hooson's threefold classification of regions the Centre and South coincide fairly closely with the 'established European core', and the Volga-Ural and North Kazakh-South Siberian regions with the 'recent expansion funnel'. The remaining regions are in the 'marginal' category.

9
Regions of the European Core

The Centre

COMPRISING THE CENTRAL, Volga-Vyatka and Central Black Earth Major Economic Regions, the Centre covers only 4 per cent of the territory of the USSR but, being highly urbanised, has a population of 44 million, some 18 per cent of the Soviet total. Thus its population density is nearly five times the all-Union average. Population growth over the past decade, however, has been slow, barely one-third of the rate for the country as a whole. Before the reorganisation of the early 1960s the three sub-divisions constituted a single, but highly diverse, economic region. The main contrast was that between the highly urbanised and industrialised Centre (hereafter referred to as the Industrial Centre) and the more southerly Black Earth Centre, which was rural and agricultural to a marked degree. The combination of these two very different areas in a single economic region before 1961 was justified as a means of maintaining a balance between the industrial and agricultural sectors; their separation reflects a greater emphasis on regional specialisation during the past decade. It is less clear on what criteria the formation of the Volga-Vyatka region was based. Its western part, particularly the Gorkiy oblast, is highly industrialised, forming an extension of the Industrial Centre, whereas most of its eastern part is thinly settled, predominantly rural territory, much of it still heavily forested. Although the contrast between the Industrial Centre and the other two sections remains evident, in recent years the last two have experienced relatively high rates of industrial growth (Table 33), reflecting a wider dispersion of industrial activity over the Centre as a whole, and there are many signs that the industrial economies of the three subdivisions are becoming more closely integrated.

Table 33

GROWTH OF INDUSTRIAL PRODUCTION, BY MAJOR ECONOMIC REGIONS 1950-70

	1950 as percentage of 1940	1960 as percentage of 1950	1965 as percentage of 1960	1970 as percentage of 1965	1970 as percentage of 1950
USSR	173	303	151	150	688
North-west	129	286	137	142	556
Centre	150	265	131	143	495
Volga-Vyatka	221	279	145	159	643
Black Earth Centre	112	390	163	152	963
Volga	259	348	161	159	890
North Caucasus	116	303	154	148	689
Urals	284	264	148	147	575
West Siberia	323	283	150	151	642
East Siberia	196	301	161	159	770
Far East	166	242	159	149	573
Donets-Dnepr	110	302	148	142	635
South-west	135	343	159	161	881
South	104	356	160	160	910
Baltic	281	397	164	162	1,049
Transcaucasus	154	239	145	152	523
Middle Asia	177	243	150	146	532
Kazakhstan	231	317	164	156	811
Belorussia	115	370	164	179	1,087
Moldavia	206	436	177	157	1,211

Source: *Narodnoye Khozyaystvo SSSR 1922-72,* 135

The Centre has long been the most important industrial region of the USSR by a considerable margin, and is still responsible for more than 20 per cent of Soviet industrial production. The region has achieved and maintained this position despite its notoriously poor resource base. Until quite recently its accessible industrial resources were restricted to lignite, peat, a limited hydro-electric potential, small quantities of iron ore in the Tula district, some mineral salts and the products of local agriculture. Over the past two decades the industrial resource base has been greatly strengthened by the opening up of the Kursk Magnetic Anomaly, which lies in the Black Earth Centre, but this remains a region that relies very heavily on other parts of the country for its industrial raw materials.

The industrial primacy of the Centre is a long-established feature. Before the nineteenth century the traditional economy, while predominantly agricultural, had some industry in the form of domestic textile manufactures based on local flax and wool, timber industries and ironworking. In the industrialisation that affected the European part of the Russian Empire in the late nineteenth century these traditional industries were modernised and greatly expanded. As a result the Centre became increasingly dependent on other regions, drawing its cotton from the newly acquired Middle Asian territories and its coal, iron and steel mainly from the Ukraine. These wider linkages were made possible by the development of the railway network, which from its inception was focused on Moscow – as were later the waterway, road, airline, pipeline and electricity transmission systems. Today Moscow lies at the centre of a spider's web of communications of all kinds, to the benefit of the central region as a whole and the Industrial Centre in particular.

Following the Revolution, and particularly during the inter-war years, Soviet development policies demanded a vigorous exploitation of such industrial raw materials as the region could provide. Lignite and peat were used on a massive scale for the generation of electricity, while agricultural products, chiefly grain and potatoes, became a major element in the chemical industry. On this basis the momentum of industrial growth was maintained. Other contributory advantages included the political and commercial significance of Moscow, the large market provided by a numerous population and the presence of a large pool of skilled labour.

In the post-war period, the centrality of the region was enhanced by the spread of oil and gas pipelines and electric power lines, which encouraged further growth and diversification of industry. This longest-established section of the 'established European core' has attracted a large share of the new industries such as chemicals, synthetic textiles and a great variety of consumer goods production. With the growth of industry in other regions, however, the dominance of the old Industrial Centre has weakened somewhat: between 1965 and 1970, when industrial output for the USSR as a whole rose by some 50 per cent, the increase was only 42 per cent in the Industrial Centre, though 52 per cent in the Black Earth Centre and 59 per cent in the Volga-Vyatka region.

Power Supplies

The special character of the region's energy base lies in the absence of bituminous coal, oil and natural gas and its resultant dependence on other regions for these commodities, which are supplemented by local lignite, peat and hydro-electricity. The chief indigenous energy source is the Moscow basin, a large lignite field lying in an arc some 200km south and west of the capital. It was first developed in the mid-nineteenth century, when it accounted for about a quarter of the Empire's very limited coal production, but the opening of the Donbass reduced the significance of the Moscow field to such an extent that its 1913 output of 300,000 tons was only 1 per cent of the Russian total. In the inter-war years, however, production rose rapidly, reaching 10 million tons in 1940, and expansion continued in the early post-war years to a peak of just below 50 million tons in the late 1950s. Since then there has been an appreciable decline, due mainly to the increasing use of oil and gas in the region, and by 1974 production was down to 35 million tons, about 5 per cent of the country's coal output. About 90 per cent of the lignite is produced in the Tula oblast and the remainder comes from mines in the Kalinin, Kaluga, Ryazan and Smolensk oblasts. In recent years an increasing proportion has been mined opencast and this will be the dominant method of extraction in future. Current plans envisage a continuing slow decline in the volume of production. Apart from its use in the chemical industry, a use now declining with the increased availability of oil and natural gas, lignite goes mainly to thermal generating plants, the most important being at Kashira on the Oka river 120km south-east of Moscow and at Novomoskovsk, Shchekino and Cherepet, all in the Tula oblast.

A second source of energy used in the generation of electricity is peat, which has been developed for this purpose entirely during the Soviet period. Major peat-fired power stations are to be found at Shatura and Orekhovo-Zuyevo, both east of Moscow, and locations near Gorkiy and Kalinin.

The Centre has a limited hydro-electric potential. In the inter-war years small stations were constructed along the Volga to the north of Moscow at Dubna, Uglich and Rybinsk, and a much larger one came into operation at Zavolzhye, near Gorkiy, in the 1950s. The region also has two of the Soviet Union's few atomic energy plants – one at Obninsk, south-west of Moscow, which was opened as early as 1954, and the second at Novovoronezhskiy, on the Don river south of Voronezh – and others are planned.

Despite these broad-ranging developments, the Centre continues to rely very heavily on other regions for its vast and growing energy demands. The importation of Donbass coal continues, primarily for use in the steel industry; for the generation of electric power and for domestic use, coal is being replaced by oil and gas piped into the region. In addition to the erection of several new gas-fired stations, lignite and coal-burning plant have been converted, especially in and around Moscow. An extensive pipeline system links the Industrial Centre with Dashava and Shebelinka in the Ukraine, with the

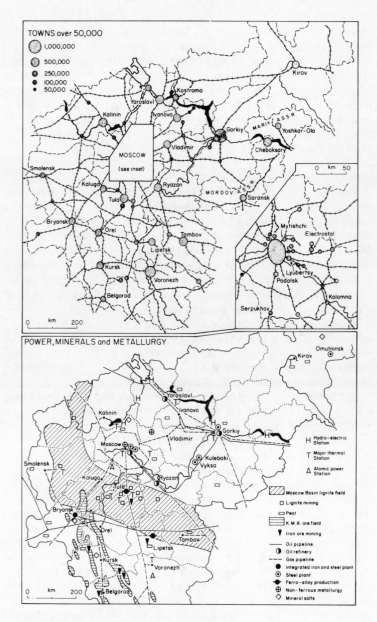

TOWNS over 50,000

- 1,000,000
- 500,000
- 250,000
- 100,000
- 50,000

MOSCOW (see inset)

Kirov
Kostroma
Yaroslavl
Ivanovo
Kalinin
Gorkiy
MARIY A.S.S.R.
Yoshkar-Ola
Cheboksary
Vladimir
Smolensk
Kaluga
Ryazan
MORDOV A.S.S.R.
Tula
Saransk
Bryansk
Orel
Tambov
Lipetsk
Kursk
Voronezh
Belgorod

0   km   200

0   km   50

Mytishchi
Electrostal
Lyubertsy
Podolsk
Kolomna
Serpukhov

POWER, MINERALS and METALLURGY

Omutninsk
Kirov
Yaroslavl
Ivanovo
Kalinin
Gorkiy
Moscow
Vladimir
Kulebaki
Vyksa
Smolensk
Kaluga
Ryazan
Tula
Bryansk
Orel
Tambov
Lipetsk
Kursk
Voronezh
Belgorod

0   km   200

H   Hydro-electric Station
T   Major thermal Station
A   Atomic power Station

▨ Moscow Basin lignite field
□ Lignite mining
▭ Peat
▤ K.M.A. ore field
▼ Iron ore mining
— Oil pipeline
◑ Oil refinery
--- Gas pipeline
● Integrated iron and steel plant
◉ Steel plant
✦ Ferro-alloy production
⊕ Non-ferrous metallurgy
◇ Mineral salts

Fig 22. THE CENTRE

Volga-Ural field and with the North Caucasus and Middle Asian fields. Pipelines now under construction will bring large additional supplies from the gasfields of the West Siberian lowland.

Although the generation of electricity from a great variety of fuels is an outstanding feature of the region, production per capita remains below the national average, especially in the Volga-Vyatka and Black Earth sections. Consequently a great deal of electric power is brought in from other regions by means of high-voltage transmission lines. At present the main source is the adjacent Volga region, but increasing use of power from Siberia seems probable in the near future.

Metallurgy

The Centre has a modest but now quite rapidly expanding metallurgical base and produced more than 8 million tons of steel in 1970, though this tonnage represents only about 7 per cent of the Soviet total, a much smaller proportion than the Centre's share of most other industries. The growth of a modern iron and steel industry, as distinct from earlier handicraft metal-working, dates from the 1890s, when blast furnaces using local iron ore were established at Tula and Lipetsk. These were considerably expanded in the inter-war years and supplied pig iron to steelworks built around Moscow, notably at Elektrostal, but steel production in the Centre continued to need large transfers of pig iron from the Ukraine. This supply is still necessary, though the region's pig iron output has much increased in recent years as a result of the exploitation of the Kursk Magnetic Anomaly ores, and this has facilitated expansion of the steel industry.

The Kursk Magnetic Anomaly was first identified in the nineteenth century, but its full extent and value were not recognised until the 1930s. Further exploration after World War II revealed the existence of two zones of iron-bearing quartzites running north-south through the Kaluga, Bryansk, Orel, Kursk and Belgorod oblasts (Fig 22). These have a metal content of 30-40 per cent, which, though low when compared with most ores previously used in the USSR, is quite high by international standards. In places the quartzites are overlain by a weathered material with a 55-60 per cent metal content. Soviet writers now claim that this is the world's largest iron ore reserve, with at least 30,000 million tons of ore in the higher grade deposit alone.[1] The development of this vast deposit was delayed by technological difficulties, particularly the waterlogged nature of the richer upper layers. Iron quartzites were first extracted at the Gubkhin mine, near Staryy Oskol (Belgorod oblast), in 1952 and a second mine was opened nearby in 1959. The overlying richer ores are also worked opencast at these sites. The main additional development during the 1960s was at

Zheleznogorsk, 75km north-west of Kursk, where both types of ore are extracted. Total output of ore from these two areas now exceeds 30 million tons a year, more than 13 per cent of Soviet iron ore production. The richer materials are fed directly into the blast furnaces, while the leaner material goes through concentrating plant near the mines.

The exploitation of the KMA ores has led to a big increase of steel production at Tula and Lipetsk, where the limited capacity of the old works has been augmented by the building of modern integrated plant. These two centres now produce 4·5 million tons of steel annually; 3 million tons of this comes from Lipetsk, which seem destined to be the biggest steel producer west of the Urals. In addition to these major plants there are also steelworks at Moscow and Elektrostal, at Gorkiy, Kulebaki and Vyksa (Gorkiy oblast) and at Omutninsk (Kirov oblast). The Centre as a whole still has a large steel deficit[2] and the construction of additional large integrated iron and steel plant, based on KMA ores, may be expected in the near future.

Engineering

The metallurgical industries support a range of engineering activities more varied than those of any other region. Soviet atlases indicate the presence of engineering of one kind or another in virtually every sizeable town, but the most important concentrations are in and around Moscow and Gorkiy and in the zone between these two leading cities. While practically every branch is represented, there is a pronounced concentration of effort on the more sophisticated types of engineering, which require a large skilled labour force and supply a very wide market. This is particularly so in Moscow and its satellite towns. The Industrial Centre employs more than a third of its workers in engineering, and supplies at least 40 per cent of the country's machine tools. Other forms of specialisation in the major cities of the region include railway equipment at Moscow, Bryansk, Kolomna, Ryazan, Tambov and Voronezh; motor vehicles at Moscow, Yaroslavl and Gorkiy; shipbuilding at Gorkiy and Rybinsk; electrical equipment at Moscow and Gorkiy; textile machinery at Ivanovo; and agricultural machinery at Bryansk, Lipetsk, Tula and Vladimir. This list is by no means exhaustive.

Textiles

The leading role played by the Centre in all branches of textile manufacture has already been discussed (Chapter 7). This activity is found mainly in the Industrial Centre, where the textile towns are heavily concentrated in a zone between the Oka and the upper Volga, in the Moscow, Ivanovo, Vladimir and Yaroslavl oblasts. Concentration is most marked in cotton textiles, which is one of the most heavily localised of all branches of Soviet industry: nearly a third of the country's output comes from the Ivanovo oblast alone. The Vladimir oblast produces a similar proportion of linen cloth, and Moscow oblast is the source of nearly 45 per cent of Soviet synthetic textiles. The woollen branch is somewhat more widely dispersed.

Chemicals

The chemical industry forms a third major element in the industrial structure of the Centre and, as with engineering and textiles, the region has long been the most important in the country, though in recent years its relative position has declined somewhat, despite a rapid growth in the volume of output. Before World War II, when the Soviet chemical industry, with the exception of a few branches such as synthetic rubber production, was at a rather low level of development, the Centre took the lead mainly on the basis of local resources, of which the most important were the edible starches, derived mainly from potatoes and grain. The chief 'imported' material was coal, both a source of energy and a chemical raw material. With the increasing relative cost of all these commodities in the early post-war years,[3] the Centre was at a distinct disadvantage in comparison with areas rich in the new chemical raw materials derived from oil and gas. During the 1960s, however, the latter have been brought to the region by pipeline, and this has entirely changed the situation, enabling the Centre to apply its skilled labour force to this rapidly growing sector. At least 15 per cent of Soviet oil-refining capacity is now situated in the region and the major refineries at Moscow, Gorkiy, Ryazan and Yaroslavl have become the basis of important petro-chemical industries.

The Industrial Centre now has the most broadly-based chemical industry of the three sections, with representatives of all the major branches. Among the most important items produced are chemical fertilisers. Phosphatic fertilisers, relying to some extent on local phosphate rock, are produced mainly at Voskresensk, Novomoskovsk and Dzerzhinsk, while nitrogenous fertiliser production, now dependent mainly on natural gas, is particularly important at Shchekino, Novomoskovsk and Gorkiy. Plastics and synthetic fibres, along with dyes, pharmaceuticals and a variety of intermediate products, are more heavily concentrated, particularly in the textile-manufacturing zone between the Volga and Oka rivers. The Black Earth Centre, in contrast, has a more limited range of chemical manufactures, among which the production of synthetic rubber and mineral fertilisers are the most important, while the Volga-Vyatka region, by virtue of its timber resources, is notable mainly for its wood-based chemical activities.

Despite the large flows of oil and gas into the region and its numerous refineries and gas-processing plants, the Centre is increasingly dependent on petroleum-based intermediates from the oil-rich Volga region. Thus even in this most recently developed sector of industry, the dependence of the Centre on its neighbours is a characteristic feature.

Other Industries

Industries based on timber are of considerable importance in the region, which is responsible for about one-sixth of Soviet timber and paper production, though its relative importance has declined over the past 20 years. Not surprisingly, these activities are most important in the north, particularly in the Kalinin, Yaroslavl, Kostroma, Gorkiy and Kirov oblasts.

Food industries are also well represented, especially in the Black Earth Centre, which plays a particularly important role in the production of sugar and vegetable oils.

Thus the outstanding characteristic of the Centre is the extremely varied nature of its industrial structure, in which only mining and metallurgy are rather poorly represented by comparison with other major industrial regions. The impact of urbanisation and industrialisation varies a good deal within the region and is at its greatest inside a line joining Kalinin, Yaroslavl, Gorkiy, Ryazan, Tula and Kaluga. Outside this zone the aspect is predominantly rural, and major industrial centres are much more widely spaced, though many of them are growing rapidly as industry is increasingly dispersed over the region.

The South

The South includes the whole of the Ukraine, now divided into three Major Economic Regions (Donets-Dnepr, South-west and South), the small Moldavian republic, sandwiched between the Ukraine and Romania, and, in the east, the Rostov oblast of the North Caucasus region, RSFSR. Reasons for attaching the latter two areas to the Ukraine are the marked similarities in environment and economy between Moldavia and the western part of the larger republic, and the fact that the Donbass coalfield extends across the Ukrainian border into the Rostov oblast. Thus defined, the South has an area (738,200sq km) equivalent to France and West Germany combined. Although this constitutes only 3·3 per cent of the territory of the USSR, the region contains 55 million people, 23 per cent of the Soviet population, and is by far the most densely settled of our nine regions. While in the eastern half of the region high population density reflects the presence of large urban-industrial agglomerations, the west, though by no means devoid of industry, is predominantly rural and agricultural.

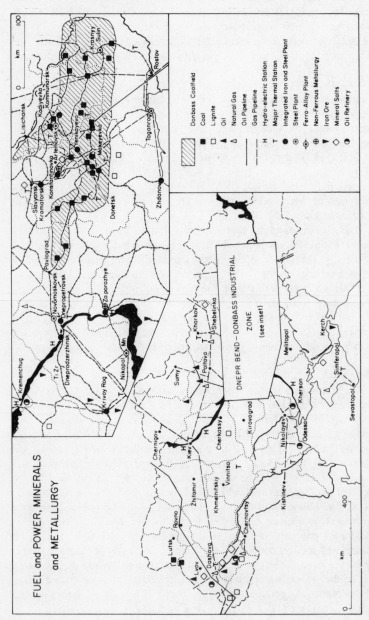

FUEL and POWER, MINERALS and METALLURGY

Legend:
- Donbass Coalfield
- Coal
- Lignite
- Oil
- Natural Gas
- Oil Pipeline
- Gas Pipeline
- H Hydro-electric Station
- T Major Thermal Station
- Integrated Iron and Steel Plant
- Steel Plant
- Ferro Alloy Plant
- Non-Ferrous Metallurgy
- Iron Ore
- Mineral Salts
- Oil Refinery

DNEPR BEND–DONBASS INDUSTRIAL ZONE (see inset)

Fig 23. THE SOUTH

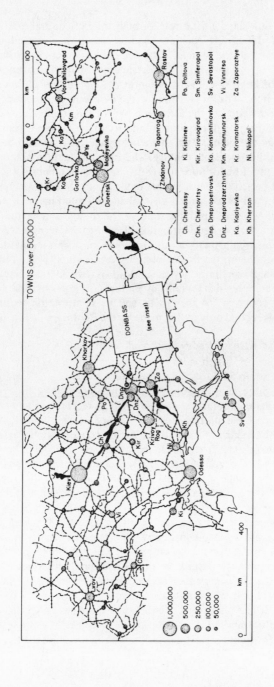

TOWNS over 50,000

DONBASS
(see inset)

1,000,000
500,000
250,000
100,000
50,000

km
0   400

km
0   100

Ch. Cherkassy   Ki. Kishinev   Po. Poltava
Chn. Chernovtsy   Kir. Kirovograd   Sm. Simferopol
Dnp. Dnepropetrovsk   Ko. Konstantinovka   Sv. Sevastopol
Dnz. Dneprodzerzhinsk Km. Kommunarsk   Vi. Vinnitsa
Ka. Kadiyevka   Kr. Kramatorsk   Za. Zaporozhye
Kh. Kherson   Ni. Nikopol

The South plays a vital role in both the agricultural and industrial sectors of the Soviet economy and is 'the best endowed and most productive of all the regions – the one the Union could least afford to lose'.[4] Its great industrial importance is mainly derived from the presence of large reserves of the most basic of all industrial resources, coal and iron. The possession of these resources, combined with a favourable location in the European part of the country, gave an early impetus to the growth of modern industry in the eastern Ukraine, which emerged as the country's first metallurgical base during the last few decades of the nineteenth century. This position it still holds, despite the development of major iron and steel complexes in other regions. During the Soviet period the development in the South of additional resources – hydro-electric power, natural gas, oil and a limited range of minerals – has permitted some diversification of the region's industrial structure and encouraged a wider distribution of industrial activities. As Table 33 shows, industrial growth during the 1960s has been a good deal more rapid in Moldavia, the South-west and the Southern region than in the Donets-Dnepr section. Nevertheless it is the Donets-Dnepr heavy industrial complex that remains by far the most important element in the industrial economy of the South and its contribution to the Soviet economy is second only to that made by the Centre.

The Donbass-Dnepr Heavy Industrial Area

The zone in which heavy industry predominates is a large one, extending some 500km from east to west and about 200km from north to south. Such an extensive piece of territory can be though of as a single industrial complex only by virtue of the economic linkages between, and the mutual interdependence of, its constitutent parts. Within this industrial zone three major concentrations of industrial activity can be identified: the Donbass coalfield, the Dnepr bend and the Azov coast. The zone is largely self-contained in the sense that it requires little in the way of raw material inputs from other regions, and is basic to the Soviet economy in supplying its products to many other parts of the country.

The biggest single resource is, of course, the Donbass coalfield, which, despite developments elsewhere, remains a major contributor to Soviet energy supplies. Its output of 220 million tons in 1974 still represented almost a third of total Soviet production and was nearly double that of its nearest rival, the Kuzbass. The great importance of the Donets field derives from its accessible location and from its wealth of coking coal and anthracite, features which have ensured its continuing expansion despite the exhaustion of the more easily worked seams and the need for progressively deeper mining in the older districts. Mining of anthracite began in the 1820s, but really large-scale development dates from the 1880s, which saw the establishment of a coke-based iron and steel industry in the eastern Ukraine. Today, as throughout the past 100 years, the majority of pits are in the Donetsk, Voroshilovgrad and Rostov oblasts (Fig 23). During the past decade there has been considerable additional development in the western limb of the coalfield in the general vicinity of Pavlograd (Dnepropetrovsk oblast). In addition to its direct use in local industry and its widespread distribution throughout the European regions,[5] Donbass coal supports a number of large thermal generating stations. These are now linked by a power grid covering the whole of the South and connected with neighbouring regions.

The coalfield is the site of one of the biggest concentrations of heavy industry in the whole of the USSR, with numerous integrated iron and steel plants founded in the nineteenth century and greatly expanded in the Soviet period, especially since World War II. Altogether there are seven major centres – Donetsk, Kadiyevka (ferro-alloys), Kommunarsk, Konstantinovka, Kramatorsk, Makeyevka and Yenikayevo – which together produce some 25 million tons of steel annually. In addition, a large integrated plant (4 million tons pa) is in operation at Zhdanov on the Azov coast, using Donbass coal and iron ore from the Kerch peninsula in the Crimea. There are also steel mills at Krasnyy Sulin and Taganrog in Rostov oblast.

These steelworks support a large heavy engineering industry. The more important products include machine tools (Voroshilovgrad, Kramatorsk), metallurgical equipment (Gorlovka, Kadiyevka, Kramatorsk), mining equipment (Donetsk, Kramatorsk, Voroshilovgrad), railway rolling stock (Voroshilovgrad, Novocherkassk, Zhdanov) and agricultural machinery (Berdyansk, Rostov, Shakhty, Taganrog).

The coalfield is also the site of an important chemical industry, which first developed in the inter-war period on the basis of coke-oven gases and the salt deposits at Artemovsk and Slavyansk. In the post-war period the raw material base for this industry has been expanded by the addition of oil from the Caucasus and natural gas from Shebelinka. In addition to several chemical plants in the main iron and steel centres, a major chemical complex has developed around Lisichansk, while at Konstantinovka a zinc smelter supports the production of sulphuric acid used in a superphosphate plant drawing apatite from the Kola peninsula.

The heavy industries of the Donbass coalfield are closely associated with those of the Dnepr bend, though it should be remembered that a distance of 300km separates Krivoy Rog from Donetsk. The Krivoy Rog iron ore deposit provides a natural complement to Donbass coal, and the two areas were linked by the exchange of these commodities in the 1880s, when the Carboniferous ironstones on which the iron industry of the Donbass was originally based proved inadequate to support further development. With the exception of the Kursk Magnetic Anomaly, still in a rather early stage of development, Krivoy Rog is the Soviet Union's biggest iron ore deposit and has been the country's leading source of iron for close on 100 years. Until the 1950s mining was wholly underground and the ores extracted were high-grade, with a metal content of 55-60 per cent. Over the past 20 years, however, with the exhaustion of the more accessible deposits of high-grade ore, the need for progressively deeper mines and a consequent rise in production costs, increasing attention has been paid to the area's lower-grade iron quartzites, which have a metal content of only 30-37 per cent but can be mined opencast. The latter now supply nearly two-thirds of the region's annual production of 120 million tons of ore. The use of these lower-grade ores has necessitated the construction of five large concentration plants on the orefield.

An additional major resource for the iron and steel industry is the manganese mined near Nikopol since the 1880s, which still accounts for nearly two-thirds of Soviet manganese production. Here too there has been a recent change from the deep mining of high-grade ores to opencast extraction of leaner materials. During the 1960s additional iron ore resources were discovered and developed at Dneprorudnyy, on the southern side of the Kakhovka reservoir, and at Komsomolskoye, a few kilometres downstream from Kremenchug. These deposits, together with the large reserves remaining at Krivoy Rog and the enormous potential of the Kursk Magnetic Anomaly, provide an assured ore supply for the future growth of the iron and steel industries of the Soviet Union and her Comecon partners, and throw doubt on the wisdom of attempting to build up an iron and steel industry in eastern Siberia.[6]

The exploitation of iron ore and managanese in this part of the Ukraine and their interchange with Donbass coal led to the establishment of iron and steel plant not only at Krivoy Rog but also at other sites along the Dnepr. There are integrated plants at Krivoy Rog, Dnepropetrovsk, Dneprodzerzhinsk and Zaporozhye, all opened in the 1880s and greatly expanded since, and steel mills at Nikopol and Novomoskovsk. These centres together produce some 20 million tons of steel annually. Major engineering industries have also been built up in the Dnepr bend area. Among the most important are the production of metallurgical and mining equipment at Krivoy Rog and Dnepropetrovsk, machine tools and railway equipment at Zaporozhye, motor vehicles at Kremenchug, Zaporozhye and Melitopol, and agricultural machinery at Kirovograd and Dnepropetrovsk.

The Dnepr bend has additional significance by virtue of its large hydro-electric potential. Stations at Zaporozhye (1932), Kakhovka (1956), Kremenchug (1960) and Dneprodzerzhinsk (1964) have a combined capacity in excess of 2 million kW. In addition, the area is quite close to the Shebelinka gasfield, which feeds a major thermal plant at Dneopropetrovsk. These power supplies have been the basis of developments in non-ferrous metallurgy and chemicals, giving the Dnepr bend a more diversified industrial structure than the Donbass. An alumina-aluminium plant was opened at Zaporozhye in the 1930s, using bauxite from Boksitogorsk; today the ore is imported from Greece. Titanium is also produced at Zaporozhye from titanium-and zirconium-bearing sands worked mainly at Volnogorsk, near Dneprodzerzhinsk. The chemical industry is most highly developed at Kremenchug, where an oil refinery was opened in 1966 to process oil from small fields in the Chernigov and Poltava oblasts. An additional power source in the same district is the brown coal deposit at Aleksandriya, now the largest producer in the Ukraine.

Other Industrial Areas

While the Donets-Dnepr industrial zone is by far the most important element in the economy of the South, the region has a number of significant second-rank industrial complexes. One of the more important of these is situated in the extreme west in the Lvov and neighbouring oblasts, a district with a variety of industrial resources. A small oilfield, opened in the late nineteenth century, now produces about 3 million tons a year. Most of this comes from the Dolina and Bytkov districts (Ivano-Frankovsk oblast), opened in the 1950s to replace the older source at Borislav. Much more important is the Dashava gasfield, which began production in the 1950s. Output from this area, together with additional sources at Rudki (Lvov oblast) and Kosov (Ivano-Frankovsk oblast), opened in the 1960s, is about 10,000 million cu m. Gas is piped to Kiev, Moscow, Minsk and Riga and across the Soviet border to Czechoslovakia. About 10 million tons of coal are mined annually in this zone, and there are important potash and sulphur deposits. The chief manufacturing centre is Lvov, which, together with the smaller towns of the area, has a very mixed industrial structure, including chemical, engineering, textile, timber and food-processing industries.

A considerable proportion of the industrial capacity of the South is distributed among its many regional centres, the majority of which have representatives of the engineering, chemical, clothing and alimentary sectors. This applies not only in such major cities as Kiev, Kharkov, Odessa and Rostov but also in the medium-sized oblast capitals. The food-processing industries are particularly strongly represented, and extend furthest down the settlement hierarchy to numerous small country towns and, increasingly, to the State and Collective farms themselves.

10

Regions of Recent Growth

The Volga-Ural Region
THIS LARGE BLOCK of territory, stretching some 2000km from the
Caspian to the northern Urals and varying in width from 1000km to
1500km, has a total area of just over 2 million sq km, nearly a tenth of
the territory of the USSR. Its population of 35 million is one-seventh of
the Soviet total. Within such a large regional unit there is considerable
diversity in the physical environment, the resource base and the
industrial economy, but the two major economic regions included in our
Volga-Ural zone have a number of common features. First, they occupy
an intermediate position between the highly developed European core –
the Centre and South discussed in the previous chapter – to the west and
the pioneer lands of Siberia to the east. Secondly, both regions have a
long history of penetration and settlement by people from the west,
despite which they have both been industrial backwaters in modern
times, the Urals from the rise of the Donbass in the nineteenth century
until their resurrection as the second metallurgical base in the 1930s,
and the Volga region until the early 1950s.

Their present-day industrial economies, though different, are both
almost entirely a product of the Soviet period, during which they have
been, at different times, among the most rapidly developing regions.
Both possess vast industrial resources. Those of the Ural region were
particularly relevant to the initial coal-and iron-based phase of
industrialisation, and those of the Volga to the later phase, with its
emphasis on oil, gas and electric power. As a result of this contrast the
Urals were developed most rapidly during the 1930s and 1940s, and the
Volga region during the 1950s and 1960s. The present situation in the
two regions is also different. In the Urals, many of the traditional
resources are nearing exhaustion and there is increasing reliance on

regions further to the east, whereas the Volga region is somewhat less developed industrially and has perhaps a greater potential for further growth. Thus, between 1940 and 1950, when industrial growth in both regions was well above the national average, it was rather more rapid in the Urals than in the Volga region. Since 1950 the reverse has been the case, with the Urals recording a rate of growth well below and the Volga region a rate well above the rate for the Soviet Union as a whole. The two sections are in some ways complementary. The Urals are notoriously deficient in energy resources, which are available in superabundance in the Volga region; the latter has virtually no metallic minerals, which are the main resource base of the Urals. Although the two regions have not in the past developed any major interchange of industrial resources, links between them have recently become stronger: electric power from the Volga, for example, is transmitted to the Urals in increasing quantities.

From the point of view of industrial geography the official boundary between the Volga and Ural regions is extremely artificial,[1] and in many ways the crest of the Urals is a more realistic dividing line,[2] despite attempts in official schemes of regionalisation to maintain a Ural region embracing both flanks of the mountain system. The resources of the east flank are primarily metallic and that section has built up various links with western Siberia and northern Kazakhstan, whereas the west flank remained less developed until, along with the Volga region, it experienced the oil-gas-hydro-electricity boom of the post-war years.

For the purposes of this volume the four westernmost oblasts of the Kazakh republic – Aktyubinsk, Uralsk, Guryev and Mangyshlak – have been attached to the Volga-Ural region. Although they cover more than 700,000 sq km, these oblasts have a combined population of only 1·6 million and contain large very thinly settled areas. Their industrial linkages are with their immediate neighbours rather than with the remainder of Kazakhstan, to which they contribute little. The developed sections of the Aktyubinsk and Uralsk oblasts are clearly a southerly extension of the Ural industrial zone, while the Guryev and Mangyshlak oblasts are important mainly for their oil resources, which make them part of the oil-rich Caspian-Volga zone.

Power Resources

A dividing line along the crest of the Urals, separating Sverdlovsk, Chelyabinsk, Kurgan and the eastern part of the Orenburg oblast from the remainder of our region, is especially significant from the point of view of power resources. The eastern section is noteworthy for its very limited energy supplies, which include a small hydro-electric potential and restricted quantities of lignite and low-grade bituminous coal.

Lignite comes mainly from two areas: mines at Volchansk and Karpinsk, to the west of Serov, produce some 20 million tons annually and a further 25 million tons are produced around Kopeysk and Korkino, south of Chelyabinsk. About a million tons of anthracite and bituminous coal are produced at Artemovskiy, 100km north-east of Sverdlovsk, and there is a small anthracite mine at Dombarovskiy, south-east of Orsk. Practically the entire output from these scattered sources is used in the generation of electricity. Although the east flank is responsible for three-quarters of the region's coal production, the great bulk is in the form of lignite, and these local resources, supplemented in several districts by the use of peat, are hopelessly inadequate for the needs of the area's metallurgical and other industries. Consequently, for the past 40-odd years, there has been a heavy dependence on fuel brought over long distances from other regions.

Foremost among these inter-regional linkages were those established in the 1930s with the Kuzbass and Karaganda fields, which continue to supply the bulk of the Urals' vital coking coal requirements. Other 'imports' of energy include oil from the Volga-Ural field via the Ufa-Chelyabinsk pipeline, and more recently from the west Siberian field as well; oil from the Guryev field piped to Orsk; natural gas from the Amu Darya fields of Middle Asia, soon to be supplemented by west Siberian gas; and electricity from hydro plants on the Volga-Kama system, especially those at Perm, Votkinsk and Kuybyshev.

When we turn to the west flank of the Urals and the Volga economic region, we find a completely different situation, for here is a zone characterised above all else by its great wealth of energy resources. The smallest of these, but the first to be developed, is the coal of the Perm oblast. The Kizel-Gubakha coalfield has been in operation since the early nineteenth century, and its output has expanded considerably during the Soviet period, though annual production is still little more than 10 million tons. This coal can be used for coking only when mixed with Kuzbass coals, so its contribution to the second metallurgical base has been of little importance. In any case it is of very minor significance when compared with the region's oil, gas and hydro-electric power.

The development of the Volga-Ural oilfield has already been outlined. Suffice it to add that, despite developments in other regions, it still produces nearly half the country's oil and 20 per cent of its natural gas. These proportions are, however, declining and the field appears to have passed the peak of its productive capacity. The oil-bearing zone is a large one (Fig 24), extending from north of Perm to the shores of the Caspian, but the great bulk of production comes from a central section stretching from the Volga bend at Kuybyshev to the Belaya valley in the Bashkir ASSR. Of the 200 million tons or more produced annually,

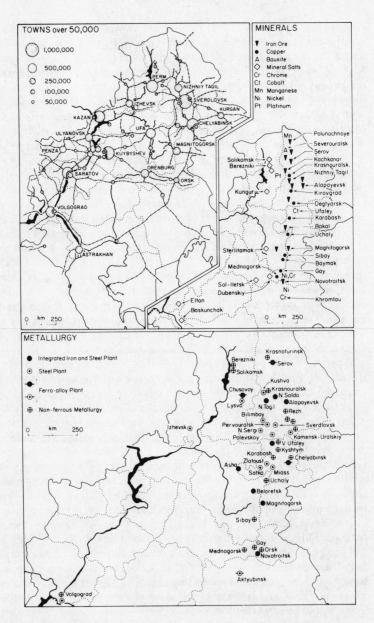

TOWNS over 50,000

1,000,000
500,000
250,000
100,000
50,000

PERM
NIZHNIY TAGIL
IZHEVSK
SVERDLOVSK
KURGAN
KAZAN
UFA
CHELYABINSK
ULYANOVSK
MAGNITOGORSK
PENZA
KUYBYSHEV
ORENBURG
SARATOV
ORSK
VOLGOGRAD
ASTRAKHAN

km 250

MINERALS

▼ Iron Ore
● Copper
▲ Bauxite
◇ Mineral Salts
Cr Chrome
Ct Cobalt
Mn Manganese
Ni Nickel
Pt Platinum

Mn — Polunochnoye
A — Severouralsk
▼ — Serov
▼ — Kachkanar
▼ — Krasnouralsk
Solikamsk — Nizhniy Tagil
Berezniki — Pt
▼ — Alapayevsk
▼ — Kirovgrad
Kungur — ● — Degtyarsk
Ct — Ufaley
● — Karabash
▼ — Bakal
▼ — Uchaly
Sterlitamak — ▼ — Magnitogorsk
▼ — Sibay
Mednogorsk — ● — Baymak
● — Gay
Ni,Cr — Novotroitsk
Sol-Iletsk — ◇ — Ni
Dubenskiy — Cr — Khromtau
Elton
Baskunchak

km 250

METALLURGY

● Integrated Iron and Steel Plant
◉ Steel Plant
◆ Ferro-alloy Plant
⊕ Non-ferrous Metallurgy

km 250

Krasnoturinsk
Berezniki
Serov
Solikamsk
Kushva
Chusovoy — Krasnouralsk
Lysva — N Salda
Bilimbay — Alapayevsk
N.Tag.l
Pervouralsk — Rezh
N Sergi — Sverdlovsk
Polevskoy — Kamensk-Uralskiy
Izhevsk — V Ufaley
Kyshtym
Karabash — Chelyabinsk
Zlatoust
Asha — Satka — Miass
Uchaly
Beloretsk
Magnitogorsk
Sibay
Mednogorsk — Gay
Orsk — Novotroitsk
Aktyubinsk
Volgograd

Fig 24. THE VOLGA-URAL REGION

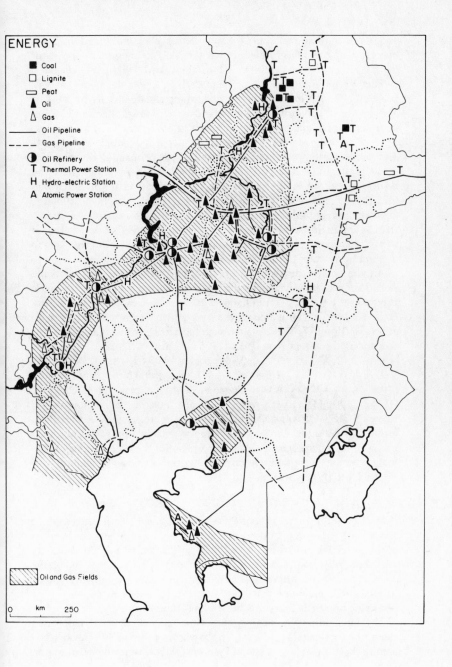

ENERGY

■ Coal
□ Lignite
▭ Peat
▲ Oil
△ Gas
— Oil Pipeline
--- Gas Pipeline
◑ Oil Refinery
T Thermal Power Station
H Hydro-electric Station
A Atomic Power Station

▨ Oil and Gas Fields

0   km   250

about 180 million tons come from the Kuybyshev oblast and the Tatar and Bashkir republics. Lower down the Volga, important deposits of natural gas have been exploited in the Saratov and Volgograd oblasts.

The Volga-Ural region as here defined contains a second oil-producing zone, in the Guryev and Mangyshlak oblasts of western Kazakhstan. The Guryev or Emba field was first exploited in 1911, but never became a major producer: output in 1970 was 2·7 million tons, most of which went by pipeline to Orsk. In the late 1950s oil was discovered further south, in the Mangyshlak peninsula, where half a dozen producing districts now supply some 10 million tons annually and further expansion is envisaged. The development of oil production in this remote and very thinly settled desert area has involved large expenditures on infrastructure, including the construction of roads, railways, pipelines and settlements. A unique feature is a desalinisation works, powered by an atomic electricity plant at Shevchenko, to product fresh water from the Caspian Sea.

Another major development of the post-war period has been the exploitation of the hydro-electric potential of the Volga and its main tributary, the Kama. During the past 20 years five major hydro-electric stations have been built along these rivers, with a total installed capacity of 7·7 million kW. These plants (with the dates at which they came into operation) are situated at Perm (1954-8, 504,000 kW), Kuybyshev (1955–7, 2,300,000 kW), Volgograd (1958–61, 2,500,000 kW), Votkinsk (1961-63, 1,000,000 kW) and Balakovo, near Saratov (1967-70, 1,400,000 kW). Together with the plant at Cheboksary (1974, 1,400,000 kW), which lies just outside the region in the Chuvash ASSR (Volga-Vyatka economic region), these have transformed virtually the whole length of the river from Gorkiy to Volgograd into a series of man-made lakes. As a result of these developments the Volga region is now in a position to transmit large quantities of electricity to its neighbours.

Minerals

In mineral resources contrasts between the eastern and western sections of the Volga-Ural region are again very pronounced. Worked deposits of metallic ores, the Urals' prime industrial resource, are almost wholly confined to the central core and eastern flank of the mountain system, while the west flank is noteworthy mainly for its variety of chemical raw materials. Apart from its oil and gas, the Volga economic region has very few mineral resources.

The Ural mountain ranges contain the most impressive and varied assemblage of metallic minerals in the whole of the USSR. Outstanding among these are the deposits of iron ore, which were the main reason for the establishment here of the second metallurgical base and supplied that base with practically all its ore requirements during its first 25 years of rapid industrial growth. An iron-smelting industry, with charcoal as its fuel, was established in the early years of the eighteenth century, and for nearly 100 years this was one of Europe's leading iron-producing districts. Its predominance in European industry was lost early in the nineteenth century, and in the 1880s the centre of gravity of Russian ironmaking shifted to the Donbass. Soviet development revivified the region, which became second only to the Ukraine as a producer of iron ore, pig iron and steel. Today the Urals retain this position in iron and steel production, but their output of iron ore – 26 million tons in 1974 – has remained stationary for some years and represents only 11 per cent of the Soviet total, a marked decline from the peak of 39 per cent in 1950.

There are six main iron-producing districts (Fig 24) – Magnitogorsk, Nizhniy Tagil, Serov, Bakal, Novotroitsk and Kachkanar – as well as numerous smaller ones. Of the areas named, the first two have been outstandingly important in the past and the last has special significance at present. The Magnitnaya Gora, a huge deposit of high-grade magnetite iron ore, near which the city of Magnitogorsk grew up in the 1930s, was for 20 years the biggest single source of iron ore in the region. In the inter-war period it not only supported the major iron and steel complex of Magnitogorsk itself, together with veral other plants in the Urals, but also supplied ore to the steelworks of the Kuzbass and Karaganda in return for coking coal. In the post-war period eastward movement of iron ore declined and eventually ceased, and the entire output, which during the 1950s and 1960s averaged 15 million tons of crude ore a year, was consumed in the blast furnaces of the Urals. As a result of this high rate of extraction, the Magnitnaya Gora deposit is nearing exhaustion and is being replaced by ores brought in from the Kustanay oblast of northern Kazakhstan. Second only to Magnitnaya Gora were the ores of the Nizhniy Tagil district, mined since the eighteenth century at Nizhniy Tagil itself and at Kushva, 50km to the north. Production during the 1960s averaged 12 million tons a year, but reserves are limited and these sources also are running out, to be replaced by lower-grade supplies from Kachkanar.

Until recently Magnitnaya Gora and Nizhniy Tagil overshadowed all other producing districts, accounting for at least 80 per cent of the entire Ural output. Most of the remainder came from Bakal, 120km west of Chelyabinsk, now producing about 5 million tons a year; from Ivdel and Bogoslovsk, near Serov (2 million tons); and from the Novotroitsk area east of Orsk (2 million tons). The main event of the past decade has been the development of the Kachkanar deposit, situated about 120km north-west of Nizhniy Tagil, which comprises enormous quantities of vanadium-bearing titaniferous magnetite with an iron content of about 17 per cent. A mining and concentrating complex that came into operation in 1963 is expected to produce about 30 million tons of ore and 6 million tons of concentrate by the mid-1970s. The fact that this deposit can be worked opencast and contains both vanadium and titanium makes it economic to use its very low grade ores which are now the chief support of pig iron production at Nizhniy Tagil.

The second major mineral resource of the Urals is copper, also found mainly in the central core and along the eastern flank. Until the 1950s the Urals were the Soviet Union's chief source of copper ores, but today, while remaining the leading producer of the metal, the region has been surpassed by Kazakhstan in ore production. Before the Revolution the main copper-mining centres were at Kirovgrad, Karabash and Baymak. Additional mines were opened in the 1930s at Krasnouralsk, Degtyarsk and Mednogorsk. In the post-war period there has been further development at Sibay and Uchaly, two somewhat isolated sites in the extreme east of the Bashkir ASSR,[3] and at Gay, north of Orsk. With the depletion of the older sources, these three districts are now responsible for the bulk of copper ore production in the region. The Gay deposit is proving particularly rich and is now believed to have reserves second only to those of Dzhezkazgan.

An extraordinarily wide range of other metallic minerals are mined in the eastern Urals. The more important items include manganese at Polunochnoye in the extreme north, bauxite at Severouralsk, cobalt at Ufaley, chrome at Khromtau and nickel near Orsk and Aktyubinsk, but there are many others.

In striking contrast to the situation on the east flank, the west flank of the Urals, together with the entire Volga region, is virtually devoid of metallic minerals. There are, however, a number of important deposits of mineral salts. The biggest of these is in the Solikamsk-Berezniki district of Perm oblast, where common salt has been extracted since the fifteenth century. In Soviet times potassium and magnesium chlorides have also been extracted in this area. Common salt is also obtained from Kungur, south-east of Perm, from Sterlitamak in the Belaya valley and from Sol-Iletsk and Dubenskiy in the Orenburg oblast. Lake Baskunchak, in the lower Volga valley, has an annual salt production of some 4 million tons, more than a quarter of the Soviet total.

Industrial Complexes

The industrial structures of the two zones on either side of the main Ural watershed reflect their contrasting resource bases. The east flank is primarily an area of heavy industry, with metallurgy, both ferrous and non-ferrous, and a wide range of engineering activities. Chemicals are an important subsidiary activity. Light industries are poorly represented, though there are important timber-based manufactures in the more northerly districts. In the Perm oblast and the Volga region, although there is some metallurgy, the most important and most widespread activities are in the chemical, alimentary and engineering sectors.

Although industrial activities are widely distributed thoughout both sections of the Volga-Ural region, a number of major industrial concentrations may be identified. In the Urals these are generally centred on groups of mines and metal works, while the Volga region has a series of industrial nodes strung out at remarkably even intervals along the river.

The *east flank* has six major industrial concentrations of which the main foci are Serov, Nizhniy Tagil, Sverdlovsk, Chelyabinsk, Magnitogorsk and Orsk. In each of these the mining of metallic minerals, metallurgy and engineering are the predominant industrial activities.

The *Serov* complex, the most northerly of these industrial concentrations, is important in both ferrous and non-ferrous metallurgy. Ironworks date back to the nineteenth century and, although the district has been overshadowed by more recent developments further south, the Serov integrated iron and steel plant now produces about a million tons of steel annually. Its iron ore is mined at several sites around Serov and Ivdel, supplemented by the manganese of Polunochnoye, which supports a ferro-alloy plant. In recent years there has been an increasing reliance on Kachkanar iron ores, which are mined about 150km to the south-west. Non-ferrous metallurgy is based mainly on bauxite, and the Severouralsk deposit, mined since the 1930s, is one of the biggest in the Soviet Union. The ore is converted to alumina and aluminium at Krasnoturinsk, and is also sent to the Kamensk-Uralskiy plant, which supplies alumina to the Siberian aluminium industry. Both platinum and gold are mined in the mountains to the west. The traditional power source is lignite, but this is now supplemented by natural gas, mainly from the Tyumen oblast, and Ivdel has important chemical industries. Many of the smaller centres in this zone have timber-processing activities.

Nizhniy Tagil, about 200 km south of Serov, is the centre of one of the most important iron and steel producing districts of the USSR, with an annual steel output of about 5 million tons. Until the 1960s the main sources of ore were, as we have seen, at Nizhniy Tagil itself and at Kushva, with smaller supplies coming from the Alapayevsk district in the east. Depletion of these reserves has been countered by the use of the Kachkanar ores. Power is derived from thermal stations based on local lignite, the biggest being that at Nizhnaya Tura, 75 km north of Nizhniy Tagil, opened in 1950. The main steel-producing centres are Nizhniy Tagil, Nizhniy Salda and Alapayevsk. Rail routes across the Urals carry ore and pig iron to steelworks in the eastern part of the Perm oblast. Non-ferrous metallurgy is represented by copper-smelting, carried on at Krasnouralsk since the 1930s. Engineering industries include a major plant for the production of railway rolling stock.

Sverdlovsk is now the largest city in the Ural region. Although, in contrast to Serov and Nizhniy Tagil, the Sverdlovsk complex lacks an integrated iron and steel plant, about 4 million tons of steel are produced annually in the steel works of Sverdlovsk and such smaller centres as Pervouralsk, Bilimbay and Nizhniy Sergi, to which pig iron is brought from both Nizhniy Tagil and Magnitogorsk. The Sverdlovsk complex is particularly noteworthy for the wide range of non-ferrous metallurgy and heavy engineering activities carried on at numerous centres within 100 km of the city. Copper smelting based largely on Degtyarsk ores is carried on at Kirovgrad and Revda and there is an electrolytic refinery at Verkhnyaya Pyshma. Bauxite from Severouralsk is converted to alumina at Kamensk-Uralskiy, and nickel is smelted at Rezh. Gold, asbestos and fluorspar are other important products. As in most parts of the Urals, the local energy base is weak, being confined to the small Artemovskiy anthracite field, and electric power is derived from a variety of long-haul fuels, including oil from the Volga-Ural and West Siberian fields, gas from Middle Asia and coal from Ekibastuz. In addition, electricity is 'imported' from the Perm and Votkinsk hydro stations. Most of the Urals chemical manufacturing centres are in this zone and, among its diverse engineering activities, electrical engineering and the production of heavy machine tools are particularly important.

Chelyabinsk is the centre of an important cluster of industrial towns in the northern part of its oblast. The cluster has a roughly cruciform shape, a fact reflected in the boundaries of the oblast itself, whose main towns lie along the north-south route from Verkhniy Ufaley to Troitsk and the route across the Urals from Asha to Kopeysk.[4] A large integrated iron and steel plant, opened at Chelyabinsk during World War II, now produces about 4 million tons of steel annually. There are smaller integrated plant at Asha and Verkhniy Ufaley, and steelworks at Satka, Zlatoust and Miass. The main source of iron ore for these plant was the Bakal deposit but, during the 1960s, they have come to rely increasingly on Rudnyy in north-west Kazakhstan, nearly 300km distant. Power is derived from the lignite deposits of Kopeysk and Korkino, supplemented by Kuzbass and Ekibastuz coal and piped supplies of oil and natural gas. Chelyabinsk is a major producer of ferro-alloys, and the main non-ferrous metal is copper. The latter is mined at Karabash, where there is also a smelter, and refined at Kyshtym. A supplementary source has been developed at Uchaly in the Bashkir republic. Tantalum and columbium are also produced in this district. The old mining towns along the railway west of Chelyabinsk are now important engineering centres whose products include machine tools, railway rolling stock and motor vehicles, making this the most important engineering zone in the Urals.

Magnitogorsk. In contrast to the industrial complexes further north, which had some industrial significance before the Revolution and have developed quite complex urban networks, Magnitogorsk is an isolated, single unit developed entirely during the Soviet period.[5] Despite its reliance on Kazakhstan for both coking coal and iron ore, the city remains the most important iron and steel centre in the USSR, with an annual steel output in excess of 15 million tons. Although there are engineering industries, these are on quite a modest scale, and the bulk of the steel produced is consumed elsewhere in the Urals and in other regions. Magnitogorsk is also the rail outlet for the eastern part of the Bashkir republic, which has iron ore deposits, a small steelworks at Beloretsk and valuable copper ores at Sibay and Baymak.

Orsk is the main centre of a more diversified industrial complex that has developed in the extreme south of the Ural region, largely since World War II. Here chemicals and non-ferrous metallurgy are the leading activities. The Orsk refinery was opened in the 1930s to process Baku and Emba oil brought by pipeline from the Caspian. Today it also refines oil from the Volga-Ural and Mangyshlak fields. Copper is particularly important in this district and a smelter has been in operation at Mednogorsk since 1939. This was originally based on ores in the immediate vicinity but, since the early 1960s, ore has come mainly from Gay, 40km north of Orsk, the largest and richest deposit in the Urals. In addition, nickel is mined at Svetlyy, in the extreme east of Orenburg oblast, and at Batamshinskiy, which, like the chrome deposit of Khromtau, lies in the adjacent Aktyubinsk oblast of northern Kazakhstan. Orsk has a nickel refinery. The Orsk complex contains one of the Urals' few hydro-electric stations, at Iriklinskiy on the Ural river, and there is anthracite mining at Dombarovskiy, to the south-east, but the area relies mainly on long-haul fuels – oil, gas and Karaganda coal. An integrated iron and steel plant was opened at Novotroitsk, a few kilometres west of Orsk, in the 1950s. This uses both local and Rudnyy iron ores to produce about 2 million tons of steel annually.

On the *west flank* of the Urals the leading industrial complexes are found around Solikamsk-Berezniki and Perm on the Kama river, and in the Belaya valley of the Bashkir republic.

The *Solikamsk-Berezniki* district has a long history of industrial activity based on local mineral salts. Saltworks were established here in the fifteenth century; modern chemical industries were set up in the 1870s and these have been greatly enlarged during the Soviet period. The main power source is coal, mined at Kizel and Gubakha since the early nineteenth century, but it is not suitable for use in iron smelting and the small steel plants at Lysva and Chusovoy are associated with the Nizhniy Tagil metallurgical complex on the other side of the Urals.

Perm. The larger industrial complex centred on Perm has much in common with those further south along the Volga in its resource base, its diversified industrial structure and its largely post-war development. Chemical industries were established at Perm in the 1920s, and a superphosphate plant there uses both Ural pyrites and Kola apatite. A large oil refinery, built in the 1950s, processes both local oil and supplies brought by pipeline from the Tatar fields. Coal-burning power stations using Kizel-Gubakha coal have been supplemented by the hydro-electric plants at Perm and Votkinsk, which have made this an energy-surplus area transmitting electricity across the Urals to Sverdlovsk. In addition to its chemical industries, the Perm complex has important synthetic textile and engineering activities, the latter including the manufacture of electrical equipment, machine tools and agricultural machinery.

Bashkir ASSR. The industries of the Bashkir republic rest mainly on its large-scale oil production, which is mostly situated in the west, along the border with the Tatar ASSR. The leading industrial areas, however, are more centrally situated, in the Belaya valley. Petro-chemicals predominate in the Ufa and Sterlitamak-Ishimbay-Salavat industrial complexes, where there are big oil refineries. The latter district has supplementary chemical resources in the form of local mineral salts.

The Volga region. Five important industrial complexes lie in the Volga valley, at intervals of approximately 300km, centred on the major cities of Kazan, Kuybyshev, Saratov, Volgograd and Astrakhan. Though differing in detail, these have a number of features in common, notably their energy orientation and their predominantly post-1940 development. Between these large complexes, smaller industrial nodes have started to develop since 1950.

The *Kazan* complex is of secondary importance, comprising only Kazan itself and its immediate satellites. A river-crossing point on the oil and gas pipelines from the Volga-Ural field to the Industrial Centre, it has a wide range of chemical and engineering activities, including shipbuilding and the manufacture of agricultural machinery. Long-established industries such as food processing, tanning and shoemaking reflect the city's importance as a regional centre and capital of the Tatar ASSR, but it has not so far seen the intensive development of a varied modern industrial structure like those of some of the cities further south.

Kuybyshev, with a population in excess of a million, is now the largest of the Volga cities and the focus of the massive Volga bend industrial complex, which extends for 150km along the river from Tolyatti to Syrzan. In many ways Kuybyshev is the capital and focal point of the entire Volga region. Situated on a major river crossing, the city was an important regional centre in the nineteenth century. Particularly concerned with the organisation of the grain traffic along the Volga, it developed major alimentary industries. Some of the earliest oil strikes in the Volga-Ural field were made nearby in the 1930s, and small refineries were built at Syrzan and Kuybyshev during World War II. Massive increases in oil production during the 1950s led to the enlargement of these refineries, the construction of additional refining capacity at Novokuybyshevsk and the establishment of major petro-chemical plants at Kuybyshev, Novokuybyshevsk, Tolyatti, Chapayevsk and Syrzan. Kuybyshev was also the site chosen for one of the biggest of the Volga hydro-electric projects, a 2·3 million kW station completed in 1957. In addition to supplying its own region, this transmits electricity by high voltage cable both eastwards to the Urals and westwards to the Industrial Centre. A favourable location, abundant power supplies and Soviet regional policy have resulted in intensive development of engineering industries, among which the production of electrical, oil-drilling and transport equipment are particularly noteworthy. Tolyatti is now the site of the one of the biggest automobile plants in the country, producing the Zhiguli, a Russian version of the Fiat, built by agreement with the Italian firm. Possibilities for the future lie in the field of non-ferrous metallurgy, and there are plans for an alumina plant, using nephelite from the Kola peninsula, to be built at Ulyanovsk, a smaller industrial node midway between Kuybyshev and Kazan.

The *Saratov* complex displays somewhat similar features, though on a smaller scale. A large refinery was built here in the 1930s to process Baku oil brought up-river from the Caspian, and there is some local oil production. Today the refinery is fed mainly by pipelines from Astrakhan and the Tatar fields and supports a petro-chemicals industry, including the production of synthetic fibres. The local energy supply comprises natural gas and a 1·4 million kW hydro-electric station opened in 1970 at Balakovo, 125km upstream from Saratov.[6] Balakovo has grown rapidly in recent years as a chemical centre roughly midway between the Saratov and Volga bend complexes.

At *Volgograd* power production and metallurgy are both important. Local resources of oil and gas are relatively small, but there is a 2·5 million kW hydro-electric station, completed in 1961, which sends power to both the Donbass and the Industrial Centre. The power station also supports a large aluminium reduction plant that draws its alumina from Hungary and the Urals. A special feature is the Volgograd steel plant, the only such enterprise in the Volga valley, which gets its pig iron from the Donbass. This supports the city's diverse engineering activities, among which the manufacture of tractors is a major item.

Astrakhan, of secondary importance when compared with the other big cities of the Volga region, is concerned mainly with the food-processing industries, particularly those based on the fisheries of the Caspian.

North Kazakhstan and South Siberia

With the sole exception of the Northlands, this is by far the largest of our nine regions. Covering about 4 million square kilometres, nearly one-fifth of the territory of the Soviet Union, it extends from the boundary of the Volga-Ural region in the west to beyond Lake Baykal, a distance of about 4000km, and stretches more than 1000km from the Turanian desert in the south to the fifty-eighth parallel. This parallel has been chosen as marking the northern limit of continuous settlement for Siberia as a whole, though in many places the limit is in fact well to the south of this line. Thus defined, the region has a population of some 25 million, about a tenth of the Soviet total, though with a density of only six per square kilometre.

This large region has a great deal of internal diversity, and contains a number of widely separated industrial complexes, but several major features impose a degree of unity and justify its treatment as a single unit. These include its great wealth of industrial resources, the predominance of power production and metallurgy in its industrial structure and the fact that its industrial economy is almost entirely a product of the Soviet period.

In the late 1950s plans for the economic development of the region appeared likely to result in a greater degree of integration among its various parts, since they envisaged the establishment of a 'third metallurgical base' in the zone between the Urals and Lake Baykal. Intensive development of the power and mineral resources of this zone was to support a big increase in its steel capacity, which would by the early 1970s amount to at least a quarter of the Soviet total, with the possibility of the region eventually rivalling the two older metallurgical bases in the Ukraine and Urals. In the event, although industrial expansion certainly took place during the 1960s, its scale was a good

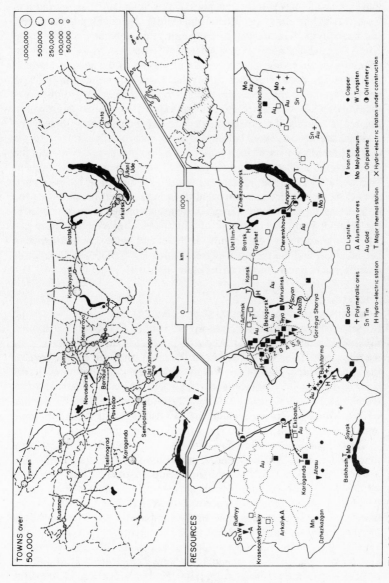

Fig 25. NORTH KAZAKHSTAN AND SOUTH SIBERIA

deal less impressive than was predicted. While low mining costs for coal and ore in the region can, to a large degree, offset the distance these materials have to be transported, this advantage has proved less than was at one time expected. Meanwhile the development of new resources in the western part of the country, notably the iron ores of the Kursk Magnetic Anomaly, has led many Soviet writers to question the necessity of investing large amounts of capital in the eastern regions. Furthermore, considerable difficulty has been experienced in building up and retaining the necessary labour force in these environmentally unattractive areas. The 1970 census revealed that population growth in the region during the preceding decade had been slightly below the national average, and well below it in many parts of Siberia.

The problem of the eastern regions is by no means resolved, and the debate continues between those who see the whole-hearted development of Siberia's power and mineral resources as essential to the continued growth of the Soviet economy and those who would prefer to see the bulk of capital investment allocated to the established industrial areas in the west, leaving the resources of Siberia as a reserve for future use when the need arises. As a result, development in the east has tended to be selective, and the region at present functions mainly as a supplier of energy, minerals and metals to the older industrial areas.

Energy

North Kazakhstan and South Siberia (Fig 25) play a major role in the Soviet coalmining industry, and in 1974 produced about 280 million tons, 40 per cent of the total. About 45 per cent of this was mined in the Kuzbass, which, as we have seen, is the main source of coking coal for the entire territory east of the Volga. A further 45 million tons of coal were produced in the Karaganda field, and 20 million tons, most of which is consumed locally, in the Cheremkhovo field of the Irkutsk oblast. Minor producers include the Minusinsk basin (5 million tons) and the Bukachacha and other small fields of the Chita oblast.

These bituminous fields have now been in operation for relatively lengthy periods, Kuzbass and Cheremkhovo since the 1890s and Karaganda since 1931. The remaining output, some 70 million tons in all, comes from a number of sources, generally of lower-grade coals, developed for the most part since World War II. The biggest of these, with an annual production now in the region of 42 million tons, is at Ekibastuz, in the Pavlodar oblast of Kazakhstan. Coal was mined here on a small scale before the Revolution, but major development began only in the mid-1950s. Steam coals are mined opencast, and although at present part of the output goes by rail to the Urals, it is intended that the entire production shall eventually be consumed in large thermal generating plants with a total capacity of 16 million kW. One such plant was opened at Yermak, near Pavlodar, in 1968 and others are nearing completion at Ekibastuz itself. Water is supplied by the Irtysh-Karaganda canal. Power from these stations will be transmitted to the European regions by 1500 kV DC lines. Similar developments have taken place on the Kansk-Achinsk lignite field, which straddles the Yenisey in Krasnoyarsk Kray. Mining began in the 1950s and output now exceeds 25 million tons a year, with plans for expansion to more than 100 million tons.[7] Large thermal stations have already been built at the mining centres of Nazarovo and Itatskiy, south of Achinsk, and others are planned.

The region is also noteworthy for its several major hydro-electric plants, all built since World War II, which include the largest such plants in the country. Some of these were clearly built in response to local requirements for electric power – for example, the Novosibirsk station, opened in 1967; those on the upper Irtysh at Ust-Kamenogorsk (1952) and Bukhtarma (1966), constructed to facilitate exploitation of that area's non-ferrous metal resources; and the station at Angarsk, which feeds the Irkutsk industrial complex. The same cannot be said of the massive 'second generation' plants opened during the 1960s at Bratsk and Krasnoyarsk, which now have installed capacities of 4·5 million and 2·4 million kW respectively, or those under construction at Ust-Ilim (5 million kW) and Sayan (6·5 million kW). All these were designed with the general objective of developing the area's power resources rather than to fulfil any specific local need. The Bratsk and Krasnoyarsk stations operated well below capacity for several years before sufficient consuming industries were established nearby. Present capacity already gives East Siberia a per capita production of electricity far in excess of any other region, and it is intended to transmit large quantities of surplus power westwards when the necessary high voltage lines are completed. This huge investment in hydro-electric power production in Siberia has been vigorously criticised by those who would prefer to see investment concentrated in the west, and a number of additional plants proposed in the 1960s, such as those on the Angara at Boguchansk and near Yeniseysk, may not materialise.

In contrast to its great wealth in coal and hydro-electric power, the region appears to lack both oil and natural gas, though it does, of course, receive oil via the trans-Siberian pipeline.

Minerals

The region contains a large number of iron ore deposits, but at present there are only four important producing districts. The first of these to be developed lies in the Gornaya Shoriya mountain country to the south of the Kuzbass, where the chief mining centres are Temirtau and Tashtogol. The area was opened up in the 1930s as a supplementary source of ore for the Kuzbass steel industry, which at that time received the bulk of its supplies from Magnitogorsk. Production expanded during and after World War II, and in the early 1950s the Gornaya Shoriya district supplied most of the ore used in the Kuzbass. Further expansion of steel capacity involved a search for additional ore supplies and mines were opened at Abaza and Teya, which lie across the watershed in the Khakass Autonomous Oblast but have been linked to the Kuzbass by rail. Since 1965 increasing quantities of ore have been brought to the Kuzbass from Zheleznogorsk on the Ilim river; this major ore field was originally intended to supply a big new steel plant at Tayshet, a major element in the proposed third metallurgical base, but this project appears to have been abandoned.

The growth of the Kazakh steel industry at Karaganda has led to the development of iron ore mining at Karazhal in the Atasu field, some 240km to the south-west, and this now supplies the bulk of Karaganda's needs; but the most important developments in Kazakhstan have occurred in the Kustanay oblast. Here the vast Rudnyy magnetite deposit, discovered in the early 1950s, has proved a welcome source of ore for the Ural steelworks, particularly those of Magnitogorsk, which were threatened with the exhaustion of local supplies. Production in this district is now about 15 million tons a year, and further growth is envisaged.

The extraction of non-ferrous metallic ores takes place mainly in the western part of the region, particularly in Kazakhstan. Details have already been given (Chapter 5) of the development of that republic's copper resources at Dzhezkazgan, Balkhash and Sayak; its lead, zinc and copper in the upper Irtysh valley; and, more recently, its bauxite at Arkalyk and Krasnooktyabrskiy. East of the Yenisey development has so far been almost entirely confined to rare items and those not available elsewhere in the Soviet Union. Gold, molybdenum and tungsten are produced in several localities (Fig 25), while the Chita oblast is noteworthy for its production of tin and such rare metals as lithium, beryllium, columbium and tantalum,[8] all of which are required in relatively small quantities and merit the cost of transportation to distant industrial areas.

Industrial Complexes

The industrial structure of North Kazakhstan and South Siberia is based largely on the production and processing of metals, and other forms of manufacturing are rather poorly represented. As previously suggested, the links between the various metallurgical and associated activities give the region a certain degree of unity, even though the third metallurgical base has not fully materialised. Several types of industrial complex can be identified, among which those based on coal, iron and steel are the oldest, most compact and most clearly defined. Outstanding among these is the Kuzbass, which has received a good deal of attention in previous chapters. With nearly 20 per cent of Soviet coal production and a steel output of some 8 million tons, the Kuzbass ranks third as a heavy metallurgical area after the Ukraine and Urals, though its steel output is less than a tenth of the Soviet total. Production comes from two large integrated plants – the Novokuznetsk works, opened in the 1930s and expanded in the post-war period, and the West Siberian plant, which came into operation near Novokuznetsk in 1964. Non-ferrous metallurgy is also important in the Kuzbass. Novokuznetsk is the site of a large aluminium reduction plant opened in 1943, which now draws its alumina from Pavlodar. Lead-zinc ores are mined at Salair, on the west side of the basin, and there is a zinc refinery at Belovo. Coke-based chemical industries are concentrated at Kemerovo, where there is a large nitrogenous fertiliser plant, while engineering activities include the manufacture of mining equipment, machine tools, railway rolling stock and agricultural machinery.

Other complexes based on ferrous metallurgy are a good deal smaller. At Karaganda a small steel plant using pig iron from the Urals was opened during World War II and the district's steel capacity was greatly increased in the 1960s by the opening of the large integrated Karaganda Metallurgical Plant in the satellite town of Temirtau. These two works together produce some 5 million tons of steel a year, the great bulk of this coming from the newer plant. The chief engineering speciality is mining machinery. Linked to Karaganda as a source of coal are the two copper-producing complexes of central Kazakhstan at Dzhezkazgan and Balkhash. Mining at Dzhezkazgan began as early as 1928 and a small smelter was opened at Karsakpay, 60 km to the west, a few years later, but large-scale development did not begin until 1940, when the district was linked to Karaganda by rail. Until the mid-1950s most of the ore was sent to the Urals, but the subsequent construction of two concentrators, a smelter and a refinery have made this a self-contained metal-producing complex. Manganese for the Karaganda plant is mined nearby at Dzhezdy and also supports a new ferro-alloy plant at Yermak in the Irtysh valley east of Ekibastuz. The Balkhash district also has a full cycle of processes from mining to metal production. Ore was first extracted at Kounradskiy in 1938, but the main source is now Sayak, 150km to the east, which began production in 1970. Kounradskiy and Sayak copper ores, together with the associated molybdenum, are smelted and refined at Balkhash itself.

Among the older industrial complexes of the region, mention should also be made of that based on the Cheremkhovo coalfield. This field has been worked since the 1890s and has a long history of chemical manufacture based on coal and local mineral salts, and of engineering, which includes the production of machine tools, mining equipment and railway rolling stock, the last at Ulan Ude, east of Lake Baykal. Among the scattered and generally small-scale industrial activities of Transbaykalia is a steel plant at Petrovsk-Zabaykalskiy. An ironworks was opened here as long ago as 1789, and the plant now consumes Kuzbass pig iron to produce some of the steel requirements of the Irkutsk region's engineering activities.

The industrial complex of the upper Irtysh basin in the East Kazakh oblast is of special interest as one of the few sizeable industrial districts of the Soviet Union based exclusively on local resources of non-ferrous metal ores. The most important metals are copper, lead and zinc, and the area is the country's leading producer of the last two. Mining dates back to the nineteenth century and there was considerable development in the inter-war years; but the most rapid growth has occurred over the past two decades, with the assistance of the power provided by the Ust Kamenogorsk and Bukhtarma hydro-electric plants. The district now has a full cycle of processes in which the biggest elements are the lead and zinc refineries at Ust-Kamenogorsk and Leninogorsk and the copper smelter at Glubokoye.

In addition to the activities described so far, two further developments have served to widen the range of industries in northern Kazakhstan and southern Siberia, particularly the latter, to diversify the structure of existing industrial complexes, to create new industrial nodes and to increase this part of the country's importance to the Soviet industrial economy. These have been the arrival of oil, brought by pipeline into a zone which as yet has no developed oil resources of its own, and the exploitation of part of the region's vast hydro-electric potential. The effect of oil has been quite obvious: in addition to providing an extra source of energy, it has led to the establishment of petro-chemical complexes around the refineries at Omsk, Pavlodar and Angarsk. The construction of large hydro-electric stations has resulted in a huge surplus of electric power, and this has proved particularly attractive to the aluminium industry. Major aluminium plants were opened during the 1960s at Shelekhov, Krasnoyarsk and Bratsk, and these three, together with the older works at Novokuznetsk, are now responsible for at least half the Soviet aluminium supply. At first the Siberian aluminium works were dependent on alumina from the Urals, but this was just a temporary phase, intended to continue only until the necessary ore and alumina supplies were made available within the region. Today, bauxite mines at Arkalyk and Krasnooktyabrskiy in Kazakhstan, opened in the mid-1960s, supply an alumina plant at Pavlodar, and nephelite from Belogorsk (Kemerovo oblast) is converted to alumina at Achinsk. In addition to their role in the aluminium industry, the Siberian hydro-electric sites support major timber-based industries, particularly the production of cellulose and associated chemical processes at Bratsk and Krasnoyarsk.

A number of other quite important industrial centres have so far received only a passing mention, among them Tyumen, Omsk, Novosibirsk, Tomsk, Barnaul, Semipalatinsk and Chita. These are major regional centres, capitals of their territories and communications nodes. Tyumen is one of the smaller cities in this group, until recently concerned mainly with timber industries; but the development of the oil and gas resources of the Tyumen oblast has led to its rapid growth over the past decade. Omsk, where railway and pipeline both cross the Irtysh and where a refinery was opened in 1955, has developed important petro-chemical industries, including the manufacture of synthetic rubber, in addition to its longer-established alimentary and engineering activities. Novosibirsk, the biggest of the Siberian cities and chief town of the West Siberian region, has major food-processing industries, especially meat packing and flour milling; it also has the biggest tin smelter in the country, which relies on concentrates from eastern Siberia and the Far East, and a steelworks using pig iron from the Kuzbass. Its highly developed engineering industry specialises in the manufacture of machine tools, electrical equipment and agricultural machinery. Tomsk, immediately north of the Kuzbass, has engineering, chemical and timber industries, Barnaul is noteworthy for its large-scale production of rayon fibres and Semipalatinsk is concerned mainly with food processing. Chita, the main organising centre for its somewhat isolated oblast, has engineering, timber and alimentary industries. All these regional centres have a much more diversified industrial structure than the various metallurgical complexes described earlier.

11
The Less Developed Regions

THE FOUR REGIONS discussed so far – Centre, South, Volga-Ural and North Kazakhstan-South Siberia – constitute little more than one-third of the territory of the Soviet Union but contain about three-quarters of the country's population. They produce about 85 per cent of the country's coal, at least 95 per cent of its steel, 75 per cent of its oil, more than 70 per cent of its natural gas and about 75 per cent of its electric power. The remaining five – Far East, North, Baltic, Caucasia and Middle Asia – are grouped together in this chapter as less developed regions lying outside the main industrialised section of the USSR and making only a secondary contribution to its industrial economy. This said, it should be emphasised that these less developed parts of the country are by no means completely lacking in industrial resources or devoid of modern industry, Indeed, in several areas, the rate of industrial growth over the last two decades has been well above the all-Union average and, in several commodities, these areas make an important and growing contribution to the Soviet industrial economy as a whole.

The less developed regions differ a good deal from each other in resources and in the nature and timing of their industrial development. While some districts, notably the Baltic region, are extremely poor in industrial raw materials and energy supplies, others, particularly in the Northlands, have vast resources that have not so far been developed, owing to their extreme remoteness and the availability of alternatives in more accessible locations. The Caucasus provides an example of a region whose relative importance was a good deal greater in the past than it is at present, while Middle Asia and the Far East have varied resources, usually on a modest scale, but have remained industrial backwaters despite fairly intensive development in the post-war period.

A common feature of all these regions, with the possible exception of the Baltic, has been the somewhat selective nature of their industrial development and particularly the marked concentration of investment in the extractive sector. The predominant role of the less developed regions has been the supply of energy and raw materials to the more developed parts of the country.

Far East

The term 'Far East' is here applied only to that section of the official Far East region lying south of the fifty-eighth parallel (Fig 26), the remainder forming part of the Northlands. With an area of 1·2 million square miles and a population of 4·3 million, our Far East covers only a fifth of the area of the official region but contains about 70 per cent of its population. While population density is extremely low, the level of urbanisation, at 74 per cent, is the highest of all our nine regions, reflecting the fact that the Russian settlers, who constitute the great bulk of the population, have not undertaken large-scale agricultural colonisation. Graphically described by Hooson as 'the Ultima Thule of inhabited Asia [occupying] a lonely position in the contemporary world',[1] the region has undergone only limited development during the Soviet period and makes only a small contribution to the Soviet economy. Indeed the range of commodities it supplies to other parts of the country is extremely limited, and it depends heavily on other regions for many of its requirements.

It is true that, in comparison with the Siberian regions to the west, the Far East has a somewhat limited resource base and this, together with its small population, does much to account for the low level of economic development. Nevertheless, the resources available could almost certainly support a much higher level of industrial production than has so far been achieved, and one senses a certain lack of interest and effort in the region on the part of Soviet economic planners, who have failed to provide the requisite level of capital investment. In the 1950s, after the establishment of the Chinese Peoples' Republic, large-scale plans were prepared for joint Sino-Soviet development of the Amur and Ussuri basins, but these were nullified by the subsequent quarrel between the two countries. The underdeveloped nature of this strategically vital frontier territory may well be viewed with disquiet from Moscow, and this could lead to a more determined effort being directed towards its industrial development. At the same time, the arguments against massive investment in central and eastern Siberia apply even more strongly to this more remote and thinly settled region. A further relevant point is the way in which the resources of the Far East are scattered throughout its territory. There are few obvious nodal

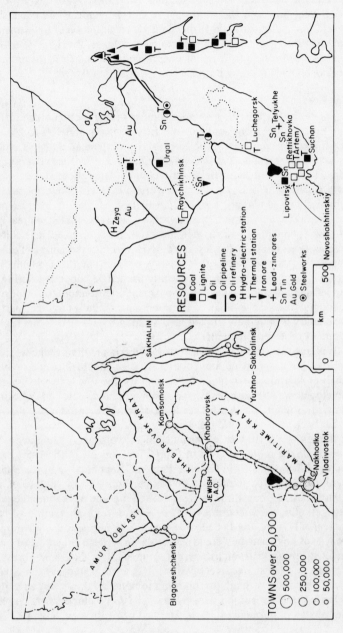

Fig 26. THE FAR EAST

RESOURCES

■ Coal
□ Lignite
▲ Oil
— Oil pipeline
◐ Oil refinery
H Hydro-electric station
T Thermal station
▼ Iron ore
+ Lead-zinc ores
Sn Tin
Au Gold
◉ Steelworks

TOWNS over 50,000

○ 500,000
○ 250,000
○ 100,000
○ 50,000

AMUR OBLAST
Blagoveshchensk
KHABAROVSK KRAY
Komsomolsk
Khabarovsk
JEWISH A.O.
SAKHALIN
Yuzhno-Sakholinsk
MARITIME KRAY
Nakhodka
Vladivostok

Zeya
H
Au
Au
T Raychikhinsk
Urgal
Sn
Sn
Sn ◉
T
Luchegorsk
T
Sn Tetyukhe
Sn +
Sn Rettikhovka
T Artem
Suchan
Lipovtsy Sn
Novoshakhtinskiy

0   500 km

points and the selection of any industrial growth centres would necessitate the assemblage of raw materials and the distribution of finished products over long distances.

Energy

This last statement applies particularly to the not inconsiderable energy resources of the Far East. Its coal production, now some 30 million tons a year, is quite large in per capita terms, but comes from a number of scattered sources, often in inconvenient locations. Of these, the largest is the Raychikhinsk district, near the Bureya-Amur confluence, which produces about 12 million tons of lignite annually; but it is some 500km from the nearest major population concentration at Khabarovsk and nearly 1200km from Vladivostok. About a million tons of coal are produced annually at Urgal, further up the Bureya valley, and at one time it was intended to use coking coal from this source for pig iron production at Komsomolsk. This project, however, appears to have been abandoned. More conveniently placed are the recently developed lignite deposits around Luchegorsk, in the Ussuri valley, now producing some 6 million tons, and the several bituminous and lignite mining centres north of Vladivostok, which have a combined output of about 10 million tons. A further 5 million tons are produced from half a dozen centres in Sakhalin. Much of the coal and lignite produced in these various districts is fed to pithead power stations, and an electricity grid linking all the main towns is now nearing completion. Nevertheless, electricity generation per capita is well below the all-Union average.

The Sakhalin oilfield has been in production since the 1920s but, although output has more than doubled during the past decade to reach 2·5 million tons, this supplies less than half the region's modest needs. The oil is carried by pipeline, river and rail to refineries at Komsomolsk and Khabarovsk. It is significant that the Trans-Siberian pipeline has, for more than a decade, terminated west of Lake Baykal. Plans to extend it to the Pacific coast, whence oil would be exported to Japan, have long been discussed but not yet put into effect. The arrival of oil in really large quantities would do much to transform the economy of the region.

The Far East has a large hydro-electric potential which, until recently, remained virtually untouched. Development of this resource along the Amur and its tributaries was a major feature of the abortive Sino-Soviet plans proposed during the 1950s, and the building of plant along the river frontier is ruled out by present political difficulties. However, a 1·5 million kW station is now nearing completion on the Zeya river and a second is planned for the Bureya.

Metallurgy

Ferrous metallurgy in the Far East is confined to a small steel mill that was opened in 1943 at Komsomolsk-na-Amure. This depends on pig iron from central Siberia and local scrap. Plans to develop an integrated iron and steel plant at this site have not been put into effect, probably because the region lacks the necessary iron ore resources. Only one field is indicated in Soviet sources – at Kimkan in the Jewish AO – but this is a very small producer.

The region has some significance in non-ferrous metallurgy, particularly as a source of tin. This is mined at a number of localities, of which the most important is at Tetyukhe, in the Sikhote Alin.

Manufacturing

The diverse but generally minor industries of the Far East are dispersed among the major regional centres – Vladivostok, Khabarovsk, Blagoveshchensk – and smaller towns, all of which have a mixed industrial structure. Engineering, alimentary industries (especially those based on fish), and timber manufactures are the main branches. Chemical industries are of some importance at the refining centres of Komsomolsk and Khabarovsk. Most of these produce only for the regional market and, apart from fish products and tin, the Far East sends little or nothing to other regions, and relies heavily on them for manufactured goods.

Baltic Region

This region comprises the three Baltic republics and the Kaliningrad oblast of the RSFSR, which together constitute the official Baltic region; the Belorussian republic; and the Leningrad, Novogorod and Pskov oblasts of the North-west region, RSFSR. Thus defined, our Baltic region (Fig 27) covers nearly 600,000sq km and has a population of about 24 million. The population density, at forty per square kilometre, is nearly four times the all-Union average. The proportion of town-dwellers is low in Belorussia, average in the Baltic republics, and high in the three Russian oblasts only because of the presence of Leningrad, a city of national rather than regional significance.

One of the outstanding characteristics of the region is the extreme poverty of its industrial resource base. In this respect it is even less well endowed than the Centre, while lacking the latter's locational advantages. This poverty alone does much to explain the limited nature of industrial development in the region and its small contribution to the industrial sector of the economy. An additional factor is that the Baltic republics and western Belorussia were detached from the USSR between 1917 and 1940,[2] and were thus not affected by Soviet inter-war

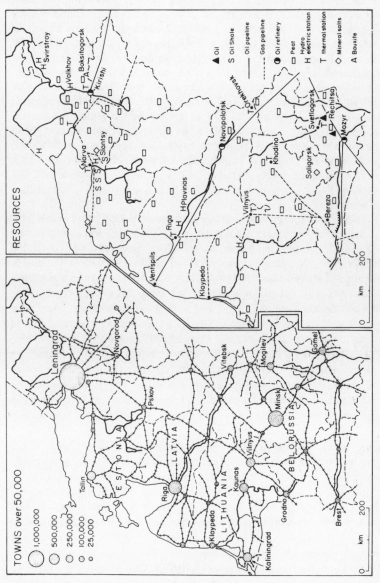

Fig 27. THE BALTIC REGION

RESOURCES

TOWNS over 50,000
- 1,000,000
- 500,000
- 250,000
- 100,000
- 25,000

▲ Oil
S Oil Shale
Oil pipeline
Gas pipeline
● Oil refinery
□ Peat
Hydro
H electric station
T thermal station
◇ Mineral salts
A Bauxite

Leningrad
Novgorod
Tallin
Pskov
ESTONIA
LATVIA
Riga
Klaypeda
LITHUANIA
Kaunas
Vilnyus
Kaliningrad
Grodno
Brest
BELORUSSIA
Minsk
Vitebsk
Mogilev
Gomel

H Svirstroy
H Volkhov
T A Boksitogorsk
Kirishi
T Narva
S Slontsy
S S S
◇
Ventspils
T Riga
H Plavinas
Klaypeda
Novopolotsk
T Otchovsk
T
Svetlogorsk
● Rechitsa
▲ Mozyr
Soligorsk
T Khodino
Vilnyus
H
T Bereza

km 0 200
km 0 200

programmes of economic development. Thus historical factors as well as the region's marginal location outside the European core have had a considerable effect. There are, of course, exceptions to these general statements. The area around Leningrad has long been an important industrial zone, which benefited from the city's role as capital of the Russian Empire from the early eighteenth century until 1918, and the republican capitals have long had some industrial importance. However, away from these few major cities, the potential for industrial growth has always been, and remains, rather limited. Nevertheless, over the past 20 years, the rate of growth in the region has greatly accelerated and a variety of major industrial plants have been established. One motive behind this trend has been the need to absorb surplus labour from the rural areas, for over much of the region high rural densities have pressed rather heavily on limited land resources.

Energy

Indigenous energy resources are particularly poor. Before World War II the only item of major importance was peat, which was extracted on a large scale and fed into numerous small local generating stations. In the 1950s peat accounted for two-thirds of all fuel burned in the power stations of Belorussia, Latvia and Lithuania. The proportion was a good deal smaller in Estonia, where there are major oil shale deposits along the coast of the Gulf of Finland, and in the Leningrad oblast, where peat and long-haul coal were supplemented by hydro-electric power from the Volkhov and Svirstroy stations. Opened in 1926 and 1933 respectively, these were among the first such plants to be built in the USSR, and are very small by present-day standards. In the early post-war years exploitation of local energy resources was particularly intensive. Peat production was stepped up and a number of large peat-fired thermal generating plants were built, notably at Khodino, Svetlogorsk and Bereza in Belorussia and at Riga in Latvia. Pre-war stations at Orekhovsk (Belorussia) and Vilnyus (Lithuania) were enlarged. There was also a big expansion in the mining of oil shale and a 1·6 million kW shale-fired generating station was opened at Narva. Hydro-electricity continues to play a relatively minor role, though it is important in the Leningrad oblast, where about half the electricity supply is derived from stations on the Volkhov, Svir and Narva rivers, and in the Karelian isthmus. Latvia now has two stations on the western Dvina and there is a small station at Kaunas in Lithuania.

As in so many other regions of the USSR, the energy supply situation was transformed during the 1960s by the advent of oil and natural gas. Oil pipelines linking the Volga-Ural field with the western USSR and the Comecon countries pass through Belorussia and Latvia, in the latter case terminating at the oil port of Ventspils, and feed refineries at Novopolotsk and Mozyr; and the pipeline to Gorkiy and Yaroslavl has been extended to a refinery at Kirishi on the Volkhov, 100km south-east of Leningrad. A gas pipeline from Dashava in the western Ukraine runs north to Vilnyus and Riga, with branches to Minsk, Grodno, Kaunas and Klaypeda, and gas from the North Caucasus fields reaches Leningrad via Moscow and Novgorod. On the Tallin-Leningrad line, which formerly carried gas derived from oil shale, the flow has been reversed to carry natural gas to the Estonian capital. Finally we may note that oil has been discovered in the upper Dnepr valley near Rechitsa, and production from this source has reached 8 million tons a year. The arrival of oil and natural gas has provided the region with a cheaper and more assured supply of energy for its older industries, has permitted a pronounced increase in the rate of industrial growth and has encouraged the development of new activities in chemical and related sectors. The bulk of the new industrial capacity installed during the last 20 years has been located in pre-existing regional centres, but some new sites have been chosen, giving a wider dispersion of industrial activity.

Industrial Complexes

Among the industries of the region, aluminium production is a special case, being one of the few activities based originally on local mineral resources and the only large-scale metallurgical operation. Bauxite, first mined at Boksitogorsk in the early 1930s, provided the raw material for the Soviet Union's first alumina and aluminium plant, which was opened at the Volkhov hydro-electric site in 1932. A second alumina plant was opened at Boksitogorsk itself in 1938, whence most of the alumina was sent to the Dneproges power site in the Ukraine. In the post-war period there has been a growing reliance on nephelite from the Kola peninsula for conversion to alumina at Volkhov and at a second plant opened nearby at Pikalevo in 1959. The alumina is reduced to aluminium at Volkhov and at plants opened during the 1950s at Nadvoitsy and Kandalaksha in Karelia. Additional raw material for this complex, to replace the nearly exhausted Boksitogorsk deposit, is a large bauxite deposit at Plesetsk in the Onega valley.

The steel industry of the Baltic region is confined to small works at Kolpino, 20km south of Leningrad, and Liyepaya on the Latvian coast, both of which run mainly on scrap metal from the region's engineering industries. The main source of steel is, in fact, the large integrated plant at Cherepovets, on the Rybinsk reservoir. Engineering, however, is well developed, particularly in and around the major regional centres.

Of these, by far the most important is Leningrad, which has several of the advantages of Moscow, in a long history of manufacturing, a skilled labour force and a large local market. Among the leading activities are shipbuilding and the manufacture of machine tools, hydro-electric turbines, tractors and railway rolling stock. Other regional centres experienced a rapid growth in engineering during the 1960s. Minsk, the Belorussian capital, which has grown particularly fast, now makes machine tools, motor cars, tractors and electrical equipment. Other major engineering centres are Riga (railway rolling stock, electrical equipment, buses, tractors, ships), Vilnyus (machine tools and agricultural machinery), Tallin (electrical equipment, ships) and Kaliningrad (railway rolling stock, shipbuilding.)

Another long-standing industry is textile manufacture, carried on in many centres. The most important material is linen and the Baltic region produces about 15 per cent of the country's linen cloth, but cotton, woollen and synthetic textiles are also produced.

The most rapid expansion in the post-war period, however, has been that of the chemical industry. Before the war this was concerned mainly with the manufacture of fertilisers, particularly necessary in a region where soils are generally poor. The large Leningrad plant, for example, was in operation before the Revolution, using imported phosphates, and later turning over to Kola apatite. More recently the production of phosphates has greatly increased near Tallin and at Kingisepp 35km east of Narva, and a major potash deposit has been opened up at Soligorsk, south of Minsk. These mineral deposits, together with oil and natural gas, have supported a massive rise in fertiliser production. In addition, the development of petro-chemicals, particularly near the new oil refineries, has widened the range of chemical products. Among these there has been a marked growth in the output of synthetic fibres, which are now produced at Mogilev, Grodno, Daugavpils and Kaunas.

Thus the Baltic region now has a wide and growing range of industrial activities – metallurgy, engineering, textiles, chemicals, food processing and timber industries are all in evidence in numerous centres. Its industrial future now appears brighter, thanks to the greater attention paid to its development over the past two decades, than at any time in the past. However, it is unlikely to become a really major contributor to the Soviet industrial economy.

The Northlands

The Northlands cover some 45 per cent of the territory of the Soviet Union – an area of 10 million sq km – but are the home of only 8 million people, less than 4 per cent of the total population. The region has vast resources of energy and minerals, whose extent has not yet been fully assessed; most of them remain virtually untouched. An extremely hostile physical environment, remoteness from the main settled area of the country, and the availability of alternative resources in more accessible locations lie behind the lack of development. In terms of resource exploitation and contribution to the Soviet economy, there is a clear distinction between the European section, where a fairly vigorous development of a wide range of industrial resources has taken place during the Soviet period, and the Siberian section, where only very limited and sporadic development has so far occurred. The last decade, however, has witnessed the opening up of the huge oil and gas fields of the West Siberian lowland, providing a further contrast between those parts of Siberia to the east and west of the Yenisey respectively. The lands beyond the Yenisey, comprising the east Siberian and Far Eastern sections of the Northlands, account for three-quarters of the region in area but for only a quarter of its population – barely 2 million people in 7 million sq km – and remain the least developed part of the whole USSR.

The European Northlands

With 5·3 million inhabitants, this area is important primarily as a source of energy and raw materials for neighbouring regions, and has experienced only a very limited development of manufacturing industry. This pattern seems likely to persist in the foreseeable future.

The energy resources of this zone include peat, coal, oil, natural gas and hydro-electricity, all of which have been developed entirely during the Soviet period. The most important single element is the Pechora coalfield. Mining began at Vorkuta in 1934 and was much expanded during the war years, when the field was linked by rail to the European network. Production continued to rise in the post-war period and now runs at about 20 million tons a year. The bulk of this coal is consumed in the north-western economic region, particularly at Leningrad, Arkhangelsk and Murmansk. Since 1955 the Pechora field has also supplied the coking coal requirements of the integrated steel plant at Cherepovets. Now that oil and gas pipelines have reached Leningrad, the demand for Pechora coal is unlikely to expand and little further growth in production is envisaged.

The Ukhta oil and gas field in the Komi ASSR was discovered in 1929, but production remained very small until the late 1950s, when additional oil and gas reservoirs came to light. The output of oil has now reached 6 million tons a year and most of this is carried by rail to the refinery at Kirishi, near Leningrad. Gas production, now in the region

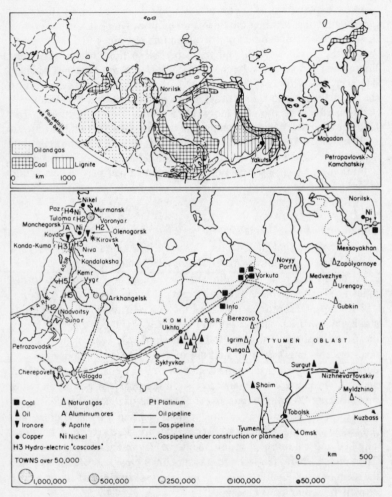

Fig 28. THE NORTHLANDS

of 10,000 million cu ms, has been considered sufficient to warrant the construction of a pipeline that joins the European network at Vologda.

Hydro-electric power is generated mainly in the Karelian ASSR and the Murmansk oblast, and in both these areas it is the main source of energy. The rivers employed are generally small but have the advantages of steep gradients regulated by numerous lakes. Consequently, development has taken the form of groups or 'cascades' of small generating plant. There are more than a score of these[3] with a combined capacity of about 1·6 million kW, little more than a quarter of the capacity of, say, the Krasnoyarsk station in Siberia, a revealing comment on the hydro-electric potential of the two areas and the way in which it has been developed.

Apart from the exploitation of these energy resources – coal, oil and gas in the Komi ASSR and hydro-electricity in the west – the most important developments have occurred in the Kola peninsula, a district rich in ferrous and non-ferrous metal ores and minerals of great importance to the chemical industry. Among the first items to be developed was apatite, a mineral used in the production of phosphatic fertilisers. Mining began in the Kirovsk district in the 1930s and was greatly expanded in the post-war period, when a second site was opened at Apatity, 20km to the west. Kola apatite is now distributed to numerous fertiliser plants in the European part of the country. A by-product of apatite mining is the production of nephelite, a source of alumina, potash and soda, which is now used in alumina production at Volkhov and Pikalevo. Some of the alumina is converted to aluminium at Nadvoitsy and Kandalaksha.

The chief metallic resource of the Kola peninsula is nickel. A mine, smelter and refinery were opened at Monchegorsk in 1938, and this site has become the focal point of a major metallurgical complex. After World War II the Petsamo district, with nickel mines at Nikel, was acquired from Finland and now sends its concentrate to Monchegorsk. Both these nickel deposits are now nearing exhaustion, but an alternative supply has been developed at Zapolyarnyy, 30km east of Nikel. A variety of other minerals are produced in small quantities, including copper, cobalt, gold, silver, columbium and tantalum. The production of iron ore in this district is an entirely post-war enterprise. Mines were opened at Olenogorsk in 1955 and at Kovdor in 1962, and concentrate from these sources is the main support of the Cherepovets steel plant.

Thus the main significance of the European Northlands is as a supplier of minerals and power to other regions. Manufacturing industry, which is of secondary importance, is carried out at a variety of scattered sites. Arkhangelsk and Murmansk, for example, have varied engineering interests, including shipbuilding, while the more southerly centres, such as Vologda, have textile plants. Lumbering and woodworking industries are, of course, important throughout the region, which produces nearly a quarter of Soviet timber.

Separate mention should be made of the integrated steel plant at Cherepovets. Opened in 1955, this plant was designed to supply the steel requirements of the north-western economic region and now produces about 2 million tons of steel annually. Its location necessitates particularly lengthy hauls of fuel and iron ore, its coal coming from Vorkuta (1800km) and its iron ore from Olenogorsk and Kovdor (1400km). Cherepovets also has chemical industries which were based initially on coke-oven gases, but are now fed by natural gas from the Volga-Ural, Saratov and Ukhta fields.

The Siberian Northlands

East of the Urals, major developments are now taking place in the vast West Siberian lowland, where oil was discovered at a number of sites in the late 1950s. The first district to be developed was the Shaim field in the valley of the Konda, a west-bank tributary of the Irtysh. Oil from Shaim was initially carried to the Omsk refinery by water, but now goes by pipeline to Tyumen, whence it is moved by rail. Subsequent developments have been mainly in the valley of the Ob, notably around Surgut and Nizhnevartovskiy, whence the oil is moved to Omsk by a pipeline through Tobolsk. Production from all three districts has increased rapidly over the past few years, total West Siberian output having reached 116 million tons in 1974, nearly four times the 1970 figure and a quarter of the Soviet total.

Natural gas is present in the middle Ob valley at Myldzhino (Tomsk oblast), whence a pipeline to the Kuzbass is under construction, but the most important fields are in the more northerly parts of the Tyumen oblast. Gas was first discovered at Berezovo, some 500km from the mouth of the Ob, in 1953, and subsequently some distance further south at Igrim and Punga. Gas from these districts is now carried by pipeline to Serov and Nizhniy Tagil. In the middle 1960s attention shifted still further north, with the discovery of major gasfields around the estuary of the Ob and in the lower reaches of the Pur and Taz valleys at Novyy Port, Medvezhye, Gubkin, Urengoy, Zapolyarnoye and Messoyakhan. With the exception of the last-named, which feeds a pipeline to Norilsk, these fields are to be linked by long-distance pipelines now under construction to the Urals via Ingrim and to the European regions via Vorkuta and Ukhta. Gas production is still in its early stages. In 1972 it reached 11,400 million cu m, about 5 per cent of the Soviet total, but this will rise very rapidly once the pipelines are completed. One cannot expect any significant development of manufacturing industry to follow the exploitation of oil and gas in the Tyumen oblast, since the harsh physical environment and the small population seem likely to fix the region's economic development at the primary stage.

The Northlands beyond the Yenisey, though rich in industrial resources, are the most empty and least developed part of the USSR. In this whole area, which covers more than 7 million sq km, there are only four towns with more than 50,000 inhabitants – Norilsk, Yakutsk, Magadan and Petropavlovsk-Kamchatskiy – and only Norilsk is a modern industrial complex of significance to the Soviet economy as a whole. Nickel mining began at Norilsk in the 1930s and was expanded during the war with the aid of equipment evacuated from Monchegorsk. Copper production was added in the 1950s, with a small chemical industry based on refinery gases. Today, while copper and nickel are the metals produced in the largest quantities, the importance of the Norilsk complex lies mainly in the by-product metals obtained in the copper-refining process, which include platinum, titanium and vana-dium. The district uses a variety of fuels. Local coalmines produce more than 3 million tons a year, there is a 440,000 kW hydro-electric station on the Khantayka river, 200km to the south, and natural gas is piped from the Messoyakhan field. The outlet is via the railway to Dudinka and thence by the Northern Sea Route.

Elsewhere, exploitation of the region's mineral resources has involved small-scale development of coal and lignite for local use and the extraction of only the more valuable minerals – tin, gold and diamonds.

Caucasia

The area under discussion here comprises the North Caucasus economic region of the RSFSR (excluding the Rostov oblast, which has close industrial ties with the adjoining Ukraine) and the three Transcaucasian republics of Armenia, Azerbaydzhan and Georgia. With an area of only 440,000sq km, 2 per cent of the territory of the USSR, this is the smallest of our nine regions (Fig 29). Its population, however, exceeds 23 million and is more than 9 per cent of the Soviet total, giving a density second only to that of the South. It is also an area of rapid population growth. The increase between 1959 and 1970 was nearly 28 per cent, a figure surpassed only by the Middle Asian region, but the level of urbanisation (48 per cent in 1970) is significantly below the all-Union average.

Oil and Gas

Caucasia's prime significance to the economy of the Russian Empire

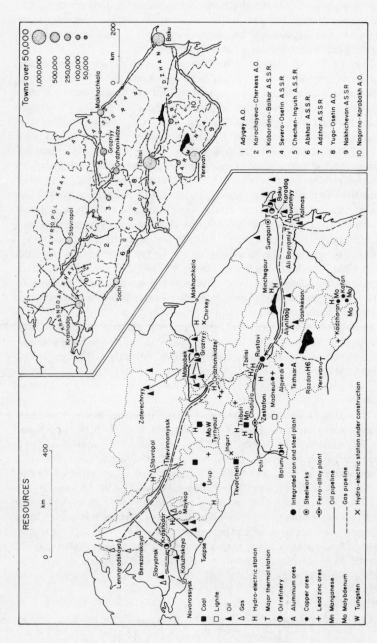

Fig 29. CAUCASIA

RESOURCES

km
0   400

Towns over 50,000

1,000,000
500,000
250,000
100,000
50,000

km
0   200

1 Adygey A.O.
2 Karachayevo-Cherkess A.O.
3 Kabardino-Balkar A.S.S.R.
4 Severo-Osetin A.S.S.R.
5 Chechen-Ingush A.S.S.R.
6 Abkhaz A.S.S.R.
7 Adzhar A.S.S.R.
8 Yugo-Osetin A.O.
9 Nakhichevan A.S.S.R.
10 Nagorno-Karabakh A.O.

■   Coal
□   Lignite
▲   Oil
△   Gas
H   Hydro-electric station
T   Major thermal station
◉   Oil refinery
A   Aluminium ores
●   Copper ores
+   Lead zinc ores
Mn Manganese
Mo Molybdenum
W   Tungsten

●   Integrated iron and steel plant
◉   Steelworks
◈   Ferro-alloy plant
─── Oil pipeline
---- Gas pipeline
×   Hydro-electric station under construction

and the Soviet Union has been as a major source of energy: the region has produced large quantities of oil since the late nineteenth century and of natural gas in the period since World War II. As we have already seen, the Baku and North Caucasus fields were the first to be exploited, and on the eve of World War II still accounted for well over 80 per cent of the modest Soviet output, about 70 per cent coming from the Baku district alone. Production began here in the 1870s, and around the turn of the century this was the world's leading oil-producing area. Output continued to increase, rising from 8 million tons in 1913 to 22 million tons in 1940. During the 1940s production fell by half, but in the 1950s and 1960s there was a marked recovery, made possible by offshore drilling and by the development of additional sources in the lower Kura valley, and output topped 20 million tons in 1970. Over the past few years, however, there has been some decline.

Production in the North Caucasus, which remained relatively minor before World War II, was derived almost entirely from the fields around Groznyy and Maykop. Output from these sources rose from about a million tons in 1913 to nearly 5 million in 1940. In the post-war period expansion has been much more rapid, and production from the whole North Caucasus region in 1970 was 34 million tons, well in excess of that of Azerbaydzhan. This increase was achieved primarily by the discovery and exploitation of several new oil pools within 100-150km of Groznyy, notably at Malgobek to the west and at Zaterechnyy in the Kuma valley to the north. These sources have been connected by pipeline to Groznyy and, along with the older sources in this district, are responsible for an annual production of more than 20 million tons. Smaller developments have also occurred in the Krasnodar Kray at Slavyansk and Kaluzhskaya. In 1974 the Baku-North Caucasus zone produced more than 50 million tons, double the 1940 figure but now representing only about 11 per cent of the Soviet total.

The production of natural gas on a large scale in Caucasia, as elsewhere in the Soviet union, is essentially a development of the postwar period. Output in 1940, though representing 80 per cent of the Soviet total, was a mere 2700 million cu m. By 1970 it had reached 44,000 million, 20 per cent of the USSR's vastly increased output. Over the last few years, however, decline appears to have set in and the 1973 production was only about 32,000 million cu m. Gas-producing districts fall into three groups, those of Azerbaydzhan, Stavropol and Krasnodar. Azerbaydzhan was one of the few areas in the USSR producing a significant quantity of natural gas before World War II, but this was just a by-product of the oil industry. In the 1950s, however, valuable supplies of gas were discovered along the Caspian coast of the south of Baku at Karadag, Duvannyy and Kalmas. These became an

important energy source for the three Transcaucasian republics, gas
being supplied to Georgia and Armenia through pipelines to Tbilisi and
Yerevan. Reserves, however, proved to be limited and the Azerbaydzhan gasfields have been overshadowed by developments north of the
Caucasus. Transcaucasian requirements are increasingly supplied by
pipelines built across the main Caucasian range and across the Soviet
frontier from Iran. Major natural gas deposits were opened up during
the late 1950s in the Stavropol and Krasnodar oblasts. The Stavropol
field was the first to be developed, and for a while was the biggest
single producer in the Soviet Union. It has now been surpassed by fields
in other regions and also by the combined output of the several
Krasnodar fields, of which the most important are those at Leningradsk-
aya, Berezanskaya and Maykop. In addition to supplying the industries
of the North Caucasus and Transcaucasian regions, the various gasfields
of Caucasia send large quantities of gas by pipeline to the European
regions.

Coal and electric power

Though oil and gas are overwhelmingly predominant, other sources
of energy have also been developed. Apart from one or two very minor
sources on the north flank of the main Caucasian range, coal production
is confined to the small Tkvarcheli and Tkibuli fields in western
Georgia, which have a combined output of 2-3 million tons. This is far
from adequate to the republic's needs, and at least half as much again is
brought in from the Donbass.

As might be expected, in a region where steep relief is widespread,
Caucasia has a considerable hydro-electric potential. More than a dozen
hydro-electric plant are in operation in the region, and a similar number
are under construction or planned. The great majority of these,
however, are small, with capacities ranging from 50,000 to
100,000kW, and it is only recently that any large-scale hydro-electric
projects have been undertaken. The biggest single plant in operation at
present is the one at Minchegaur on the Kura, which has an installed
capacity of 360,000kW and was built in connection with a scheme to
irrigate large areas in the lower Kura valley. About 540,000kW are
installed in a cascade of six stations along the Razdan valley in
Armenia, where the river drops more than 1000m in less than 100km
between Lake Sevan and Yerevan. These form part of a larger scheme
that has not been completed owing to difficulties experienced in
maintaining a steady flow from the lake. Major plants under
construction at present are a good deal larger. These include a 1·6
million kW station on the Inguri river in western Georgia and a 1
million kW plant at Chirkey on the Sulak in Dagestan. All the plants

completed so far are a good deal smaller than some of the region's major thermal stations, including the two oil-fired stations at Baku and the gas-fired plants at Ali Bayramly, Tbilisi, Yerevan and Nevinnomyssk, each of which has a capacity in excess of half a million kilowatts.

Metallurgy

Transcaucasia is exceptional among the less developed regions in having an integrated iron and steel plant.[4] This is at Rustavi in eastern Georgia, and now produces about 1·4 million tons of steel annually. Iron ore is drawn from Dashkesan in western Azerbaydzhan, and coking coal comes from the Tkvarcheli field and the Donbass. There is also a steel mill at Sumgait, near Baku, which uses local scrap and Donbass pig iron to produce steel pipes for the oil industry. Possibly Georgia's greatest contribution to the industrial economy of the USSR is that made by the large manganese deposit at Chiatura, which is responsible for about a third of Soviet output. This supports a ferro-alloy plant at Zestafoni, but much of the output is shipped via the Black Sea port of Poti to the European regions and abroad.

Caucasia, and particularly the Transcaucasus, is of considerable importance in the production of non-ferrous metals, its resources including ores of aluminium, copper, lead, zinc, molybdenum and tungsten. The devlopment of a large-scale aluminium industry in this part of the country depends on the exploitation of two indigenous sources of ore – alunite at Alunitdag, near Dashkesan, in western Azerbaydzhan, and nephelite syenite at Tezhsar, in western Armenia. The use of both these has meant completely new processes, and this has delayed the growth of the industry. Alumina plants to use these ores have been built at Alunitdag, Kirovabad and Razdan, and these will eventually supply the aluminium reduction plants at Sumgait and Yerevan. The latter were completed before the alumina plants and have until recently relied on alumina from the Urals and the European USSR. Copper is produced mainly in Armenia, where the chief sources of ore are at Kadzharan and Kafan, in the extreme south-east, and in the Madneuli-Alaverdi district, which straddles the boundary with Georgia. Both have been in operation since well before the Revolution and both send concentrate to the large smelter at Alaverdi. A third source of copper ores is in the early stage of development at Urup, in the Kabardino-Balkar ASSR. Ordzhonikidze, midway along the northern flank of the main Caucasus range, has a lead smelter and zinc refinery which process both lead-zinc ores mined in the vicinity and smaller quantities of concentrate from scattered mining sites in the Transcaucasus. The chief sources of molybdenum and tungsten are Tyrnyauz in the Kabardino-Balkar ASSR and the Kadzharan-Kafan district of south-eastern Armenia.

Manufacturing Industries

Oil, natural gas, coke-oven by-products and smelter gases from non-ferrous metallurgy supply a widely dispersed and very varied chemical industry. Among the more important sites are those associated with the oil refineries at Baku, Gronznyy, Krasnodar, Taupse and Batumi, the coke ovens at Rustavi and the Alaverdi copper smelter. Other major centres include Yerevan, where the industry was originally based on acetylene derived from local limestone by the calcium carbide process but now depends mainly on natural gas, and Nevinnomyssk in the Stavropol Kray, where a chemical complex based on Stavropol natural gas was built up during the 1960s. Among the region's wide range of chemical products, the most important are nitrogenous and phosphatic fertilisers, synthetic rubber, synthetic fibres and plastics.

Special mention should also be made of the alimentary industries, which are particularly well developed in this region and occupy an unusually large number of centres. Local specialisation reflects the varied nature of Caucasian agriculture and its concentration on high value crops. Krasnodar oblast, which corresponds with the rich mixed farming zone of the Kuban, has flour milling, meat processing, sugar refining and the production of vegetable oils as its main alimentary activities. Tea and tobacco-processing plants are numerous in western Georgia, and eastern Georgia and Armenia are noteworthy for their wineries and distilleries. Fruit and vegetable canning are widespread in the Caucasus and in the towns along the northern hill-foot of the main Caucasus range.

Middle Asia

For our purposes Middle Asia includes not only the four republics of Kirgizia, Tadzhikistan, Turkmenia and Uzbekistan, which constitute the official Middle Asian economic region, but also the five southern oblasts of Kazakhstan – Kzyl-Orda, Chimkent, Dzhambul, Alma-Ata and Taldy-Kurgan (Fig 30). The latter are somewhat isolated from the remainder of Kazakhstan by the Turanian desert and have strong affinities with their southern neighbours in their physical, human and economic geography, the type of economic development they have experienced and their role in the Soviet economy. Thus defined, the region covers about 2 million sq km and has a population of more than 24 million, one-tenth of the Soviet total. Population growth is more rapid here than in any other region, with an increase of more than 40 per cent between 1959 and 1970, reflecting the numerical predominance of

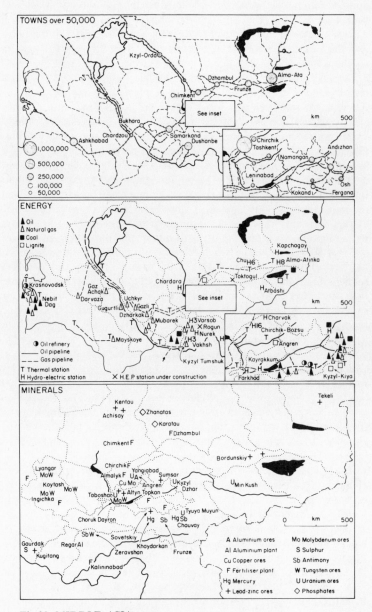

Fig 30. MIDDLE ASIA

non-Russian ethnic groups with a Moslem cultural and historical background. The great bulk of the population is concentrated in a narrow piedmont zone between the great Turanian desert to the north and the formidable mountain barriers that close the region in on its southern side.

For many centuries the peoples of Middle Asia depended primarily on intensive irrigated agriculture, supplemented by nomadic or transhumant stock rearing in the desert and mountains. Until recently such industrial development as did occur took place almost entirely within the piedmont zone where, apart from the products of agriculture, raw materials for industry were limited in range and quantity. Since World War II, however, and particularly since the late 1950s, the power and mineral resources of the region have been exploited more intensively. This has brought about developments in both the desert and mountain zones, thus spreading industrial activity, at least at the extractive stage, more widely throughout the region. Despite the fact that numerous important industrial developments have taken place over the past 20 years, during which the pace of industrial growth has been more rapid than at any other time in the region's history, Middle Asia remains less industrialised and more heavily dependent on agriculture than any other major division of the USSR. This is to be seen, for example, in the level of urbanisation, which, at 40 per cent, is lower than in any other region. In several oblasts, mainly those where irrigated agriculture supports large rural populations, the urban element is less than 25 per cent. A special feature of the region is the way in which recent urban growth has to a large degree been supported by immigration from the European regions, so that the urban population has a large and growing proportion of Russians. The indigenous peoples, despite their rapid growth in numbers, have been slow to move from rural-agricultural to urban-industrial areas and, as a reaction to this situation, small enterprises in the light and food-processing sectors have been established in small country towns and on the farms themselves.

The present industrial structure comprises two fairly distinct elements. The element that is more important to the Soviet industrial economy is composed of the extractive industries, which supply increasing quantities of energy and of minerals, mainly non-ferrous metals, the great bulk of which go to support the continued growth of older industrial complexes in the main industrial zones of the USSR. Most of the extractive industries have been developed since World War II, largely in previously empty or thinly settled desert and mountain areas. The second element comprises the diverse manufacturing industries, aimed mainly at local and regional markets and found chiefly in the older cities, whose origins were as trading and administrative rather than as industrial centres. In any case, manufacturing industry, though much expanded in the post-war years, is still relatively minor in relation to the region's population, and Middle Asia continues to rely heavily on other parts of the country for manufactured goods. Throughout the Soviet period the region has occupied a marginal or peripheral position in the Soviet industrial economy, in economic as well as in locational terms. Its essential role is, and seems likely to remain, that of a supplier of energy and raw materials to the more highly developed parts of the country.

Energy

Among the various developments that have taken place in Middle Asia since the Revolution, none has been more important than the exploitation of its energy resources, particularly its natural gas. An early start in oil production took place in the extreme west of the region, where the Turkmen oilfield was first exploited around Nebit Dag before World War I. Production remained low through the inter-war period, and in 1950 was only 2 million tons. During the 1950s, however, several new oil pockets were found and output rose more rapidly, reaching 16 million tons in 1974. The latter figure still represented less than 4 per cent of the Soviet total, and the Turkmen field seems likely to remain only a minor producer.

The various oil-producing districts are now linked by pipeline to a refinery at Krasnovodsk, on the Caspian, but this cannot cope with the entire output, and Turkmen crude oil is shipped to refineries in the Caucasus and the Volga region. Plans for a pipeline to a proposed refinery at Shagal, near Chardzhou on the Amu Darya, were announced several years ago but have not yet been put into effect. Consequently, though some Turkmen oil is moved eastwards by rail, the greater part is consumed outside the Middle Asian region. Additional supplies amounting to about 2 million tons annually are derived from a number of more centrally located districts. Most of these are in the Fergana basin, where half a dozen small producing units, some of which have been in operation since the early years of this century, support two refineries. One of these, at Khamza-Khakimadze, 25km from Fergana, was opened as long ago as 1908. A much larger refinery, opened at Fergana itself in 1958, processes Turkmen as well as Fergana basin oil. Reserves in the Fergana basin are small and no significant expansion of output is envisaged. The same can be said of the small oilfield in the Surkhan Darya valley of south-eastern Uzbekistan, which has been in operation since the 1930s.

Middle Asia has no major coalfield but contains several small coal and lignite deposits, the combined output of which is about 10 million tons a year. Most of this comes from two main areas. The Fergana basin, where small-scale coalmining began before the Revolution, produces about 4 million tons from four or five sources, the largest of which is at Kyzyl-Kiya, south-east of Fergana. The biggest single producing unit, however, is at Angren, in the valley of the same name south-east of Tashkent. Production began here in the 1940s and has greatly expanded in the post-war period. The Angren opencast mines yield about 5 million tons of lignite a year. Most of the coal and lignite produced in Middle Asia is consumed in thermal generating plant in the cities.

Before the 1950s hydro-electric development was confined to several clusters of small-capacity plants, usually constructed in association with irrigation projects, which supplied power separately to the major cities of the region. More than thirty such plants had a combined capacity of less than 700,000kW.[5] Somewhat larger plants have been associated with more recent irrigation projects. Control of the Syr Darya for the Hungry Steppe irrigation scheme included the Farkhad and Kayrakkum barrages, each with a capacity of 126,000kW, and the Chardara station (100,000kW) was built on the same river in connection with the Pakhta Aral irrigation project. All these stations are, however, very small when compared with those on the major European and Siberian rivers and are also overshadowed by the Middle Asian thermal generating plant, particularly those built recently on the basis of the region's natural gas resources.

The 1960s marked a new phase, during which a number of major hydro-electric plants were under construction, and others were planned, as part of a more thorough and co-ordinated development of the region's potential. Several of these have a capacity in excess of all the pre-1960 stations combined and, together with the big gas-fired thermal plants, are linked by a regional electricity grid now nearing completion. Of these new major hydro-electric plants, the biggest at present is the Nurek station on the Vakhsh river in Tadzhikistan. With a planned final capacity of $2 \cdot 7$ million kW, this came into operation in 1972, and a second, $3 \cdot 2$ million kW, station is under construction on the same river at Rogun. A 600,000kW plant was opened at Charvak on the Chirchik river north-east of Tashkent in 1970. Major developments are also under way on the Naryn river in Kirgizia. A 40,000kW plant was opened on the upper reaches of the river Atbashi in 1970 and a $1 \cdot 2$ million kW station is nearing completion at Toktogul. Despite these and other developments, total output of electricity per capita in the Middle Asian region remains well below the national average, an indication of the region's relatively low level of industrialisation. At the same time, it should be noted that total electricity output has increased nearly fourfold over the past decade.

Of all recent developments in Middle Asia, however, none has been as striking as the rapid growth of natural gas production. Output in the four southern republics rose from 722 million cu m, less than 2 per cent of the Soviet total, in 1960 to 77,600 million some 30 per cent, in 1970. The great bulk of this development has occurred in western Uzbekistan and in Turkmenia, previously among the least developed parts of the region. The gas is carried by pipeline to the major cities of the region as far east as Alma-Ata, feeding large thermal generating plants en route, and also to the Urals and European Russia. Natural gas now accounts for about 60 per cent of the electricity generated in Middle Asia. Thus the exploitation of this resource has not only given added impetus to the industrialisation process in the Middle Asian region but has provided a major additional source of energy for the older industrial areas. Apart from the relatively small quantities of gas produced in the west Turkmen and Fergana oilfields, the first discoveries were made in the late 1950s at Gazli, Dzharkak and Uchkyr in the Bukhara oblast and at Mubarek in the Surkhandarya oblast. The first to be developed were the Dzharkak and Mubarek fields and gas from these sources goes mainly into the regional pipeline system. Additional supplies developed during the 1960s and used mainly within Middle Asia are those of Kyzyl Tumshuk in southern Tadzhikstan, Shibarghan in Afghanistan and the Mayskoye field in Turkmenia, whence there is a pipeline to Ashkhabad. Major producing districts in the Amu Darya valley – Gaz Achak, Gazli, Gugurtli and Uchkyr – together with the Darvaza field in central Turkmenia, send the bulk of their output to the Urals and Europe. Of all the gas produced in the various Middle Asian fields about 21 percent is consumed within the region, 26 percent is piped to the Urals and 53 percent to the European regions.[6]

Minerals

Middle Asia is moderately well endowed with a wide range of minerals, but little use was made of these before World War II. One notable deficiency is the apparent absence of any major source of iron ore, a fact which, together with the lack of coking coal, militated against the development of a ferrous metallurgical base. Ferrous metallurgy is restricted to a small steel plant at Bekabad (formerly Begovat), about 120km south of Tashkent; this relies on long-haul pig iron and scrap from the region's engineering industries to produce about 400,000 tons of steel a year, less than a fifth of the region's requirements.

A number of quite important non-ferrous metallurgical centres have been established in Middle Asia, and this activity has grown rapidly in the post-war period. A major item is the lead smelter at Chimkent, opened in 1934. The original sources of ore were at Kentau and Achisay, 150km to the north, but today the Chimkent plant consumes ores and concentrates from numerous other mining districts of Middle Asia. Of these, the most important are at Tekeli in the Taldy-Kurgan oblast; Bordunskiy, south-east of Frunze; Altyn Topkan, north of Leninabad; and Kugitang in the south-east corner of the Turkmen republic; all opened during the 1960s. Zinc ores and concentrates produced in these districts were, until recently, sent outside the region for refining in the Ukraine and Caucasus, but are now dealt with by a large electrolytic refinery opened in 1970 at Almalyk, in the Angren valley. The Angren valley is now emerging as a major non-ferrous metallurgical complex. Local resources include the Angren lignite, lead-zinc ores in the mountains to the south and a large copper-molybdenum source near Almalyk, where a copper concentrator, refinery and rolling mill were all built during the 1960s. This district is also destined to play an important role in the aluminium industry. A plant is being built at Almalyk for the extraction of alumina from the kaolin clays that occur as overburden in the Angren lignite field. The alumina will provide the raw material for the aluminium plant at Regar, west of Dushanbe, which at present processes alumina from the Urals, and there are plans for a second aluminium plant at Angren. Middle Asia is also the source of several relatively rare metallic minerals, notably molybdenum, tungsten, antimony, mercury and uranium[7] (Fig 30). In addition, there is a major sulphur deposit at Gaurdak in south-east Turkmenia and phosphates at Karatau and Zhanatas near Dzhambul.

Manufacturing Industry

Before World War II, the bulk of Middle Asia's limited industrial capacity was concerned with the processing of agricultural commodities, and such activities are still a major component of the region's industrial structure. The modern textile industry is almost entirely a product of the Soviet period, though there is of course a long tradition of domestic textile manufacture. Cotton ginning is carried on in a large number of centres, and big cotton textile plant have been built in the major cities of Tashkent, Fergana, Ashkhabad and Dushanbe. Despite this, and despite the fact that they grow some 90 per cent of the country's cotton, the Middle Asian republics produce less than 10 per cent of Soviet cotton cloth. Similarly, although this is an important sheep-rearing area, woollen textile production is only about 5 per cent of the Soviet total. Silk is a traditional speciality, the initial winding process being carried out in Ashkhabad, Bukhara, Chardzhou, Dushanbe, Leninabad, Margilan (near Fergana) and Osh, but most of the silk thread produced goes to other textile areas, especially the Centre. Middle Asia has so far played only a minor role in the Soviet Union's rapidly expanding synthetic textiles industry. Viscose rayon fibres are produced from cotton linters at Namangan and nitron fibres are manufactured at Navoi, in the Bukhara oblast, but the output of cloth is very small. In view of the large and rapidly increasing surplus of labour in the densely populated rural areas, expansion of all types of textile manufacture would appear to be highly desirable, and is taking place, but it will be a long time before the region has a share in textile production commensurate with its output of textile raw materials.

The chemical industry is another obvious field for industrial expansion in view of the region's resources of gas, oil, phosphates and sulphur, and the growing availability of the by-products of non-ferrous metallurgy. So far development has been mainly in the manufacture of chemical fertilisers. There are now six large superphosphate plants at Almalyk, Chardzhou, Chimkent, Dzhambul, Kokand and Samarkand, all dependent on the major phosphorite source at Karatau. Sulphuric acid is derived from a variety of sources, including gases from the Chimkent lead smelter and native sulphur from Gaurdak. Nitrogenous fertiliser plants, now using hydrogen derived from oil and natural gas, have been built at Chirchik, Fergana, Navoi and Kalininabad.

Engineering, particularly the lighter branches, has grown rapidly in recent years. About the more important items are the manufacture of machine tools at Tashkent, Frunze and Chimkent, and of tractors, combines, agricultural machinery and equipment for the food and chemical industries. However, none of these activities is of any great importance in the all-Union context and Middle Asia continues to import large quantities of machinery from other regions.

As might be expected in a region of great agricultural importance, the alimentary industries are well represented. They include not only flour milling and meat processing but also sugar refining, fruit and vegetable canning and wine making.

Conclusion

IN ADDITION TO painting a fairly detailed picture of the present-day industrial geography of the USSR, this volume has tried to place contemporary patterns of industrial activity within a time perspective of industrial growth and locational change. In conclusion we must attempt some assessment of the progress achieved so far and the prospects for the future. Such an assessment poses a number of questions, few of which can be answered with real precision but all of which require consideration. How does the Soviet achievement to date compare with those of other industrial powers over the past 50 years? How does the present rate of economic growth in the USSR compare with those in other countries? Can present growth rates be maintained in the years ahead? What changes are likely to occur in the structure and location of Soviet industry in the short-and long-term future?

Some mention has already been made of the difficulties of comparing growth rates in the USSR with those of other countries. There are considerable discrepancies between official Soviet figures and those calculated by western economists, the former giving a consistently more favourable picture than the latter. While the figures appearing in Soviet statistical handbooks may be designed to impress, they do not necessarily reflect any desire to deceive, and differ from western assessments mainly because of different methods of computation.[1]

However optimistic they may be, even Soviet data show a progressive decline in the rate of industrial growth during the post-war years. Figures published regularly in *Narodnoye Khozyaystvo SSSR* indicate an average annual increase in gross industrial production of about 16 per cent in the 1930s,[2] 10 per cent in the 1950s and about 8·5 per cent[3] in the 1960s, the latter rate being little more than half that of the pre-war decade. Incidentally, it is a striking comment on the poor performance of the agricultural sector that the corresponding figures for gross agricultural production were 2·3 per cent, 5·2 per cent and 3·5 per cent respectively. When data from agriculture, industry and other economic activities are combined in a measure of national income, steady decline in the rate of growth is again apparent (1930s, 14 per cent per annum; 1955-60, 9·2 per cent; 1960-65, 6·6 per cent) though with some recovery in the late 1960s (1965-70, 7·7 per cent). Separate western calculations of Gross National Product[4] give much lower figures of about 6 per cent per annum in the 1930s and just over 5 per cent in the 1960s. It will be observed that the discrepancy between the Soviet and western figures quoted has become much smaller in recent years.

Given that Soviet economic planning has persistently concentrated on the industrial sector at the expense of agriculture and other activities, it is not surprising that rates of growth should have been highest in that sector. Nor is it surprising that, even in this most favoured sector, the rate of growth has declined in the post-war period. A fall below the high rates recorded in the 1930s was inevitable for the very simple reason that the latter were, to a large degree, a function of the low starting point, in terms of absolute levels of production, at the beginning of the first Five Year Plan. It is a familiar truism that, the greater the total production the smaller is the rate of growth, in percentage terms, represented by a given volumetric increase in output. For this reason alone the maintenance of pre-war growth rates was hardly to be expected.

Turning to the matter of comparisons between Soviet growth rates and those of the capitalist world, there can be little doubt that in the 1930s the former were a good deal higher than the latter, owing in part to the impact of depression in the capitalist world and in part to a time lag in the development of Soviet industry. Soviet performance in the 1930s was akin to that of other industrial countries some 50 years earlier, in the latter part of the nineteenth century.

What of the situation in more recent years? The data set out in Table 34 indicate that, in the industrial sector at least, Soviet growth during the 1960s was well in excess of that achieved by the larger capitalist economies, with the noteworthy exception of Japan, where growth occurred at nearly double the Soviet rate. In terms of Gross National Product, however, Soviet performance is much less impressive according to western observers. Between 1958 and 1964 'Soviet growth . . . was less than both West Germany and France, economies with higher per capita incomes. It also fell below Italy, a country with a slightly lower per capita income, and far behind Japan, a country with 80 per cent of the Soviet per capita income level. This slowdown in

Table 34

GROWTH OF INDUSTRIAL PRODUCTION IN THE SOVIET UNION AND
SELECTED CAPITALIST COUNTRIES, 1963-71
Index numbers: 1963=100

	1964	1965	1966	1967	1968	1969	1970	1971
USSR	107	116	127	139	151	162	175	189
USA	106	117	128	131	138	145	139	139
UK	107	111	113	113	120	123	124	125
West Germany	109	114	116	114	128	144	154	157
France	107	110	118	122	127	142	152	160
Italy	102	107	119	128	136	141	150	146
Japan	116	120	136	162	190	222	258	270

Source: *United Nations Statistical Yearbook*, 1972

growth [was] a major concern of the leadership as the golden
anniversary of the revolution approached.'[5] With the decline in growth
rates in many parts of the capitalist world in the late 1960s and early
1970s, Soviet performance appears in a better light, but there is no
reason to suppose that this situation is in any way permanent or that the
Soviet system as such is capable of producing more rapid long-term
economic expansion than its rival. On the other hand, it is clear that a
centrally directed economy like that of the USSR, is capable, by
channelling effort in a particular direction, of achieving very rapid
short-term growth in selected sectors. Discussion has been confined so
far to gross industrial production and overall GNP with no mention of
per capita measures. It should be remembered that, throughout much of
its existence,[6] the Soviet Union has experienced population growth rates
significantly above those of most major industrial countries. Thus per
capita growth rates have been a good deal lower than gross rates, a point
which should be borne in mind when comparisons are made.

Mention of the population factor leads us to consider population as a
resource and the efficiency with which it is used as expressed in the
productivity of labour. Comparisons in this sphere, even those based on
Soviet sources, show the USSR in a much less favourable light. Labour
productivity in agriculture is particularly low – a reflection of the low
priority given to agricultural development throughout most of the Soviet
period – but even in the favoured industrial sector it is well below that of
most advanced capitalist powers.[7] Much of the rapid increase in
industrial production in the inter-war years was achieved with the aid of

massive transfers of population from rural to urban employment.
Between 1929 and 1939, while the total population grew by about 11
per cent, the urban population doubled. In the post-war period this
factor has again been important: between 1950 and 1970 total
population increase amounted to 41 per cent and urban population
doubled again.

Such a process cannot, of course, continue indefinitely, and the rural
population cannot be looked upon as an inexhaustible reservoir of
labour to support industrial growth. At the same time, as we have seen,
changing vital rates have brought a marked decline in the rate of
population growth. It is highly significant that, between the censuses of
1959 and 1970, the population of working age[8] grew less rapidly than
the population as a whole (9 per cent as against 16 per cent), a trend that
will continue during the 1970s as the children born during the 1960s
enter employment. Ever since the Revolution the proportion of the
population of working age who are actually employed has steadily
increased, and this 'participation ratio'[9] is now well in excess of 75 per
cent. Consequently, the volume of untapped labour resources has
diminished and is likely to diminish still further, emphasising the need
to increase labour productivity as the chief means of raising output.
Soviet planners are well aware of the situation. The current Five Year
Plan aims at an increase of 36-40 per cent in labour productivity in
industry. It lays stress on this target as one 'of crucial importance for
our whole economic development programme. A rise in living
standards directly depends on the growth of labour productivity. In the
five-year period we must obtain 80-85 per cent of the total national
income increment through higher labour productivity'.[10]

There are of course associated problems regarding the sectoral and
regional distribution of labour. A growing emphasis on more complex
and technologically advanced industrial processes demands a progressively higher proportion of skilled labour, and this will necessitate
further large-scale investment in education, training and research. The
regional problem has been mentioned in several places in this volume.
Areas of labour surplus lie mainly in Middle Asia while much of Siberia
suffers from labour shortage, but current migration flows are doing
nothing to restore the balance. In any case, where surpluses do still
occur, they come in the form of untrained rural labour, whereas the
need is for skilled industrial workers.

Although in general terms a more rapid rate of population growth
may appear desirable, the chief need is for a more efficient use of
existing population resources. Since this policy is being forced upon the
USSR by current demographic trends, the population supply should
prove adequate to support sustained economic growth.

If human resources are adequate, physical resources of most types can only be described as abundant. There can be little doubt that industrial resources were used extravagantly in the past, and the current Five Year Plan calls for 'economies in raw and other materials' to reduce the 'material intensiveness of industry', so that it may 'cut the costs of production and considerably reduce requirements of manpower and capital investment.'[11] Generally speaking, in the period since the Revolution, industrial development has rarely been hindered by raw material shortages and, where it has been, the fault has lain with inadequate extraction rates rather than genuine deficiency. In many instances the main problems facing Soviet planners have been those of establishing priorities and choosing between alternatives – which resources in which regions should be developed immediately and which should be set aside for possible utilisation at some future date? Energy production is a case in point.

In the interwar and early post-war years high priority was allotted to the development of the country's coal resources as the main source of energy, and oil and gas were relatively neglected; but over the past two decades oil and gas resources have been much more vigorously developed than those of coal. Incidentally, this is a sphere in which the USSR is especially favoured, for if, in the coming decades, oil and gas reserves should become depleted, very large reserves of coal will still be available. A second aspect of energy supply demanding a choice of priorities has been the debate concerning the relative importance to be attached to hydro and thermal electricity generation. The country's vast hydro-electric potential is another major resource which could be more' fully developed should the need arise.

Despite the superabundance of energy resources within the borders of the USSR, there have, as with other types of resource, been problems of regional imbalance resulting from the great distances separating major deposits from main consuming areas. The problem of transport has led to the intensive exploitation of such low-grade fuels as peat and lignite in areas of high energy demand like the Centre, while major high-grade fuel resources in remote inhospitable areas of northern Siberia have remained virtually untouched.

On numerous occasions the great size of the Soviet Union and its plentiful resources have ensured that, when an established source of supply has shown signs of exhaustion, alternatives have been available. One major example has been the shift of the main oil-producing area from the Caucasus to the Volga-Ural field and its potential movement beyond the Urals to the West Siberia lowland. Another case has been that of iron ore, where threatened exhaustion of the Nizhniy Tagil and Magnitnaya Gora deposits in the Urals has been countered by the exploitation of alternative, though lower-grade, deposits both within the Urals at Kachkanar and in the adjacent Kustanay oblast of northern Kazakhstan. More recently the development of the Kursk Magnetic Anomaly ores has transformed the situation in the European part of the country, and has been a major weapon in the armoury of those who argue for the concentration of industrial development in the European sector rather than in the eastern regions.

In other cases the general desire to supply all the country's requirements from within its own frontiers has led to the substitution of one raw material for another. An example is provided by the aluminium industry, where an apparent shortage of bauxite resulted in the use of other ores, a substitution which necessitated the development, not without difficulty, of the appropriate alternative technologies.

Thus, with an adequate population and an abundance of resources, the future of the USSR as one of the world's greatest industrial powers would seem to be assured. Such problems as do exist – and they are not inconsiderable – are concerned with the best means of utilising the great natural wealth at her disposal. The sheer size and growing complexity of the Soviet economy present a major challenge to centralised economic planning, which has yet to prove that it can achieve results superior to those of the other systems. If sustained economic growth is to be the sole criterion of success, there can be little doubt that the Soviet Union will be successful. If, as is claimed, the purposes of economic growth include 'a considerable rise in the people's material and cultural level',[12] ie an improved standard of living, then much has still to be achieved. Greater efficiency in the use of resources and changes in the industrial structure to provide more for the consumer must now be major objectives. Both these trends are already visible, and there is little reason to doubt that by the end of the century the living standards of the Soviet citizen could be among the highest in the world.

One aspect of the efficient use of resources is what Soviet writers refer to as the 'optimal location of productive forces', that is the geographical distribution of capital, labour and equipment that will achieve the highest returns. The nature of this optimal pattern, which is of particular interest to the economic geographer, has been a matter of debate over much of the period since the Revolution and will no doubt continue to be so in the years to come. As we have seen, economic development over the past 50 years has led to major locational changes, particularly in the form of industrial, and for that matter agricultural, development outside the old European core area. The extent to which this 'drang nach Osten' will continue is a major issue of the presen day. Current population trends do not favour the establishment of large additional capacity east of the Urals, still less beyond the Yenisey, and a lively debate continues between the supporters of investment in Siberia and Europe respectively. In recent years, the resource potential of the west has been reassessed and the emphasis on investment in the east has lessened. This may, however, only be a temporary phase. Presumably a time will come when the vast resources of the east must be more fully utilised to replace the diminishing resources of the west. Whether this will necessarily mean large-scale movements of population and manufacturing industry towards the east is a separate issue. We are brought back to the aspects of the physical environment discussed at the beginning of this book, which are likely to ensure that industry in large parts of Siberia does not develop beyond the extractive stage. The division will persist between the ecumene, containing the great bulk of the population, and the non-ecumene, supplying raw materials to the settled zone.

References

The titles of the works by the authors cited are to be found in the Bibliography, pages 231–248.

CHAPTER 1

Environment and Resources, pages 3-14

1 Texts with a thorough treatment of the physical environment include J.P. Cole, 1967; J.C. Dewdney, 1965; J.S. Gregory, 1968; G.M. Howe, 1968; D.J.M. Hooson, 1966; G. Jorré, 1967; R.E.H. Mellor, 1964; W.H. Parker, 1969; S.P. Suslov, 1961.
2 D.J.M. Hooson, 1966, 40.
3 R. Hutchings, 1971.
4 R. Hutchings, 1971, 11.
5 W.H. Parker, 1969, 7.
6 J.A. Hodgkins, 1961, 150.
7 Where the term 'European section' is used, this should be taken to include the Ural economic region unless otherwise indicated.
8 For details of the distribution of iron ore resources, see P.E. Lydolph, 1972, 508. The importance of the European section has increased with the reassessment of the Krivoy Rog and Kursk Magnetic Anomaly ores (see pp 168 and 158).

CHAPTER 2

Population and Transport, pages 15-33

1 P.E. Lydolph, 1970, 551.
2 For a fuller discussion of the effects of physical factors on the

223

transport system, see R.E.H. Mellor, *Adv. Sci.* 20, 1964; 1964, 322-27, and 1969, 5-12.

3   *New Directions in the Soviet Economy,* 579.
4   *Soviet News* 5745, 16 July 1974, 268, and V. Biryukov, *Sov. Geog.* XVI (4), 1975, 225-230.
5   R.E.H. Mellor, 1969, 20.

CHAPTER 3

Industrial Development, pages 34-55

1   D.J.M. Hooson, 1966, 49.
2   A. Nove, 1969, 12.
3   W.H. Parker, 1968, 300.
4   W.H. Parker, 1968, 299.
5   J.P. Nettl, 1967, 76.
6   A. Nove, 1969, 74.
7   J. Miller, 1955, 16.
8   R.W. Campbell, 1967, 15.
9   P.E. Lydolph, 1970, 473.
10 Hooson's terms, see Chapter 8.
11 P.E. Lydolph, 1970, 474.
12 In many sectors it may be assumed to have been much lower in 1941-4, but precise data are not available, these years being omitted from most annual series in Soviet statistical publications.
13 Quoted by M. Dobb, 1966, 313.
14 R.E.H. Mellor, 1970, 10.
15 For example, D.J.M. Hooson, 1964 and 1966; P.E. Lydolph, 1970; R.E.H. Mellor, 1970.
16 D.J.M. Hooson, 1966, 95-100.
17 Figures for regional shares of industrial production are based on value-added data given in L. Dienes, 1972, 443 (see also Table 13).

CHAPTER 4

Fuel and Power, pages 62-85

1   J.A. Hodgkins, 1961, 5-6.
2   The pattern of 'proven' reserves is rather different: 30 per cent of these are in the European USSR and another 47 per cent in the southerly, more accessible parts of Siberia. This is because these are the areas where the most detailed geological exploration has been carried out (Hodgkins, op cit).

3 Proven reserves of coalfields now being mined amount to about 225,000 million tons (Hodgkins, op cit).

4 Hodgkins, op cit.

5 *Petroleum Press Service*, XXXVIII (7), July 1971, 246.

6 Ibid, 245.

7 An area lost to Poland after World War I and finally regained only in 1945.

8 *Petroleum Press Service*, XXXVII (9), September 1970, and XXXVIII (7), July 1971.

9 L. Dienes, *Sov Studies*, XXIII (1), July 1971.

10 *Geog Mag*, XLVI (8), May 1974, quoting *Oil and Gas Journal*, December 1973.

11 This is equivalent to more than twice the total oil reserves (12,200 million tons of coal equivalent) quoted by the *Oil and Gas Journal*, December 1973.

12 T. Shabad, 'News Notes', *Sov Geog*, XIV (5), 1975, 338

13 In 1970 nuclear plant produced 2500 million kWh, only 0.3 per cent of total Soviet output and equivalent to about one-tenth of British or United States nuclear production. Roughly 10 per cent of the additional capacity to be installed in the USSR during the 1971-5 Plan will be nuclear, and nuclear plant should account for about 2.5 per cent of total production in 1975.

14 P.E. Lydolph, 1970, 498.

CHAPTER 5

The Metallurgical and Engineering Industries, pages 86-109

1 V. Ya. Rom, *Sov Geog*, XV(3), 1974, 123.

2 See, for example, the total of 10,556 million tons quoted in P.E. Lydolph, 1970, 508.

3 N.P. Nikitin *et al*, 1966, quoted by J.P. Cole and F.C. German, 1970, 183, estimate the total reserves of the Kursk Magnetic Anomaly alone at 40,000 million tons, while V.P. Novikov, *Sov Geog*, X(2), 1969, states that the Kursk Magnetic Anomaly has 30,000 million tons of high-grade and 'many trillions of tons' of lower-grade ores.

4 *Narodnoye Khozyaystvo SSSR, v 1970 godu*, 193.

5 The four exceptions, all in the extreme west, are Belorussia, Moldavia and the South-western and Southern regions of the Ukraine.

6 See, for example, the views expressed by V.P. Novikov, op cit, 1969; V. Ya. Rom, op cit, 1974; and S.A. Nikitina, *Sov Geog*, XV(3), 1974, 128-34.

7   Two of the best in this respect are *Atlas Razvitiya Khozyaystva i Kultury SSSR*, 1967, and *Atlas SSSR*, 1969.

8   For the position up to the 1950s, see J. Kowalewski, *Optima*, 9(4), 1959, 209.

9   In fact post-war development here, as in other cases, has shown resources to be much greater than was realised in the 1930s.

10   T. Shabad, 1969, Fig 8, 60.

11   T. Shabad, 1969, 62.

12   See, for example, A.G. Omarovskiy, *Sov Geog*, I(3), 1960, 42-56.

13   Particularly those cited in note 7 above.

14   Such data would appear to be available only to Soviet geographers working in the USSR, who would appear to have easier access to unpublished statistical data than their British counterparts.

15   A.N. Lavrishchev, 1969, 219.

16   L. Symons, *Geography*, 58(4), 1973.

CHAPTER 6

The Chemical Industries, pages 110-121

1   L. Dienes, 1969, 16.

2   G.W. Hemy, 1971.

3   Strictly speaking, Sterlitamak, which lies in the Bashkir ASSR, is within the Volga economic region but, geographically, it is in the Urals.

4   T. Shabad, 1969, 77.

5   Ibid, 301.

6   Imports of natural rubber in the 1960s averaged about 250,000 tons a year.

7   T. Shabad, 1969, 82-3.

8   Ibid.

9   Ibid.

10   Ibid, 86.

11   An exhaustive list of chemical sites, including those producing these lesser items, appears in G.W. Hemy, 1971.

12   R.E.H. Mellor, 1964, 285.

CHAPTER 7

The Timber Industries, Light Industries and Food Industries, pages 122-134

1   The two sets of figures do not, of course, add up to 100 per cent, owing to the exclusion of the important building materials industry

together with other sectors, which are not separately tabulated in
published Soviet data (see Tables 14 and 16).
2   P.V. Vasilyev in I.P. Gerasimov *et al*, 1971.
3   In 1940 the Centre produced 87 per cent of all cotton cloth.
4   P.R. Pryde, 1968, 591.

CHAPTER 8

Regionalisation pages, 137–152

1   P.M. Alampiyev, 1964, 25.
2   There is a single exception to this rule. The Kaliningrad oblast,
    annexed by the USSR in 1945 as a detached part of the Russian
    republic, has been allocated to the Baltic economic region, which
    also contains the Lithuanian, Latvian and Estonian republics.
3   C. Thomas, *SGM*, 88 (3), 1972, 207. The minimum size of a city
    also varies between republics. It is 12,000 in the RSFSR, 10,000
    in the Ukraine and 5,000 in other republics.
4   Yu.G. Saushkin, *Econ Geog*, 38, 1962, 28-37.
5   P.M. Alampiyev, *Sov Geog*, IV (10), 1963, 60.
6   T. Shabad, *Geog Rev*, 43, 1953, 217.
7   P.M. Alampiyev, 1964, 35-7.
8   Yu.G. Saushkin, *Econ Geog*, 38, 1962, 29.
9   Z. Mieczowski, *Can Geog*, IX (1), 1965, 20.
10 To be precise, there were seventeen major economic regions, the
    Belorussian and Moldavian republics being considered as units
    outside the system. In 1974 there were eighteen major economic
    regions and Moldavia was a republic outside the system of such
    regions.
11 P.M. Alampiyev, 1964, 43.
12 Quoted by Yu. G. Saushkin *et al*, *Sov Geog*, V (10), 1964, 20.
13 Ibid.
14 D.J.M. Hooson, 1964 and 1966, 121-4.
15 In March 1973 the Guryev oblast was divided into the Guryev and
    Mangyshlak oblasts.
16 In March 1973 the Karaganda oblast was divided into the
    Karaganda and Dzhezkazgan oblasts.
17 It will be observed that Kazakhstan as a unit has completely
    disappeared in this scheme of regions. Of all the official major
    economic regions, this is perhaps the least satisfactory. See P.E.
    Lydolph, 1970, 31, 217.

CHAPTER 9

Regions of the European Core, pages 153–168

1   V.P. Novikov, *Sov Geog*, X (2), 1969.
2   G.I. Gladkevich, *Sov Geog*, XII (9), 1971.
3   L. Dienes, 1969, 174.
4   D.J.M. Hooson, 1966.
5   In 1970 there was a net 'export' of about 80 million tons of coal and coke from the Donet-Dnepr and North Caucasus regions, of which about a quarter went to other parts of the South. *Transport i Svyaz SSSR*, 1972, 71.
6   V.P. Novikov, op cit.

CHAPTER 10

Regions of Recent Growth, pages 169-189

1   Witness the anomalous situation of the Bashkir ASSR. Until 1961 it was part of the Ural economic region. It was then transferred to the Volga economic region, ostensibly to bring the bulk of the Volga-Ural oilfield within a single economic unit. In terms of structure, relief and location it is clearly as much part of the Urals as the neighbouring Perm oblast, which remains within the Ural economic region. Two outstanding features of the Perm oblast are its important oil-producing districts (part of the Volga-Ural field) and its hydro-electric power (part of the Volga-Kama development), both of which would suggest its attachment to a still larger Volga economic region.
2   The crest-line of the Urals is in fact so used in Hooson's scheme, where it is the dividing line between Volga-Ural and Ural-Ob regions.
3   Thus these sites are officially in the Volga economic region.
4   In broader terms these are part of the north-south rail route along the entire eastern flank of the Urals from Polunochnoye to Orsk, completed during the Soviet period, and the main link between the European railway system and the Trans-Siberian line.
5   Unlike the other centres, there was no railway here before the 1930s. Magnitogorsk lies off the main north-south Ural line and still has no direct rail link to the west.
6   Somewhat confusingly, this is referred to in Soviet sources as the Saratov hydro-electric station.
7   A recent report (*Sov News*, 5738, 21 May 1974) suggests that production could be as much as 350 million tons a year by 1990.
8   T. Shabad, 1969, 265.

CHAPTER 11

The Less Developed Regions, pages 190-215

1 D.J.M. Hooson, 1966, 295.
2 Estonia, Latvia and Lithuania were detached from the USSR by the Treaty of Brest Litovsk and became independent at the end of World War I. They were re-annexed by the Soviet Union in 1940 but occupied by Germany from 1941 until 1944-5. The western half of Belorussia became part of Poland in 1921 and was one of the least developed parts of that country. This area was returned to the USSR on the partition of Poland in 1939 but was occupied by Germany from 1941 to 1944. Kaliningrad oblast was part of German East Prussia and the Sub-Carpathian oblast part of Czechoslovakia until 1945. Thus this whole western zone was not finally incorporated into the Soviet Union until after World War II.
3 The various hydro-electric systems are as follows: in Karelia the Suna (two stations, 60,000kW), Vyg (five stations, 230,000kW), Kem (five stations, 250,000kW) and Kovda-Kuma (three stations, 300,000kW); and in the Murmansk oblast the Paz (four stations, 133,000kW), Tuloma (two stations, 265,000kW) and Voronya (two stations, 225,000kW) systems (T. Shabad, 1969, 112-14).
4 The only other such plant is the one at Cherepovets, on the Rybinsk reservoir. This lies just within the Northlands as we have defined them, but is only a short distance from the boundary of the Industrial Centre.
5 These were the Alma-Atinka system (eight stations, 45,000kW) supplying Alma-Ata, six stations (20,000kW) in the Chu valley supplying Frunze, sixteen stations (320,000kW) on the Chirchik river and Bozsu canal near Tashkent, and six stations (280,000kW) on the Varsob and Vakhsh rivers in Tadzhikstan (T. Shabad, 1969, 304, 324, 335).
6 T. Shabad, 'News Notes', *Soviet Geog*, XVI (5), 1975, 336.
7 T. Shabad, 1969, 330, 338-9, 345.

CONCLUSION, pages 216–222

1 For comments on this problem see, *inter alia*, A. Nove, 1961; 1968, 346-54; 1969, 381-8; S.H. Cohn in V.G. Treml and R. Farrell (eds), 1968, 24-54.
2 Within this average there were marked fluctuations between a minimum of 5·2 per cent in 1933 and a maximum of 28·7 per cent in 1936.
3 At this stage annual fluctuations were much less marked. The

minimum was $7 \cdot 1$ per cent in 1969 and the maximum $10 \cdot 0$ per cent in 1967.

4   For example, those given by S.H. Cohn in E. Mieckiewicz, 1973, 93.

5   S.H. Cohn in Treml and Farrell, op cit, 30.

6   Obvious exceptions were the periods of the Civil War and World War II. Even with the birth-rate decline of the 1960s, natural increase remained above the west European level.

7   Soviet sources now claim that productivity in industry has reached 60 per cent of the U S level. This may be an exaggeration.

8   Defined in *Itogi Vsesoyuznoy Perepisi Naseleniya 1970 goda,* Tom II, Tablitsa 3, as males aged 16-59 and females aged 16-54.

9   Treml and Farrell, op cit, 35.

10   A. Kosygin, *Directives of the Five-Year Economic Development Plan of the USSR for 1971-75,* Moscow, Novosti, 1971, 26.

11   Ibid, 20.

12   Ibid.

Bibliography

THE ARRANGEMENT OF the bibliography follows that of the main body of the text, beginning with a list of general works, followed by works relevant to the General, Sectoral and Regional sections of the book respectively. References for each section are broken down by chapter headings. All the works in the general section of the bibliography are, of course, relevant to the later sections but are not repeated. However, where an item is relevant to both the sectoral and regional sections, it is repeated, appearing first in full and later in an abbreviated form.

In view of the large literature available, the bibliography is highly selective. References to books include a number of standard works in Russian and other languages as well as in English, but references to journals are confined to those available in English, including translations published in *Soviet Geography* and elsewhere.

References are given by author's name in alphabetical order, and date, followed by title and location. This should facilitate identification of citations included in the chapter references on pp.223-230.

GENERAL

Academy of Sciences, Institute of Geography (1955-66). A series of regional economic geographies of the regions and republics of the USSR, sometimes referred to as the 'Blue Series' (30 volumes), Moscow.

Balzak, S.S., Vasyutin, V.F., Feygin, Ya G. (1949). *Economic Geography of the USSR*, New York, Macmillan.

Baransky, N.N. (1956). *Economic Geography of the USSR*, Moscow, Foreign Languages Publishing House.

Breyterman, A.D. (1965). *Ekonomicheskaya Geografiya SSSR*, Leningrad University.

Cherdantsev, G.N., Nikitin, N.N., Tutykhin, B.A. (1956-58). *Ekonomicheskaya Geografiya SSSR*, 3 vols, Moscow, Gosizdat.

Cole, J.P. (1967). *A Geography of the USSR*, Harmondsworth, Middx, Penguin.

Cole, J.P. and German, F.C. (1961, 1970). *A Geography of the USSR*, London, Butterworth.

Cressey, G.B. (1962). *Soviet Potentials: An Economic Appraisal*, Syracuse Univ Press.

Dewdney, J.C. (1965, 1970). *A Geography of the Soviet Union*, Oxford, Pergamon.

Gregory, J.S. (1968). *Russian Land, Soviet People*, London, Harrap.

Hooson, D.J.M. (1964). *A New Soviet Heartland?*, Princeton, Van Nostrand.

Hooson, D.J.M. (1966). *The Soviet Union*, Univ of London Press.

Howe, G.M. (1968). *The Soviet Union*, London, Macdonald & Evans.

Jorré, G. (1961, 1967). *The Soviet Union: The Land and Its People*, London, Longman.

Kalesnik, C.V., ed. (1968-). *Sovetskiy Soyuz: Geograficheskoye Opisaniye*. A series of regional texts on the regions and republics of the USSR still in the course of production. Moscow, Mysl.

Khrushchev, A.T. (1969). *Geografiya Promyshlennosti SSSR*, Moscow, Mysl.

Kovalskaya, N.Ya and Khrushchev, A.T. (1970). *Ekonomicheskaya Geografiya SSSR*, Moscow University.

Lavrishchev, A. (1969). *Economic Geography of the USSR*, Moscow, Progress Publishers.

Lyalikov, N.I. (1960). *Ekonomicheskaya Geografiya SSSR*, Moscow.

Lydolph, P.E. (1964, 1970). *Geography of the USSR*, New York, Wiley.

Mathieson, R.S. (1975) *The Soviet Union: An Economic Geography*, London, Heinemann

Mellor, R.E.H. (1964). *Geography of the USSR*, London, Macmillan.

New Directions in the Soviet Economy (1966). Studies prepared for the Sub-committee on Foreign Economic Policy of the Joint Economic Committee, Congress of the United States, Washington, Govt Printing Office.

Nikitin, N.P., Prozorov, E.D., Tutykhin, B.A. (1973). *Ekonomicheskaya Geografiya SSSR*, Moscow, Prosveshcheniye.

Parker, W.H. (1972). *The Super-Powers: The United States and the Soviet Union Compared*, London, Macmillan.

Saushkin, Yu. G., Nikolskiy, I.V., Korovitsy, V.P. (1967). *Ekonomicheskaya Geografiya Sovetskogo Soyuza*, Moscow University.

Shabad, T. (1961). 'The Soviet Union' in *A Geography of Europe*, Hoffman, G.W. (ed), New York, Ronald Press, 638-728.

Shabad, T. (1969). *Basic Industrial Resources of the USSR*, New York, Columbia University Press.

Shabad, T. 'News Notes' in *Sov Geog*.

Shuvalov, E.L. (1965) *Ekonomicheskaya Geografiya SSSR*, Moscow.

Soviet News, Press Department, Soviet Embassy, London; weekly.

STATISTICAL HANDBOOKS

Narodnoye Khozyaystvo SSSR, annual, Moscow, Statistika.

Narodnoye Khozyaystvo RSFSR, annual, Moscow, Statistika.

Promyshlennost SSSR, irregular, Moscow, Statistika.

Transport i Svyaz SSSR, Statisticheskiy Sbornik, annual, Moscow, Statistika.

NB. A full listing of statistical abstracts published during the preceding year appears annually in *Soviet Studies;* see also:

Clarke, R.A., (1972). *Soviet Economic Facts, 1917-1970*, London, Macmillan.

Mickiewicz, E. (1973). *Handbook of Soviet Social Science Data*, London and New York, Collier-Macmillan/Free Press.

ATLASES

Atlas Mira, Glavnoye Upravleniye Geodezii i Kartografii MVD SSSR, Moscow, 1954.

Atlas Razvitiya Khozyaystva i Kultury SSSR. Glavnoye Upravleniye Geodezii i Kartografii pri Sovete Ministrov SSSR, Moscow, 1967.

Atlas SSSR (Vtoroye Izdaniye), Glavnoye Upravleniye Geodezii i Kartografii pri Sovete Ministrov SSSR, Moscow, 1969.

Fiziko-Geograficheskiy Atlas Mira, Akademiya Nauk i Glavnoye Upravleniye Geodezii i Kartografii GGK SSSR, Moscow, 1964.

MAPS

Elektrifikatsiya SSSR, 1:5,000,000, Glavnoye Upravleniye Geodezii i Kartografii pri Sovete Ministrov SSSR, Moscow, 1973.

Mestorozhdeniya Poleznykh Iskopayemykh SSSR, 1:5,000,000, Glavnoye Upravleniye Geodezii i Kartografii pri Sovete Ministrov SSSR, Moscow, 1973.

Soyuz Sovetskikh Sotsialisticheskikh Respublik, 1:4,000,000, Glavnoye Upravleniye Geodezii i Kartografii pri Sovete Ministrov SSSR, Moscow, 1974.

USSR and Adjacent Areas, 1:8,000,000, Directorate of Surveys,

Ministry of Defence, United Kingdom (GSGS, Series 5104, Edition 3) 1964.

USSR and Adjacent Areas, Administrative Map, 1:8,000,000, Directorate of Surveys, Ministry of Defence, United Kingdom (GSGS, Series 5103, Edition 3) 1969.

CHAPTER 1   ENVIRONMENT AND RESOURCES

Berg, L.S. (1950). *Natural Regions of the USSR*, New York, Macmillan.

Borisov, A.A. (1965). *Climates of the USSR*, Edinburgh and London, Oliver & Boyd.

Burkhanov, V.F. (1970). 'Criteria for determining an engineering-geographic boundary of the north of the USSR', *Sov Geog*, XI (1), 24-32

Dewdney, J.C. (1970). *Physiography (Geography of the USSR)*, Wellington, NZ, Hicks Smith.

Dyankonov, F.V. (1973). 'On economic-geographic approaches to an evaluation of the use of natural resources', *Sov Geog*, XIV (6), 363-71.

Gerasimov, I.P., Armand, D.L., Preobrazhenskiy, V.S. (1964). 'Natural resources of the Soviet Union: their study and utilization', *Sov Geog*, V (8), 3-14.

Gerasimov, I.P., Armand, D.L., Yefron, K.M. (1971). *Natural Resources of the Soviet Union: Their Use and Renewal*, San Francisco, Freeman.

Gladkevich, G.I. and Khrushchev, A.T. (1974). 'Principles of an economic evaluation of mineral deposits for purposes of geographical prediction', *Sov Geog*, XV (1), 12-19

Gvozdetskiy, N.A., *et al* (1962-3). *Fizicheskaya Geografiya SSSR*, 2 vols, Moscow.

Hooson, D.J.M. (1970). *Climate and Man (Geography of the USSR)*, Wellington, NZ, Hicks Smith.

Hutchings, R. (1971). *Seasonal Influences in Soviet Industry*, London, Royal Inst Internat Affairs/Oxford Univ Press.

Lopatina, Y.B. (1971). 'The present state and future tasks in the theory and method of an evaluation of the natural environment and resources', *Sov Geog*, XII (3), 142-52.

Newey, W.W. (1970). *Mineral Resources (Geography of the USSR)*, Wellington, NZ, Hicks Smith.

Newey, W.W. (1970). *Water (Geography of the USSR)*, Wellington, NZ, Hicks Smith.

Parker, W.H. (1969). *The World's Landscapes: 3. The Soviet Union*, London, Longman.

Privalovskaya, G.A. (1975) 'The physical factor in the system of conditions determining the location of industrial production in the U.S.S.R.', *Sov. Geog.* XVI (5) 279-290.

Pryde, P.R. (1972). *Conservation in the Soviet Union*, Cambridge Univ Press.

Runova, T.G. (1973). 'A natural-resource regionalization of the USSR', *Sov Geog*, XIV (8) 506-18.

Suslov, S.P. (1961). *The Physical Geography of Asiatic Russia*, London, Freeman.

CHAPTER 2 POPULATION AND TRANSPORT

POPULATION

Brook, S.I. (1972). 'Population of the USSR – Changes in its demographic, social and ethnic structure', *Geoforum*, 9, 7-21.

Demko, G.J. and Casetti, E. (1970). 'A diffusion model for selected demographic variables: an application to Soviet data', *AAAG*, 60 (3), 533-9.

Dewdney, J.C. (1969). *Population (Geography of the USSR)*, Wellington, NZ, Hicks Smith.

Dewdney, J.C. (1971). 'Population changes in the Soviet Union, 1959-1970', *Geography*, 56 (4), 325-30.

Dewdney, J.C. (1974). 'Inquiry into people: the Soviet Union', *Geog Mag*, XLVI (7), 350-54.

French, R.A. (1966). 'Recent population trends in the USSR' in Kaser, M. (ed), *Soviet Affairs No. 4, St. Anthony's Papers No. 19*, Oxford Univ Press.

Harris, C.D. (1971). 'Urbanization and population growth in the Soviet Union, 1959-1970', *Geog Rev*, 61 (1), 102-24.

Konstantinov, O.A. (ed), (1964). *Geografiya Naseleniya v SSSR: osnovnye problemy*, Moscow, Nauka.

Kovalev, S.A. and Kovalskaya, N.Ya (1971). *Geografiya Naseleniya*, Moscow University.

Lewis, R.A. (1969). 'The post-war study of internal migration in the USSR', *Sov Geog*, X (4).

Lewis, R.A. and Rowland R.H. (1969). 'Urbanization in Russia and the USSR, 1897-1966', *AAAG*, 59 (4) 776-96.

Lorimer, F. (1946). *The Population of the Soviet Union: History and Prospects*, Geneva, League of Nations.

Lydolph, P.E. (1972). 'Manpower problems in the USSR', *TESG*, 63, 331-44.

Lydolph, P.E. and Pease, S.R. (1972). 'Changing distributions of population and economic activities in the USSR', *TESG*, 63, 244-61.

Mellor, R.E.H. (1957). 'The population of the Soviet Union', *Geography*, 42 (2), 114-15.

Perevedentsev, V.I. (1969). 'Contemporary migration in the USSR', *Sov Geog*, X (4), 192-208.

Pokshishevskiy, V.V. (1963). 'Prospects of population migration in the USSR', *Sov Geog*, IV (1), 13-25.

Pokshishevskiy, V.V. (1971). *Geografiya Naseleniya SSSR*, Moscow, Prosveshcheniye.

Pokshishevskiy, V.V. (1972). 'Urbanization in the USSR', 'Socioprofessional structure of the population of the USSR and its employment pattern', 'Population migration in the USSR', *Geoforum*, 9, 83-5.

Pokshishevskiy, V.V. *et al* (1964, 1970). 'On basic migration patterns', *Sov Geog*, V (10); also in Demko, G.J., Rose, H.M., Schnell, G.A. (eds) *Population Geography: A Reader*, New York, McGraw-Hill.

Roof, M.K. and Leedy, F.A. (1959). 'Population redistribution in the Soviet Union', *Geog Rev*, 49 (2), 208-21.

Sheehy, A. (1966). 'Population trends in Central Asia and Kazakhstan', *Cent As Rev*, 14 (4), 317-29.

Stanley, E. (1968). *Regional Distribution of Soviet Industrial Manpower, 1940-60*, New York, Praeger.

Thomas, C. (1972). 'Urbanization and population change in European Russia, 1959-1969', *SGM*, 88 (3), 196-207.

Urlanis, B.Ts. (1974). *Problemy Dinamiki Naseleniya SSSR*, Moscow, Nauka.

Zayonchkovskaya, Z.A. and Perevedentsev, V.I. (1969). 'The present state and basic problems in the study of migration in the USSR', *Sov Geog*, X (4), 167-78.

Zayonchkovskaya, Z.A. and Zahkarina, D.M. (1972). 'Problems of providing Siberia with manpower', *Sov Geog*, XIII (10), 671-83.

TRANSPORT

Armstrong, T.E. (1955). 'The northern Soviet sea route', GJ, CXXI (2), 136-48.

Belousov, I.I. (1964). 'Transportation and the formation of economic regions', *Sov Geog*, V (9), 19-23.

Biryukov. V. (1975) 'The Baykal-Amur Mainline: a major national construction project'. *Sov Geog* XVI(4) 225-30.

Galitskiy, M.I., Danilov, S.K., Korneyev, A.I. (1965). *Ekonomicheskaya Geografiya Transporta SSSR*, Moscow.

Gudkova, G.N. and Moskin, B.V. (1974). 'The development of motor roads in the U.S.S.R' *Sov Geog* XV(9), 573-81.

Hanson, P. (1963). 'Soviet inland waterways', *Journ Transport History* (Leicester), 6 (1), 3-13.

Hilton, C. (1969). 'Market potential and potential transportation costs: an evaluation of the concepts and their surface patterns in the USSR', *Can Geog*, 13 (3), 216-36.

Izyumskiy, O.A. (1970). 'Transport development of the middle Ob oil district', *Sov Geog*, XI (8), 655-9.

Kazanskiy, N.N. and LASIS, Yu. V. (1963). 'Methods of forecasting freight flows in planning a transport net', *Sov Geog*, IV (7), 3-18.

Kibalchich, O.A. (1963). 'The distribution of population and related indicators in long-term planning of passenger traffic', *Sov Geog*, IV (7), 26-35.

Kish, G. (1958). 'Soviet air transport', *Geog Rev*, 48 (3), 309-20.

Kish, G. (1963). 'Railroad passenger transport in the Soviet Union'. *Geog Rev*, 53 (3) 363-76.

Krasheninnikov, V.G. (1973). 'The role of river transport in the development and location of productive forces in the eastern regions of the USSR', *Sov Geog*, XIV (5), 295-308.

Mellor, R.E.H. (1964). 'Some influences of physical environment upon transport problems in the Soviet Union', *Adv Sci*, 20.

Mellor, R.E.H. (1969). *Transport (Geography of the USSR)*, Wellington, NZ, Hicks Smith.

Nikolskiy, I.V. (1960). *Geografiya Transporta SSSR*, Moscow.

Nikolskiy, I.V. (1961). 'The geography of transportation of Kazakhstan', *Sov Geog*, II (3), 44-53.

Nikolskiy, I.V. (1961). 'Railroad freight traffic of the USSR', *Sov Geog*, II (6), 39-92.

Nikolskiy, I.V. (1972). *Geografiya Transporta SSSR*, Moscow University.

Pavlenko, V.F. (1963). 'The transport geography situation and inter-regional links of Central Asia', *Sov Geog*, IV (9), 27-33.

Polyakov, Y.A. (1963). 'Selection of an optimal form of surface transportation in the northeast of the USSR', *Sov Geog*, IV (9), 34-42.

Popova, Ye. I. (1974). 'The transport industry in the western and eastern zones of the USSR', *Sov Geog*, XV (4), 187-243.

Rom, V.Ya. (1961). 'The Volga-Baltic waterway', *Sov Geog*, II (9), 32-43.

Symons, L.J. (1973). 'Soviet civil air services', *Geography*, 58 (4), 328-30.

Symons, L.J. and White, C. (Eds) (1975) *Russian Transport: An Historical and Geographic Survey*, London, Bell.

Taaffe, R.N. (1960). 'Rail transportation and the economic development of Soviet Central Asia', *Research Papers, No 64, Dept of Geog, Univ of Chicago*.

Taaffe, R.N. (1962). 'Transportation and regional specialization: the example of Soviet Central Asia', *AAAG*, 52, 80-98.

Taaffe, R.N. (1964). 'Volga river transportation – problems and prospects' in Thoman, R.S. and Patton, D.J. (eds), *Focus on Geographic Activity*, New York, McGraw-Hill.

Varlamov, V.S. (1969). 'Problems of transport development of the West Siberian plain in conjunction with the formation of a new economic complex in its territory', *Sov Geog*, X (6), 312-26.

Varlamov, V.S. and Kazanskiy, N.N. (1963). 'Forecast of average length of haul on Soviet railroads', *Sov Geog*, IV (7) 19-25.

Vorobyev, A.A. (1964). 'Problems in the location of transportation in the southern part of eastern Siberia, *Sov Geog*, V (5), 3-12

Westwood, J.N. (1964). *Soviet Railways Today*, New York, Citadel Press.

Wood, D.S. (1963). 'Connecting five seas', *Nat Geog Journ India*, 9 (1), 25-31.

Yegrova, V.V. (1964). 'The economic effectiveness of the construction of pioneering railroads in newly developed areas', *Sov Geog*, V (4), 46-55.

CHAPTER 3   INDUSTRIAL DEVELOPMENT

Bergson, A. (ed) (1953). *Soviet Economic Growth: Conditions and Perspectives*, Evanston, Ill, and White Plains, NY, Row, Peterson.

Bernard, P.J. (1966). *Planning in the Soviet Union*, Oxford, Pergamon.

Bowles, W.D. (1962). 'Soviet Russia as a model for underdeveloped areas', *World Politics* (Princeton), XIV (3), 483-504.

Budtolayev, N.M., Novikov, V.P., Saushkin, Yu. G. (1964). 'Problems of economic development of the west and east of the Soviet Union', *Sov Geog*, V (1), 3-14.

Campbell, R.W. (1967). *Soviet Economic Power: Its Organization, Growth and Challenge*, London, Macmillan.

Conolly, V. (1967). *Beyond the Urals: Economic Developments in Soviet Asia*, London, Oxford Univ Press.

Dienes, L. (1972). 'Investment priorities in Soviet regions', *AAAG*, 62 (3).

Dobb, M. (1948, 1966). *Soviet Economic Development since 1917*, London, Routledge & Kegan Paul.

George, P. (1968). 'Cinquante ans d'expérience économique socialiste:

centralisme, régionalisme, décentralisation économique', *Ann Geog*, 77, 576-89.

Hutchings, R. (1971). *Soviet Economic Development*, Oxford, Blackwell.

Krotov, V.A. (1964). 'Geographical aspects and problems of the industrialization of Siberia', *Sov Geog*, V (9), 50-56.

Lonsdale, R.E. (1961). 'Industrial location planning in the USSR', *Prof Geog*, XIII (6), 11-15.

Lydolph, P.E. and Pease, S.R. (1972), op cit (see POPULATION).

Mazanova, M.B. (1972). 'The role of the eastern regions in the economy of the USSR', *Sov Geog*, XIII (10), 655-71.

Mellor, R.E.H. (1970). *Industrial Development (Geography of the USSR)*, Wellington, NZ, Hicks Smith.

Miller, J. (1955). *Soviet Russia*, London, Hutchinson.

NATO (nd) *Prospects for Soviet Economic Growth in the 1970s: Main findings of a symposium held 14-16th April, 1971 in Brussels*, Brussels, NATO Directorate of Economic Affairs

Nettl, J.P. (1967). *The Soviet Achievement*, London, Thames & Hudson.

Nove, A. (1961, 1968). *The Soviet Economy*, London, Allen & Unwin.

Nove, A. (1969). *An Economic History of the USSR*, London, Lane/Penguin.

Orlov, B.P. (1970). 'Tendencies of economic development in Siberia and promotion of the region's role in the national economy', *Sov Geog*, XI (1), 1-13.

Parker, W.H. (1968). *An Historical Geography of Russia*, Univ London Press.

Powell, R.P. (1968). 'Economic growth in the USSR', *Scientific American*, 219 (6), 17-23.

Rodgers, A. (1974). 'The locational dynamics of Soviet Industry', *AAAG*, 64, 226-40.

Schwartz, H. (1965). *The Soviet Economy since Stalin,*. Philadelphia, Lippincott.

Treml, V.G. and Farrell, R. (eds) (1968). *The Development of the Soviet Economy: Plan and Performance*, New York, Praeger.

CHAPTER 4   FUEL AND POWER

Barr, B.M. and Bater, J.H. (1969). 'The electricity industry of Central Siberia', *Econ Geog*, 45 (4), 349-69.

Bulatov, V.S. (1972). 'On possible pipeline routes for Tyumen gas', *Sov Geog*, XIII (3), 153-62.

Bulatov, V.S. (1974) 'An analysis of factors determining the level of natural gas extraction in the north of Tyumen oblast' *Sov Geog*, XV (8), 484-90.

Campbell, R.W. (1968). *The Economics of Soviet Oil and Gas*, Baltimore, Johns Hopkins.

Dienes, L. (1971). 'Issues in Soviet energy policy and conflicts over fuel costs in regional development', *Sov St*, XXIII (1), 26-58,

Elliot, I.F. (1974). *The Soviet Energy Balance*, New York, Praeger

Economist (1974). 'Energy: is Siberia really the answer?', *Economist*, 23 Feb 1974.

Gonchar, V.I. (1974). 'Electric power in the southern part of the Central economic region', *Sov Geog*, XV (3), 135-41.

Hodgkins, J.A. (1961). *Soviet Power: Energy Resources, Production and Potentials*, London, Prentice-Hall.

Lydolph, P.E. and Shabad, T. (1960). 'The oil and gas industries in the USSR', *AAAG*, 50 (4), 461-86.

Michel, A.A. and Klain, S.A. (1964). 'Current problems of the Soviet electric power industry', *Econ Geog*, 40, 206-20.

Naymushin, I. and Gindin, A. (1960). 'Problems of the Angara series of hydro-electric power stations', *Sov Geog*, I (6), 61-7.

Padick, C. (1965). 'Re-orientation in power generation in the Volga basin, USSR', *Yearbook of the Association of Pacific Coast Geographers*, 27, 27-37.

Petroleum Press Service (1970). 'Russia plans its future', XXXVII (9), 321-3; (1971). 'Spotlight on Russia', XXXVIII (7); (1972). 'Soviet trade in slow decline', XXXIX (5), 162-3.

Rodgers, A. (1964). 'Coking coal supply: its role in the expansion of the Soviet steel industry', *Econ Geog*, 40, 113-50.

Shimkin, D.B. (1962). *The Soviet Mineral Fuels Industry, 1928-1958; A Statistical Survey*, Washington, US Dept of Commerce.

White, S. (1974). 'The energy equations: The Soviet factor', *New Scientist*, 21 Feb 1974, 472-4.

Zaytsev, M.K. (1968). 'The development of the oil and gas industry of Turkmenia', *Sov Geog*, IX (6), 503-10.

Zvonkova, T.V. (1972). 'Geomorphic methods in oil and gas prospecting', *Sov Geog*, 13 (6) 353-63.

Zvyagintseva, K.M. (1974) 'On the three fuel and energy supply zones of Siberia' *Sov Geog*, XV (8) 491-98.

CHAPTER 5   THE METALLURGICAL AND ENGINEERING INDUSTRIES

Adamchuk, V.A. (1964). 'The problem of creating a Kazakhstan metallurgical base', *Sov Geog*, V (6), 20-35.

Buyanovskiy, M.S. (1961). 'On the question of iron and steel plant location in Kazakhstan', *Sov Geog*, II (9), 44-9.

Gladkevich, G.I. (1971). 'Determination of an optimal location for an iron and steel plant based on iron ore of the Kursk Magnetic Anomaly', *Sov Geog*, XII (9) 604-10.

Kapitanov, Y.I. (1963). 'The Kursk Magnetic Anomaly and its development', *Sov Geog*, IV (5), 10-15.

Khrushchev, A.T. (1975) 'The formation of the industrial complex of the Kursk Magnetic Anomaly', *Sov Geo*, XVI (4) 239–48.

Kowalewski, J. (1959). 'The Soviet Union's struggle for self-sufficiency in metals'. *Optima* (Quart Journ Anglo-American Corpn of S. Africa), 9 (4), 209-15.

Matrusov, N.D. (1970). 'Geographical problems in the development of machine-building in the Ob-Irtysh complex', *Sov Geog*, XI (1), 464-71.

Nikitina, S.A. (1974). 'The iron and steel industry of the Lipetsk industrial node', *Sov Geog*, XV (3), 128-34.

Novikov, V.P. (1969). 'The Kursk Anomaly – a promising iron ore base for the iron and steel industry of the Urals (based on a territorial model of the Soviet economy)', *Sov Geog*, X (2), 43-86.

Omarovskiy, A.G. (1960). 'Changes in the geography of machine building in the USSR', *Sov Geog*, I (4), 42-55.

Rodgers, A. (1964), op cit (see FUEL AND POWER),

Rom, Ya. (1974). 'Geographical problems in the iron and steel industry of the USSR, *Sov Geog*, XV (3), 121-8.

CHAPTER 6   THE CHEMICAL INDUSTRIES

Dienes, L. (1969). 'Locational factors and locational developments in the Soviet chemical industry', *Research Papers, No 119, Dept of Geography, Univ of Chicago.*

Hemy, G.W. (1968). The Soviet chemical industry', *Chemistry and Industry*, 207-15.

Hemy, G.W. (1968). 'Chemical minerals in the USSR', *Chemical and Process Engineering.*

Hemy, G.W. (1970). 'Alkalis and chlorine in the USSR', *Chemical and Process Engineering.*

Hemy, G.W. (1971). *The Soviet Chemical Industry*, London, Hill.

Meshcheryakova, M.N. (1967). 'The integrated development and location of the petrochemical industry in industrial nodes of the Middle Volga region', *Sov Geog*, VIII (2), 81-6.

Shabad, T. and Lydolph, P.E. (1962). 'The chemical industries in the USSR', *TESG*, 53, 169-79.

Sokoloff, M.G. (1968). 'L'industrie chimique en URSS', *La documentation française; Notes et études documentaires*, 3473-4.

CHAPTER 7   THE TIMBER INDUSTRIES, LIGHT INDUSTRIES AND FOOD INDUSTRIES.

Barr, B.M. (1971). 'Regional variations in Soviet pulp and paper production', *AAAG*, 61 (1), 45-64.

Bone, R.M. (1966). 'The Soviet forest resource', *Can Geog*, X (4), 94-116.

Gorovoy, V.A. and Privalovskaya, G.A. (1966). *Geografiya Lesnoy Promyshlennosti SSSR*, Moscow, Nauka.

Pryde, P.R. (1968). 'The areal deconcentration of the Soviet cotton textile industry', *Geog Rev*, 58 (4), 575-92.

Rodgers, A. (1955). 'Changing locational patterns in the Soviet pulp and paper industry', *AAAG*, 45, 85-104.

CHAPTER 8   REGIONALISATION

Alampiyev, P.M. (1960a). 'Tendencies in the development of major economic-geographic regions', *Sov Geog*, I (4), 43-52.

Alampiyev, P.M. (1960b). 'Problems of general economic regionalization at the present stage', *Sov Geog*, I (8), 3-15.

Alampiyev, P.M. (1964). *Economic Areas in the USSR*, Moscow, Progress Publishers.

Aleksandrov, Yu.K., Kistanov, V.V. and Epshteyn, A.S. (1974). 'A quantitative approach to designing a system of economic regions of the USSR', *Sov Geog*, XV (9), 543-53.

Altman, L.P. (1965). 'Economic regionalization of the USSR and new methods in economic-geographic research', *Sov Geog*, VI (9), 48-55.

Chambre, H. (1959). *L'Aménagement du Territoire en URSS: Introduction à l'Etude des Régions Economiques Soviétiques*, Paris, Mouton.

Dewdney, J.C. (1967). 'Patterns and problems of regionalisation in the USSR', *Research Papers Series* No 8, Dept of Geography, Univ of Durham.

Dewdney, J.C. (1970). *The Regions (Geography of the USSR)*, Wellington, NZ, Hicks Smith.

Feygin, Ya. G. (1964). 'Problems of improving the regionalisation of production and consumption of industrial output', *Sov Geog*, V (10), 33-8.

Kalashnikova, T.M. (1969). *Ekonomicheskoye Rayonirovaniye*, Moscow University.

Kantsebovskaya, I.V. and Runova, T.G. (1974) 'Problems in the methodology of measuring and mapping the level of economic development of the USSR, *Sov Geo*, XV (9), 566-72.

Khrushchev, A.T. (1971). 'Industrial nodes of the USSR and principles for a typology', *Sov Geog*, XII (2), 91-102.

Kistanov, V.V. (1960). 'Aspects of the formation of economic regions in the eastern USSR', *Sov Geog*, I(4), 52–9.

Kistanov, V.V. (1965). 'On indicators of regional specialization and integration', *Sov Geog*, VI (8), 16-25.

Kistanov, V.V. and Epshteyn, A.S. (1972). 'Problems of optimal location of an industrial complex', *Sov Geog*, XIII (3), 141-52.

Kolosovskiy, N.N. (1961). 'The territorial-production combination (complex) in Soviet economic geography', *Journ Reg Sci*, 3(1), 1-25.

Komar, I.V.(1960). 'The major economic-geographic regions of the USSR', *Sov Geog*, I(4), 31-43.

Konstantinov, O.A. (1960) 'The present status of economic-geographic studies on the economic regionalization of the USSR', *Sov Geog* I (8), 36-59.

Kurakin, A.F. (1975) 'Problems in the spatial concentration of industry' *Sov Geog*, XVI(3), 145-53.

Lis, A.G. (1975). 'On the question of the composition of economic territorial complexes', *Sov Geo*, XVI(1), 20-27.

Lonsdale, R.E. and Thompson, H. (1960). 'A map of the USSR's manufacturing', *Econ Geog*, 36, 36-62.

Melezin, A. (1968). 'Soviet regionalization: an attempt at the delineation of socio-economic integrated regions', *Geog Rev*, 58(4), 593-621.

Mieczkowski, Z. (1965). 'The major economic regions of the USSR in the Khrushchev era', *Can Geog*, IX (1), 19-30.

Mieczkowski, Z. (1967). 'The economic-administrative regions in the USSR', *TESG*, 58(4), 209-19.

Mints, A.A. and Kakhanovskaya, T.G. (1975). 'An attempt at a quantitative evaluation of the natural resource potential of regions of the U.S.S.R.', *Sov Geog*, XV(9), 554-65.

Moshkin, A.M. (1962). 'What is a territorial-production complex?', *Sov Geog*, III(9), 49-55.

Nekrasov, N.N. (1971). 'Scientific principles of the general outline for the location of productive forces in the USSR for the period up to 1970', *Sov Geog*, XII (4), 219-26.

Nikolsky, I.V. (1973). 'A typology of regional production complexes', *Sov Geog*, XIV(2), 92-100.

Pociuk, S.G. (1961). 'The territorial pattern of industrialisation in the USSR', *Sov St*, XIII (1), 69-95.

Pokshishevskiy, V.V. (1960). 'The role of population geography in problems of economic regionalization of the USSR', *Sov Geog*, I(8), 28-35.

Pokshishevskiy, V.V. (1966). 'Economic regionalization of the USSR: a review of research during 1962-64', *Sov Geog*, VII (5), 4-32.

Pokshishevskiy, V.V., Dolgopolov, K.V., Mints, A.A. (eds), (1964). *Geograficheskiye Problemy Krupnykh Rayonov SSSR*, Moscow, Mysl.

Praesidium of the Supreme Soviet of the USSR (annual). *Administrativno-Territorialnoye Deleniye Soyuznykh Respublik*, Moscow.

Probst, A. Ye. (1962). *Razmeshcheniye Sotsialisticheskoi Promyshlennost*, Moscow.

Probst. A. Ye. (1966). 'Territorial production complexes in the USSR', *Sov Geog*, VII (7), 47-55.

Rodoman, B.B.(1972). 'Principal types of geographical regions', *Sov Geog*, XIII (7), 448-54.

Saushkin, Yu. G. and Kalashnikova, T.M. (1960). 'Current problems in the economic regionalization of the USSR', *Sov Geog*, I(6), 50-9.

Sdasiuk, G.(1962). 'The history of regionalisation in the USSR', *Nat Geog Journ India*, 8(2), 145-56.

Soviet Geography, (1966). Bibliography on Economic Regionalization, 1962-64, *Sov Geog*, VII (5), 65-96.

Zaytsev, I.F. (1969). 'A territorial model of productive forces', *Sov Geog*, X(9), 507-22.

CHAPTERS 9-11   REGIONS

Since several of the items listed here refer to more than one of the regions used in the text, they are classified by major geographical divisions only.

EUROPEAN USSR

Altman, L.P. and Dolkart, M.L.(1968). 'Problems of economic development in the North-west economic region during the new five-year plan (1966-70)', *Sov Geog*, IX (1), 11-22.

Buyanovsky, N.S. (1960). 'On the question of the prospects of development of the Pechora basin', *Sov Geog*, I(3), 9-19.

Gladkevich, G.I.(1971), op cit. (THE METALLURGICAL AND ENGINEERING INDUSTRIES).

Gonchar, V.I. (1974), op cit (FUEL AND POWER).

Gorovoy, V.L. (1961). 'The timber industry of northern European Russia', *Sov Geog*, II(4), 53-9.

Hooson, D.J.M. (1960). 'The Middle Volga: an emerging focal region of the Soviet Union', *GJ*, CXXVI, 180-90.

Kapitanov, Y.I. (1963), op cit (THE METALLURGICAL AND ENGINEER-
ING INDUSTRIES).

Khorev, B.S. (1962). 'Prospects of development of the industrial
complex of the Volga-Vyatka major economic region', Sov Geog,
III(9), 39-48.

Khrushchev, A.T. (1975) op, cit. (THE METALLURGICAL AND
ENGINEERING INDUSTRIES).

Kurnikov, F.D. (1967). 'The basic tendencies of development of the
industrial complex of the Volga region', Sov Geog, VIII (2), 107-16.

Nikitina, S.A. (1974), op cit (THE METALLURGICAL AND ENGINEERING
INDUSTRIES).

Novikov, V.P. (1969), op cit (THE METALLURGICAL AND ENGINEER-
ING INDUSTRIES),

Rom, V. Ya. (1961), op cit (TRANSPORT).

Rom, V.Ya. (1974) 'Historical geography of industry in the Cherepovets country', 'Sov. Geo, XV(5), 299-310.

Saushkin, Yu. G. and Shcherbakov, A.S. (1967). 'The industrial nodes
of the Middle Volga', Sov Geo, VIII(2), 70-81 (1961).

Savenko, Yu. N. (1961). 'The fuel balance of the Kuybyshev oblast',
Sov Geog, II(6), 8-13.

Shaposhnikov, A.S. (1967). 'The Middle Volga economic region –
outpost of the chemical industry', Sov Geog, VIII (2), 87-93.

Stepanov, P.N. and Savenko, Yu N. (1961). 'Some problems of
electric power development in the Kuybyshev economic-
administrative region', Sov Geog, II (3), 73-9.

Taaffe, R.N. (1964), op cit (TRANSPORT).

Taskin, G.A. (1961). 'The Soviet north-west: economic regionalization', Geog Rev, 51, 213-35.

Wood, D.S. (1963), op cit (TRANSPORT)

Zolotarev, Yu. F. (1967). 'Formation of the oil-gas-power-chemical
complex of the Kuybyshev industrial node', Sov Geog, VIII (2),
101-6.

SIBERIA AND THE FAR EAST

Armstrong, T.E. (1955), op cit (TRANSPORT).

Barr, B.M. and Bater, J.H. (1969), op cit (FUEL AND POWER).

Belorusov, D.V. (1969). 'Specific peculiarities of the West Siberian
complex', Sov Geog, X(6), 271-85.

Belorusov, D.V. (1972). 'The effectiveness of integrated development
of productive forces in the new pioneering areas of western Siberia',
Sov Geog, XIII (10), 684-91.

Biryukov, V. (1975) op cit (TRANSPORT)

Budkov, S.T. (1970). 'The forest products industry: a specialized activity of the Sosva valley section of the Ob basin', *Sov Geog*, XI (9), 767-74.

Bulatov, V.S. (1972), op cit (FUEL AND POWER).

Bulatov, V.S. (1974) op cit (FUEL AND POWER).

Burkhanov, V.F. (1970), op cit (ENVIRONMENT AND RESOURCES).

Cole, J.P. (1956). 'A new industrial area in Asiatic USSR', *GJ*, CXX(3), 354-9.

Conolly, V. (1967), op cit (INDUSTRIAL DEVELOPMENT).

Dyakonov, F.W. (1964). 'Productive forces and productive territorial complexes in the north-east of the USSR', *Sov Geog*, V (1), 40-52.

Dyakonov, F.V. (1969). 'The development of new areas and economic complexes in the West Siberian plain', *Sov Geog*, X(6), 327-37.

Economist (23rd Feb 1974), op cit (FUEL AND POWER).

Izyumskiy, O.A. (1970), op cit (TRANSPORT).

Kirby, E.S. (1971). *The Soviet Far East*, London, Macmillan.

Krasheninnikov, V.G. (1973), op cit (TRANSPORT).

Krotov, V.A. (1964), op cit (INDUSTRIAL DEVELOPMENT).

Krotov, V.A., *et al* (1968). 'The role of eastern Siberia in solving some of the economic problems of the Pacific basin', *Sov Geog*, IX (3), 142-4.

Levintov, A. Ye. (1972). 'Transport-economic links and the formation of the territorial-production structure of the Ob-Irtysh region', *Sov Geog*, XIII (1), 26-40.

Matrusov, N.D. (1970), op cit (THE METALLURGICAL AND ENGINEERING INDUSTRIES).

Mazanova, M.B. (1972), op cit (INDUSTRIAL DEVELOPMENT).

Mosalova, L.M. (1973). 'Regional peculiarities in the formation of industrial nodes in the Middle Ob region', *Sov Geog*, XIV (8), 519-25.

Naymushin, I. and Gindin A. (1960), op cit (FUEL AND POWER).

Orlov, B.P. (1970), op cit (INDUSTRIAL DEVELOPMENT).

Shotskiy, V.P. (1973). 'Geographical pre-planning studies of economic complexes in the south of Krasnoyarsk Kray', *Sov Geog*, XIV (9), 572-81.

Thiel, E. (1957). *The Soviet Far East*, London, Methuen.

Tideman, A.M. and Ronkin, G.S. (1971). 'Regional planning problems in the Soviet Far East', *Sov Geog*, XII (2), 124-31.

Varlamov, V.S. (1969), op cit (TRANSPORT).

Yegrova, V.V. (1964), op cit (TRANSPORT).

Zayonchkovskaya, Z.A. and Zakharina, D.M. (1972), op cit (POPULATION).

Zvyagintseva, K.M. (1974) op cit (FUEL AND POWER)

KAZAKHSTAN AND CENTRAL ASIA

Adamchuk, V.A. (1964), op cit (THE METALLURGICAL AND ENGINEERING INDUSTRIES).

Belyayev, N.A. (1968). 'Industrial development in the desert of west Turkmenia', *Sov Geog*, IX (6), 511-18.

Buyanovskiy, M.S. (1961), op cit (THE METALLURGICAL AND ENGINEERING INDUSTRIES).

Buyanovskiy, M.S. (1965). 'Balkhash-Ili, a potential major industrial complex', *Sov Geog*, VI (8), 3-15.

Conolly, V. (1967), op cit (INDUSTRIAL DEVELOPMENT).

Feygin L.Ya. (1964). 'Problems of improvising inter-regional productive relationships of the Central Asian economic region', *Sov Geog*, V (6), 3-10.

Imshchenetskiy, A.I. (1972). 'Some aspects of the development and location of industry in the Central Asian economic region', *Sov Geog*, XIII (10), 706-15.

Kosov, V.F. and Dvoskin, B.Y. (1972). 'The territorial structural organization of the productive forces of Kazakhstan', *Sov Geog*, XIII (10), 691-706.

Nikolskiy, I.V. (1961), op cit (TRANSPORT).

Nove, A. and Newth, J.A. (1967) *The Soviet Middle East*, London, Allen and Unwin.

Pavlenko, V.F. (1963), op cit (TRANSPORT).

Probst, A. Ye. (1964). 'Further productive specialization of the Central Asian region', *Sov Geog*, V (6), 11-19.

Sheehy, A. (1966), op cit (POPULATION).

Taaffe, R.N. (1960), op cit (TRANSPORT).

Taaffe, R.N. (1962), op cit (TRANSPORT).

PERIODICALS CITED

Adv Sci   *Advancement of Science*, London, British Association

AAAG   *Annals of the Association of American Geographers*, Washington

Ann Geog   *Annales de Géographie*, Paris, Société de Géographie

Cent As Rev   *Central Asian Review*, London

Can Geog   *Canadian Geographer*, Toronto, Canadian Association of Geographers

Econ Geog   *Economic Geography*, Worcester, Mass

Geoforum   *Geoforum, Journal of Physical, Human and Regional Sciences*, Braunschweig, Pergamon/Vieweg

Geog Mag   *Geographical Magazine*, London

Geog Rev   *Geographical Review* New York, American Geographical Society

GJ   *Geographical Journal*, London, Royal Geographical Society

Journ Reg Sci   *Journal of Regional Science*

Nat Geog Journ India   *National Geographical Journal of India*, Varanasi, National Geographical Society of India

Prof Geog   *Professional Geographer*, Washington, Association of American Geographers

SGM   *Scottish Geographical Magazine*, Edinburgh, Royal Scottish Geographical Society.

Sov Geog   *Soviet Geography: Review and Translation*, New York, American Geographical Society.

Sov St   *Soviet Studies*, Glasgow

TESG   *Tijdschrift voor Economische en Sociale Geografie*, Rotterdam, Nederlandse Vereniging voor Economische en Sociale Geografie

Index